LECTURES ON POLITICAL ECONOMY

VOLUME II: MONEY

LECTURES ON POLITICAL ECONOMY

By

KNUT WICKSELL

EDITED WITH AN INTRODUCTION BY

LIONEL ROBBINS

Professor of Economics in the University of London

VOLUME TWO

MONEY

LONDON
ROUTLEDGE & KEGAN PAUL LTD
BROADWAY HOUSE: 68–74 CARTER LANE, E.C.4

First published 1935
Second Impression 1946
Third Impression 1950
Fourth Impression 1956
Fifth Impression 1962

PRINTED IN GREAT BRITAIN BY
LUND HUMPHRIES
LONDON · BRADFORD

CONTENTS OF VOLUME II

INTRODUCTION

B

I. THE CONCEPTION AND FUNCTIONS OF MONEY

Bibliography.—The literature on the subject of money is abundant. According to an estimate of C. Menger (in his article "Geld" in Conrad's *Handwörterbuch*) an approximately complete bibliography would fill an octavo volume of over 300 pages. Yet its importance is not proportionate to its scope; of course, the innumerable special treatises on the money of different countries and different ages have their value, but the standard works which have advanced our knowledge of the nature and laws of money are comparatively few. As regards the general theory of money, the views of the classical school are represented by the works of Adam Smith, and especially of Ricardo and J. S. Mill (*Principles*, book iii, ch. vii–xiii and xix–xxiv). Mill's presentation is, however, marred by his attempt to combine two fundamentally opposite outlooks.

For a general survey of modern money and monetary theories we recommend the excellent essay by E. Nasse, in Schönberg's *Handbuch* (supplemented by W. Lexis, and by C. Menger's essay in the *Handwörterbuch*, which is more theoretical). Jevons's *Money and the Mechanism of Exchange* (which is available in several languages) is substantial and very readable, though without great originality. A new, exhaustive, and in every respect valuable work is Helfferich's *Das Geld*, in the Frankenstein collection, *Hand- und Lehrbuch der Staatswissenschaften*. G. F. Knapp makes some noteworthy contributions to terminology in his *Staatliche Theorie des Geldes* (1905), and his account is attractively written, though somewhat one-sided.

The chapters relating to money in T. H. Aschehoug's *Socialökonomik* (ch. 58 et seq.) are of special interest for Scandinavian readers.

Further references will be given under the main headings.

In the introduction to the first volume an account was given of the plan and general arrangement of these lectures.

In that plan the theory of the *medium of exchange*, money and credit, occupied the fifth and last of the sub-divisions of the general or theoretical part, of which three have been treated in Volume I.[1] Similarly, this volume is primarily *theoretical.*

To preserve continuity, however, we shall, in passing, also deal with certain technical questions relating to currency and credit, although, strictly speaking, these belong to the next section, which is devoted to applied economics. Meanwhile, it is to be noted that we are concerned here only with one part or phase of the extensive field of credit; namely that which is indissolubly bound up with money, in so far as credit forms, in common parlance, a *substitute* for ready money (or, as we prefer to express it, a means of accelerating the real or virtual velocity of circulation of money—since, for the present, we mean by money only metallic money). The other phases of credit will be more suitably treated in the various sections on practical economics—e.g. under agriculture and industry (agricultural and industrial credit) and especially under trade; for not only does trade regularly employ credit, but it also has a special branch which consists of trade in credit; dealing in shares, the issuing system, and the stock exchange, with which a large part of banking is concerned.

The theory of money, delimited in this way, constitutes a complete and rounded whole, which eminently belongs to the province of economic science. In all other economic spheres other circumstances, such as technique, natural conditions, individual or social differences, play a role which science can only imperfectly survey and control. But, with regard to money, everything is determined by human beings themselves, i.e. the statesmen, and (so far as they are consulted) the economists; the choice of a measure of value, of a monetary system, of currency and credit legislation—all are in the hands of society, and natural conditions (e.g. the scarcity or abundance of the metals employed in the currency, their chemical properties, etc.) are relatively unimportant. Here, then, the rulers of

[1] [It will be remembered that the subdivision dealing with population was omitted from Volume I.—Ed.]

society have an opportunity of showing their economic wisdom —or folly. Monetary history reveals the fact that folly has frequently been paramount; for it describes many fateful mistakes. On the other hand, it would be too much to say that mankind has learned nothing from these mistakes. Undoubtedly, we have advanced far in the theory and practice of money in the last 100 to 150 years. Meanwhile there still remain in this field a number of dark places which must be illuminated; there are still different, even diametrically opposed, opinions on the most vital questions, which is the more to be regretted since transactions involving money and credit daily gain ground at the expense of the old system of barter. Consequently even smaller errors may nowadays have serious consequences, since every disturbance makes itself felt in a much higher degree and over a much wider area than formerly.

For various reasons, it is impossible to give an account here of all the different views which have been held concerning money. Even a summary review of them would, I fear, produce in most readers a sense of confusion and insecurity. I shall therefore content myself in the main with a connected account of the view which seems to me most correct. Only on certain specially important points, in which the conflict between opposing theories has been of epoch-making and world-wide importance, will a full and exhaustive account be given.

1. *The Economic Importance of Money*

We have hitherto considered production, distribution, and exchange as if they were effected without the assistance of money; in other words, as if labourers, landowners, and capitalists received an apportionment of the product in kind—as regards the two first categories, moreover, an apportionment in advance, from a pre-existing supply or stock of similar goods—and then exchanged among themselves the products so acquired. In such a case, we are not concerned with any other price than the relative prices of the commodities. Interest was regarded as the direct expression of the marginal productivity of real capital itself, or as the difference between the marginal productivity of saved and current (present) labour and land; or, more correctly, as the marginal productivity of "waiting", in which it was of no importance whether the owner of productive capital was himself regarded as the entrepreneur or whether he was regarded as having lent his capital to another entrepreneur. We did not, in principle, take any *entrepreneur's profit*, strictly so-called, into consideration, but assumed that as soon as the field of production was large anough to permit full and free competition between entrepreneurs, it would tend towards zero. This simplification of the problem is absolutely necessary in a preliminary treatment of economic phenomena, because actual economic life is usually too complex to be examined directly with any chance of success. It is also permissible—as a first approximation—because there can be no doubt that, in many cases, transactions which are made with the assistance of money can be conceived as having been made without its intervention. Among the many similes which have been employed to illustrate the nature and functions of money that which describes it as the oil in machinery is, from many points of view, the most appropriate. Oil is not a component part of a machine; it is neither a motive force nor a finishing tool; and in an absolutely perfect machine a minimum of lubrication would be required. Naturally, however, our simplification is only provisional. Economists frequently go too far when they assume that the economic laws which they have deduced on barter assumptions may be applied without qualification to actual conditions, in which money actually effects practically all exchanges and investments or transfers of capital. The ideal machine, running without friction, and therefore without a lubricant, has not yet been invented, even though we have perhaps approached nearer to perfection in the economic field than in the mechanical field. The use—or the misuse—of money may, in fact, very actively influence actual exchange and capital transactions. By means of money (for example by State paper money) it is possible—and indeed this has frequently happened—to destroy large amounts of real capital and to bring the whole economic life of society into hopeless confusion. On the other hand, by a rational use of money, it is possible actively to promote the accumulation of real capital and production in general. Not that either money or credit is a substitute for, or can really replace, real capital; but by its aid it is possible to facilitate the process of saving, the restriction of present consumption which is the source of the accumulation of real capital or even to enforce it—by no means always an unqualified gain. Credit, in its widest sense, contributes to the greatest possible productivity of capital. Broadly speaking, a closer study of money and its functions will reveal a number of more or less unexpected relationships, both in the field of production and in that of consumption. And in so far as money, *qua* money—at least in metallic form—can be made superfluous, it is only by a study of its laws that the necessary conditions can be ascertained.

2. *Money as a Measure and Store of Value*

The conception of money is involved in its functions and it is usual to distinguish three such functions: as a *measure of value*, as a *store of value*, and as *a medium of exchange*. Sometimes more or less distinct variations, such as the medium of savings, loan medium, medium of payment (the latter for unilateral payments such as taxes and so on) are added to these. Of the three main functions, only the last is in a true sense characteristic of money; as a measure of value any commodity whatever might serve. Indeed, compared with the two others, this is not really a function at all, for it has no relation to the thing itself or to any of its external physical properties. The only quality which is essential in a commodity which is to serve as a measure of value is that it should have, as nearly as possible, a constant value: what this implies we shall examine later. And however desirable it may be that the commodity which is adopted as the medium of exchange should have such a constant value, this is not indispensable; still less is it inherent in the conception of a medium of exchange. For a long time past one class of commodities, the precious metals, has been employed as a medium of exchange, whilst another, such as grain, has been used as a measure of value, especially in the fixing of wages and taxes. (Until quite recently the stipends of the country clergy in Sweden were reckoned partly in grain, although they were paid in money in accordance with the so-called *Markegång* scale; and this is still true of existing free-farm rents.) A remedy for fluctuations in the value of money proposed in more recent times is that in agreements extending into a more or less remote period of time the measure of value (unit of value) should be something other than money, for example the average price of a number of commodities (the so-called multiple standard). It is clear, however, that a commodity which serves as a medium of exchange naturally comes to be used also as a measure of value for transactions in goods and service which are near or simultaneous in time; and since it then becomes difficult or undesirable to prescribe any fixed limit, money has gradually been transformed into a general measure of value, even for valuations which are separated by a considerable period of time. Commodities which are subject to violent fluctuations in value have therefore proved unsuitable as media of exchange wherever they have been so employed. The establishment of a greater, and if possible absolute, stability in the value of money has thus become one of the most important practical objectives of political economy. But, unfortunately, little progress towards the solution of this problem has, so far, been made.

Similarly, the function of acting as a *store of value* is not essentially characteristic of money. One might even go so far as to say that, from the social point of view, money never has this function, but only from the individual or private point of view. Society as a whole only requires to preserve *useful things*, certain utilities for the future. It is true that the precious metals, if carefully preserved, are almost indestructible, since they are not destroyed by the acids in the air. Their utility as ornaments, or for certain technical purposes, can therefore be preserved indefinitely. This utility is, however, too limited and specialized. It is never this utility which is contemplated by those who hoard money (and seldom by those who hoard ornaments) but the object in view is nearly always that of procuring *something else* for it at a future time. In other words, it is the exchange value which it is desired to preserve; it is money as a future medium of exchange which is hoarded. On further reflection it will appear that this is only possible or effective on certain definite assumptions. In so far as somebody else at the same time hoards a sum equal to that which I withdraw from my hoard, for immediate use as a medium of exchange, the amount of money in circulation and, presumably, the price level, will remain much the same. From the economic point of view of the individual the saving achieves its purpose, since the person saving will at a future date consume what he now forgoes and which somebody else will then forgo. From the social point of view, the only result will be that some part of the supply of money will habitually be withdrawn from circulation; or, as we prefer to express it, that the velocity of circulation of all existing money will be retarded. Again, if everybody adopted the same procedure at the same time, this result would not be achieved. So long as saving is continued the price of commodities falls, and if everybody saves uniformly, everybody will continue to obtain just as many commodities for their remaining income as if they had not saved and were in fact not compelled to restrict their consumption. But when once the money so accumulated is returned to circulation, the prices of all commodities will rise, and nobody will be able to increase his consumption. Thus saving will not have involved any sacrifice, and the result will prove to be exactly nothing. Thus it follows that the accumulation of money *in concreto*, which was once so common, may have been a good means—at least as long as none better was discovered—of protecting one's children, for example, or one's old age, against want. Over against those age groups which were bent on saving there were, in the nature of things, other classes which were obliged to encroach on pre-existing savings. But on the other hand, this was clearly useless as a protection against a general calamity such as famine, especially in olden times when grain could not easily be transported from one country to another. In less progressive countries, such as India, this custom of hoarding money, *qua* money, still persists. Even the poorest have some bits of silver buried in the ground beneath their beds, or else wear them on their persons as ornaments. Their object is primarily to possess a reserve during the oft recurring crop-failures. If the failure is only local and a neighbouring district has a good harvest, the means is good and effective ; but if the failure is general, over a wider area, these accumulated stocks of money are (and were still more so before the building of railways in India) quite useless and serve only to drive up the prices of foodstuffs to a dizzy height.

We are reminded of how common this hoarding was all over the world, even in comparatively modern times, by a story in Macaulay's *History of England.* A London merchant of the name of Pope, the father of the famous poet, retired from business towards the end of the seventeenth century to one of his country estates, taking with him the sum of £20,000 in gold and silver coin—a considerable sum, especially in those days. From time to time during the remainder of his life he withdrew from this reserve the amounts he required for his own maintenance and that of his family.

In France, the custom of keeping large amounts of ready cash has been preserved until the present day. A witness before the English Gold and Silver Commission in 1887 said that he had spoken with a hotel-owner in the South of France whose annual turnover amounted to a million francs or more. When he was asked his banking connections, he is reported to have pointed to a safe in the corner of the room and to have said, "That is my bank."

The hoarding regularly practised in earlier times by princes, chiefly with the object of creating a reserve for future wars, was of a somewhat different character. In peace time, the taxes imposed on subjects, for the accumulation of these funds, were probably not too oppressive, in so far as the reduced personal incomes were more or less counterbalanced by cheaper prices of commodities. On the outbreak of war, when the state war-treasuries were broken into and came into circulation, the consequent rise in prices compelled all the population to restrict their consumption, whereby supplies became available for the unproductive consumption of the opposing armies, thus assuming the character of a disguised war tax. The state issues of paper money, so common during war periods in the eighteenth and nineteenth centuries, had substantially the same effect, but were the more dangerous because they could be expanded indefinitely; for which reason also the promise of a future withdrawal of such paper money was rarely fulfilled.

Similarly, from the individual point of view the use of money as a standard of future payments over longer periods is unsatisfactory and incomplete, since the capital saved is not employed in production and thus does not, as a rule, yield any interest. Owing to the development of credit, private hoarding has fallen almost entirely into desuetude in the more progressive countries and has been replaced by a more economic method of storing value. The money capital saved, usually through the medium of banks and savings banks, is loaned as quickly as possible and is thereby returned to circulation. From the individual's point of view, this means the transformation of dead capital into fruitful capital, with an interest-bearing claim guaranteed by the bank. Even if the money bears no interest there is still the advantage that the individual is spared the anxiety of guarding his hoard.

On the other hand, the question may be raised whether the general economic advantage of this arrangement is, broadly speaking, very considerable. At first sight it might appear as if it would be restricted to making all existing stocks of money available for circulation. That, of course, would be a great advantage to any individual country, for the money which was not required in circulation could be, and in fact automatically would be, sent abroad in exchange for goods or as interest-bearing loans. But this again would only be to the economic advantage of individuals. In a closed economy, the result, it may be supposed, would be—if we may assume it in anticipation—that the increased volume of money would bring about a corresponding rise in the prices of commodities. There would be no direct gain since the larger volume of money with higher prices performs the same service as the smaller volume with lower prices. Yet even in this case there would be an ultimate gain in so far as the production of the precious metals would become less profitable—so that the labour and capital employed in this fundamentally unproductive activity would find more useful employment.

In reality, however, the economic significance of the change from hoarding to the modern forms of saving and (private) accumulation of capital is more fundamental than that. Anyone who saves a part of his income and locks it away, thereby withdrawing it from circulation, to that extent exercises a depressing influence on prices, even though it may be infinitesimal as regards each individual. Other individuals thereby obtain more for their money; in other words they divide among themselves that part of consumption which is renounced by those who save. The subsequent use of these savings, say in old age, involves sharing in the consumption of others. The total effect may thus be compared with a sort of consumption loan which those who save give to their contemporaries and of which they subsequently claim the capital (though without interest), from the same generation or from the next.

By saving in the modern sense a man entrusts his savings as they are accumulated to a bank, which lends them as quickly as possible to some enterprise which employs them *productively* in one way or another. Money is thus withdrawn from circulation only for a moment, if at all. No drag on prices need then arise. The commodities of which the saver forgoes the consumption will not, in a properly ordered system, be produced at all, since the units of labour and natural resources which would have been employed in their production will now be employed in preparations for *future* production. Apart from some inevitable economic friction everything else will remain unchanged at the moment of saving, but production will have become more capitalistic, i.e. directed more towards the future, and consequently, as a rule, more fruitful. When, at some future time, the saver claims the return of his capital, he will therefore receive an additional sum in the form of interest—which can be, and usually is, paid in the interim. He does not deprive the future generation of anything, but has rather assisted generally in increasing its real income and consumption, because of the effect of more intensive capitalistic production in raising wages and rents.

The view so frequently expressed by the classical economists, such as Mill, that savings *immediately* furnish other persons with increased means of subsistence in proportion to the consumption which is renounced thereby, is, however, untenable with the modern form of saving—which the classics also assumed. The benefits which saving confers only become visible at a future time, when, thanks to those savings, the production of society is increased.

If we imagine an *organic and progressive* accumulation of capital and expansion of production, the payments to the original factors in production, wages and rents, would no doubt as a rule increase from the beginning, though certainly not by an amount equal to the new savings.

Reverting to the highly simplified example of the laying down of wine in Volume I (p. 175), if we increased the original capital of 314 million shillings, then the price of the grape juice V_0, which was previously 67 shillings per hectolitre, would immediately rise, and with it wages (and rent); whilst, at the same time, interest—still assuming a four years' storage-period—would fall till V_0 equalled 68·30 shillings and interest had sunk 10 per cent, for which reason a five year storage-period would have been as profitable as a four year. At the same time, capital, both new and old, with V_0 unchanged—or rather under the pressure of an infinitesimal rise in the price of grape-juice—would be diverted more and more to five-year storage, until it was all so invested, whereupon V_0 would again begin to rise and interest to fall, etc.

If, alternatively, we assume an organic extension of production, wages would of course rise uninterruptedly with the growth of capital. In the highly simplified instance of the laying down of wine alluded to above, we also found that a growth of capital due to new savings from 314 to 422 million shillings, or an increase of 108 million shillings, produced an increase in the annual sum of rent and wages of only a bare 3 million shillings. Thus the workers were very far from " sharing in the consumption which existing savers renounced ".

The principal error committed by the older economists was that they constantly regarded production as taking place in *one* year and neglected to take into consideration the lengthening of the period of production. In the present case, the new capital is absorbed mainly in the gradual laying down of a further year's vintage, by which no additional labour, but only a year's postponement of the sale of the four years' wine, is required.

In the second part of Marx's *Capital* (p. 490 et seq.) this error of the classical economists is rightly pointed out. The figures there cited by Marx, and quoted subsequently by Tugan-Baranowsky, and others, are, however, unsuitable in so far as they assume not only the growth of capital but also a simultaneous growth in *all three* factors of production: labour, capital, and natural resources.

The transition from hoarding to modern forms of saving introduces further peculiar phenomena. If banks are opened in a country which formerly possessed none, and in which the greater part of the money was hidden in " safes and coffers ", then this money is put into circulation, and the consequence is, apart from increased enterprise, a more or less marked rise in prices. The latter is, in fact, a necessary condition of the former, for the enforced general reduction of consumption which results from it constitutes just that accumulation of real capital which is the indispensable preliminary to a higher degree of capitalistic production. In other words, increased enterprise withdraws some labour and natural resources from the production of present commodities in order to employ them in preparation for future production, and this would be impossible in the long run if present consumption were not restricted in the same degree. As we shall see later on, the banks can achieve the same result independently, without obtaining control of already existing stocks of money, by increasing the volume of credit.

The only substantial accumulations of money which exist in our days in the economically most progressive countries are, as is well-known, the metallic cash reserves of the banks ; though in countries still using metallic currency to any large extent this does not prevent the *aggregate* of the small sums in the hands of the public from exceeding—in some cases very greatly exceeding—the amount of precious metals in the hands of the banks. This latter circumstance is indeed of great importance in judging the monetary and interest policy of the banks. In such countries, the primary function of the banks is to control the supplies of metallic money for current needs or to prevent a surplus from arising, thus regulating prices and the value of money. These reserves can scarcely be called standards of future payment, for in reality they neither bring to nor withdraw from society any real values.

At the same time, it is well-known that the metallic reserves of the banks constitute reserves for *international payments*, and to that extent they are undoubtedly to be regarded as standards of future payment. But, when these supplies of money in any country as such are taken into account, that country appears to some extent as an individual *vis-à-vis* other countries, so that even this function of money, seen from the world point of view and that of international currency, assumes fundamentally a private or individual economic character. In recent times, attempts have often been made and proposals put forward to render this last remnant of the old hoarding practice superfluous. We shall deal in another place with the conditions of its successful achievement.

3. *Money as a medium of exchange. The exchange value of money and the "need" for money*

There remains the function of money as a medium of exhange or a means of payment, which includes, as has been said, the storing of value over a short period; i.e. the period between a sale and a subsequent purchase or, more generally, between a payment received or advanced and a payment by the receiver. What is meant by a medium of exchange? It is an object which is taken in exchange, not on its own account, i.e. not to be consumed by the receiver or to be employed in technical production, but to be exchanged for something else within a longer or shorter period of time. Now this is also true of a merchant's goods, but in that case it is a question of *continued production*, since commerce and distribution may be regarded as a part of production, as the final phase of the process of production; or—in the case of trade in raw materials or semi-manufactures, as well as machinery or tools—as an intermediate link in the process. Fundamentally, therefore, these commodities are means of production, and not *mere* media of exchange. But even with this limitation our definition is still too wide to describe money accurately. Something more must be added, namely the quality of being general or *conventional*. We shall illustrate the importance of this latter qualification by means of an example and shall thus discover the essence of the nature of money.

For this purpose, we shall revert to the case described in Volume I on p. 64, in which three or more kinds of goods, A, B, C, etc., are exchanged for each other on the same market. Once again, we ignore, for the present, the *time*-element, though in fact it enters into every exchange transaction. If there are two kinds of commodities on the market they can be exchanged directly against each other without any medium of exchange, and the use of such a medium would not, under these assumptions, confer any benefit, though it might, of course, still serve—and in exchanges in kind does, in fact, serve—as a *measure of value*. If, on the other hand, there are more than two kinds of goods, then, as Walras has shown, there cannot be any general equilibrium in the market so long as the owners of the goods are constrained to exchange their supplies directly with one another. It is true that, even under such conditions, the influence of supply and demand in the market would bring about a certain equilibrium : one unit of *A* would be exchanged for so many units, or for such and such a fraction of a unit, of *B* ; and, similarly, one unit of *B* for *C*, etc. But these prices would not generally be *correlated*. Whereas, in ordinary price formation, the price of *A* in terms of *C* must always be the same as the product of the price of *A* in terms of *B* and the price of *B* in terms of *C*—or, if it be preferred, the quotient between the prices of *A* and *C*, both expressed in terms of *B*—this is generally not the case here, but *A* can have an exchange value in terms of *C* either more or less than the said product or quotient. If, for example, 1 lb. of *A* is exchanged for 3 lb. of *B* and 1 lb. of *B* for 2 lb. of *C*, it might happen that 1 lb. of *A* would nevertheless *not* exchange for 6 lb. of *C*, but for, say, 5 or 7 as the case might be.

But should this happen, the operation which in the international money and exchange market is known as *arbitrage* would necessarily appear in the market ; this is more or less the function of a middleman. If, for example, the price of *A* in terms of *C* is higher than the said product or quotient, then it will be to the advantage of the owner *C*, as can easily be seen, to obtain his requirements of *A* in an indirect manner by first acquiring *B* for *C* and then *A* for *B*. In other words, in such circumstances an *indirect exchange* always develops, to a larger or smaller extent, out of the direct exchange ; and only in this way is there established that general market equilibrium by which all prices are correlated in such a manner that one exchange relation can always be expressed by the quotient or product of two or more of the others. This relationship becomes most marked in extreme cases, also described in the passage referred to above ; as in the case where the owner of *A* has no demand for *C* but only for *B*, the owners of *B* only want *C*, but not *A*, and the owner of *C* only *A* and not *B*. In this example, suppose that *A* represents forest products, *B* fish, and *C* corn, and that the owners are the populations of the three Scandinavian countries. In such circumstances, no direct exchange is, of course, possible, though an indirect exchange is. For example, the owners of *A*, the population of Sweden, might obtain in exchange for their staple goods (timber), a certain quantity of *C*, Danish corn, not in order to consume it themselves but in order to exchange it for *B*, Norwegian fish, and in this manner to acquire this latter commodity, which is in demand.

In this transaction, the commodity *C* clearly plays the role of a medium of exchange and is, in contrast to commodities intended for further production, or for trade in the ordinary sense, a real medium of exchange. The sole purpose of the process was to facilitate an exchange which would otherwise have been impossible, even though the required commodities existed in the immediate vicinity of the consumers. But it is not a *general* medium of exchange; it is a medium only for intermediaries, whilst remaining for producer and final consumer a commodity, like any other. For this reason the whole operation is very clumsy and incomplete. The medium of exchange must be obtained and transported in quantities equal to the total value of the commodities offered or demanded—an entirely unnecessary double transport of what may be perishable and fragile goods.

Conditions are quite different where we have available a *general* medium of exchange, i.e. a commodity which is habitually, and without hesitation, taken by anybody in exchange for any commodity—especially if it is at the same time durable, easily transported and of high value in proportion to its bulk. An owner of *A* having in his possession a quantity of this commodity, which we will call *P*, sends the latter in exchange for the quantity of commodity *B* which he requires. The owner of *B* exchanges it in turn for a quantity of the commodity *C* from whose owner it passes in exchange for a quantity of *A*; thus it comes once again into the hands of an owner of A. The latter will generally be a different person from the one who first put the medium of exchange into circulation. The last seller, with the help of the medium of exchange, now effects his purchases of B, whereupon the new seller of B makes his purchases of C etc., until the commodity P (the medium of exchange, or money) after a larger or smaller number of revolutions in its coil-like movements, returns to its original starting-point. It will now have facilitated the exchange of a quantity of the commodities A, B, and C equal to its exchange value *multiplied* by the number of times it has circulated. Owing to the peculiarity that, at the conclusion of one purchase or sale, it is immediately ready to effect a new one, returning after a longer or shorter period of time to its starting point, money is differentiated from all other commodities, even if the latter can sometimes incidentally serve as (individual) media of exchange in carrying trade.

In real life, at any rate in larger communities, it is true that a coin once spent returns less often *in corpore* to its former owner; and, naturally, still less frequently does it return before he requires to make a new payment. But, sooner or later, he obtains in its place another coin of the same size and value, so that the circulation of money is complete on this occasion so far as he is concerned. Money possesses in the highest degree—and this is one of its most important characteristics—the quality of a *res fungibilis.* It behaves in much the same way as the circulation of the blood, to which, as has often been pointed out, the circulation of money bears a resemblance, even if only a superficial one. Broadly speaking, the whole volume of the blood circulates incessantly through the blood vessels, but it must be very unusual for the same drop of blood to pass the same capillary vessel twice, least of all twice in succession.

That, however, constitutes an imperfection from the point of view of money, and logically there would be nothing—provided that we could disregard the time-element required for purchase and payments—to prevent all money transactions in a country or in the whole world from being effected *with one and the same penny piece.* The paradox in this idea will be less unfamiliar to the imagination if we remember that the greater part of international trade, at any rate, is conducted by payments in which money is not, in fact, used at all.

It has been said that other goods, considered as goods, and not as exchange media, only reach the market in order to leave it again. They move as a rule in a simple path, easily traced out from producer to consumer, with a few, if any, intermediaries; for which reason the expression "circulation of goods", which is sometimes employed, is rather unreal. Money, on the other hand, always remains in the market, though in different hands. Indeed, its function is to pass from hand to hand. The well-known Dutch economist, N. G. Pierson, has very happily likened money to a shunting locomotive at a railway station: at one moment it pulls one line of trucks, at the next it pushes another; its function being to bring each truck on to the right rails in order that it may be able to reach its destination. But the locomotive never leaves the station.

These observations may appear simple and even trivial, though in nine cases out of ten they are forgotten when reasoning about money. But one of their consequences is that the characteristics of money as a commodity (its concrete qualities) are forced more and more into the background when it is used as a medium of exchange. They may emerge again, but only when it ceases to be money and becomes an ordinary commodity. Money is thus converted into an abstract symbol, a mere quantity of value. Even the Roman jurist Paul knew that money performed its services "non tam ex substantia quam ex quantitate". It would perhaps be more correct to say that, economically speaking, money is a quantity in two dimensions, quantity of value on the one hand and velocity of turnover or circulation on the other. These two dimensions multiplied together give the efficiency of money (Helfferich) or its power to facilitate the turnover of goods during a given time, in the course, for example, of one consumption year. Greater velocity of circulation achieves, from the point of view of the community, the same result as a larger quantity or, what is exactly the same from the point of view of society, a more valuable substance of money; and vice versa.

Consequently, the laws determining the exchange value of money, or, what is the same thing seen from the obverse side, the laws governing the general level of concrete commodity prices and its changes, are quite different from the laws determining the exchange value of the commodities themselves. It is a great, and unfortunately a common, error to forget this and to imagine that what applies to commodities in general and to commodities in terms of each other can also be applied without qualification to "the commodity money" and its relation to commodities proper. This is not true, simply because money is not a commodity like other commodities.

The formulæ by which we endeavoured to express the laws of price formation in the previous volume and which all relate to the exchange value of commodities in terms of one another, become meaningless when we consider the exchange value of money or the actual level of commodity prices. It is true that the exchange of goods effected by money is regulated in the main by those laws: in equilibrium, the supply of, and demand for, every commodity must still coincide; the marginal utility of a commodity, to every individual consumer, will still remain proportional to its price. But money itself has no marginal utility, since it is not intended for consumption, either directly or at any ascertainable future time. It has, perhaps, an *indirect* marginal utility, equivalent to the goods which we could obtain in exchange for it, but this depends in turn on the exchange value, or purchasing power, of the money itself and and it thus does not itself regulate the latter. Similarly, "supply" and "demand", expressions so conveniently applied to almost everything under the sun, become obscure and, in reality, meaningless when applied to money. The individual seller who offers his goods at a certain price may, it is true, be said to "demand" money to an amount equal to the selling price; and the buyer who demands goods can be said to offer or "supply" a corresponding amount of money. But these individual offers or demands constitute in combination only an abstract value, not a total demand or supply of society for *a definite physically determined quantity of money*; for the same pieces of money may function, from one day to the next, several times over in sales and purchases and thus constitute the object of both supply and demand. In this sense, therefore, the demand for money can neither exceed nor fall short of the supply. However small the quantity of money, it could in a given time effect any number of transactions, at whatever price, if only it could circulate with sufficient velocity; and, on the other hand, the quantity of money required for the annual turnover of goods may assume any magnitude if only it circulates slowly enough.

It is very common to seek to establish a difference between "money on the wing" and "money in hand" because the latter lies idle for longer periods in the till. This is done by C. Menger, in the article "Money" in the *Handwörterbuch der Staatswissenschaften* (but cf. 3rd edition, pp. 606 and 909). Only the first kind of money, it is said, influences prices. This view, however, is unscientific, and in any case it is quite impossible to draw the line between circulating and non-circulating money. A fund, in order to fulfil its functions, must be so large that it is never exhausted and only rarely falls below a certain minimum amount. For that reason, some money may often lie untouched for years in the same till, though it has not, on that account, ceased to serve as a means of circulation. If we liked we could, from time to time, change it for other money, so that in the end every coin would have the same velocity of circulation as every other, i.e. the average velocity of the whole volume of money, upon which everything depends.

In the case of hoarding in the strict sense, which is becoming more and more rare in civilized countries, it is of course possible to say that certain parts of the stock of money in a country are withdrawn from circulation, but even this is unnecessary; in any case, there is no objection to including the whole monetary stock of a country in the conception of the general velocity of circulation of money. If commodity prices should change so much that a favourable opportunity arose for the purchase of *durable goods*, such as real property, we should soon see the hoarded money become effective as an automatic regulator of the velocity of circulation and hence of commodity prices.

Attempts have sometimes been made to render the definition

of demand for money more precise by taking into account only those sums which are due for payment at certain agreed or statutory dates for payment, the end of a month or of a quarter, etc. But little is gained thereby, for of the persons who must make payments on those dates many, and perhaps most, will certainly have arranged their affairs in such a way that at those dates money is due to them in the form either of payment or of a loan; for which reason the velocity of circulation is much greater at such fixed payment dates than during the intervening intervals.

In a word, there is nothing in the act of exchange as such which can determine the value of money or concrete commodity prices. This is the more obvious since, at bottom, it is only goods. which are exchanged against each other. To the individual, it is of no importance whatever if he has to pay three or four times as much money as usual for the goods he demands provided that he will receive payment for his own goods in the same proportion; for the result will be, as before, that the money will return to him after the exchanges are effected. This will happen in any case if we do not take into account the *time* required for the exchange transactions. To society, as a whole, the matter is of even smaller importance. Nothing, at least so far as internal trade is concerned, can be of less importance to a country than the question whether it has little or much money, or whether this is of great or little value. The quantity of money, the velocity of circulation, and the prices of commodities always adjust themselves in such a way that all money intended for circulation, that is, all the money in the country will be exchanged against all the goods which are turned over.

We have assumed, however, that the goods which are finally exchanged against each other by the mediation of money are in the market *simultaneously*, in the widest sense of the term: i.e. are turned over at the same time. In such a case there is, strictly speaking, no other limit to the velocity of circulation of money, and thus no other minimum limit to the demand for money with a given turnover and a given price level than that determined by the time interval necessary for its actual payment or its transport. This latter is not without importance as regards payments between remote places, but with modern communications such transport does not, as a rule, often require more than a few days. Furthermore, the virtual circulation of money, especially in international payments, is greatly increased by the familiar procedure of cancelling out debits and credits.

The above assumption, however, seldom holds true in practice. In reality the seller is seldom transformed into a buyer; rather he remains a seller and leaves the market without buying anything himself. The money he acquires then remains in his hands both as ready money for anticipated future purchases or payments, and as a reserve for unforeseen liabilities. His money thus becomes his means of storing value (though usually only for a shorter period), his potential purchasing power, or future medium of exchange. In other words, it becomes a pledge or guarantee—*de facto* not *de jure*—for the future performance of counter-services to which he is economically entitled by virtue of the services he has performed. And since the money in his possession cannot, at the same time, serve as a medium of payment or exchange for somebody else, *the real limit to the velocity of circulation of money*, at any given moment, is to be found here. It is the total of individual *cash balances* which regulates and limits the demand for money, and thereby modifies the value of money. In this sense it may be said that money has by no means exhausted its function as a store of value, but that the latter remains of vital importance, expecially as a factor influencing its exchange value or purchasing power. In countries using a metallic currency, especially where banking technique is imperfectly developed, these private reserves, though small individually, nevertheless constitute a considerable total. They tend to increase with the growth of population and the development of the monetary system. Moreover, if the production of the precious metals does not keep pace with the increasing demand for cash, the inevitable consequence must be an increase in the value of money and pressure on commodity prices.

On the other hand, there exists a persistent, and in many cases very successful, endeavour to employ credit, to supersede the last remnant of the ancient function of money as a means of storing value. Theoretically, this process may proceed to any desired extent, since a promise to pay—if properly secured and redeemable at will—is just as good a pledge or reserve as is a supply of the medium of exchange. Thus, in this case also, the limits of the velocity of circulation and of demand for money are at first sight very indefinite and variable, and their close examination requires thorough investigation.

4. *The Relation between Money and Credit*

Clearly, there is a close connection between money and credit, in so far as credit is the best lever for increasing the velocity of circulation and thus diminishing monetary requirements. But this connection has another and very important aspect, in so far as the granting of credit or the transference of capital is itself frequently made in the form of money—which is also the way in which capital accumulations, or savings, are made. Money is usually said to constitute a *means of saving* and of *transferring capital* (loans). By capital here we mean only real capital employed in production, including trade, and this can, as we have already shown, always be referred back to one or both of the two elements: accumulated labour and accumulated natural resources. The simplest imaginable form of capital accumulation and capitalistic production would be where the possessors of labour and natural resources employed them themselves in the creation of objects destined for future production and consumption. But, especially as regards labour, this is practically never the case. Labour usually constitute *one* group and the entrepreneurs who employ it in the service of production constitute another. A third group consists of those who accumulate capital (savers) who voluntarily postpone the present consumption which they are economically in a position to enjoy, and thereby render production for the future possible. Capital accumulation and transfer are almost always effected by means of money, usually in accordance with the following simple scheme.

A landowner who saves a part of his income subscribes and pays for shares or bonds in a neighbouring railway which is under construction. With the money so obtained, the railway board pays a number of workmen, who provide themselves with milk and other foodstuffs from the landowner's land. The landowner, in proportion as the money flows back to him, re-invests it in shares or bonds; and so on. The landowner might, if he so wished, directly consume the product of this labour, if, for example, he employed the same workmen as beaters in a hunt. Instead, the labour is now used in a saved-up form in order to render future railway traffic possible. This is the *accumulation of real capital.* If we add to our illustration horses, which in the one case may be used for hunting and in the other may be hired out by the landowner for a cash payment as beasts of burden for building the railway, we shall thereby include another element in capital, *saved up natural resources,* in so far as we regard the value of pasturage, hay, oats, etc., used for the feeding of such horses, as essentially representing the rent of land. Even the most complex forms of capital accumulation and transfer, as well as the transformation of existing capital, may be analysed in the same way. Here, too, as we have seen, money transactions only represent the *form* of real economic phenomena; any quantity of money, however small, would evidently be adequate to effect any amount of capital accumulation or capital transfer whatever. In other words, the quantity of money and the quantity of capital in a country bear no necessary relation to each other whatever.

In this respect the well-known Danish economist, W. Scharling, is of the opposite opinion. In his view, money, in addition to acting as a medium of exchange, also "represents capital". "It is too often thought," he says (*Bankpolitik*, ch. 1, p. 43) "that every increase in gold production increases the volume of money in circulation correspondingly—but in reality only a part of this quantity of metal comes into circulation, often only an infinitesimally small part, in so far as the constant increase in the supply of capital requires a constant increase of money, capital, etc." In support of this opinion Scharling adduces that the total metallic holdings of the great metallic banks increased in the years 1873–1886 from 3,329 million reichsmarks to 6,044 million, whereas the amount of notes issued against this metallic reserve at the same time went down from 11,328 millions to 10,389 millions. Since the amount of notes always exceeded the metallic cover, it is scarcely possible to maintain that some part of the latter had been "withdrawn from circulation". Scharling appears also to have overlooked the immense simultaneous increase in the use of cheques which, in most cases, perform exactly the same services as paper or metallic currency; the "idle capital" may therefore be said to have been in circulation just as much as if a corresponding note issue had been based upon it.

A fact which might appear to lend support to Scharling's view is that, in a period of depression, metallic currency usually accumulates in the banks while at the same time large stocks of goods accumulate in the hands of manufacturers (accumulated real capital). When better times arrive the money flows out into circulation, and the accumulated stocks begin to be consumed by the labourers and other producers of fixed capital; in other words, some circulating capital becomes fixed. But this relation is more apparent than real. It is usually incipient unemployment, low wages, and decreased consumption, as well as falling prices, which reduce the demand for metallic currency; whereas just the contrary is evidently true of better times.

On several occasions, moreover, Scharling has stated that the metallic cover in the central banks is superfluously large, which would scarcely be the case if it were required to represent the, in all probability, vastly greater volume of real capital in process of accumulation.[1]

But since the various phases of credit, both of the kind which constitutes a transfer of capital and of the kind which replaces money as a store of value and thereby increases the velocity of circulation, constantly overlap, and can never be differentiated fully, the money market and the capital market (credit market) will always—not only in popular opinion and speech but also to a large extent in reality—be one and the same;

[1] In my book, *Geldzins und Güterpreise* (Jena, 1898), I had already brought forward my objections to Scharling's views (p. 106). K. Helfferich subsequently criticized them from the same point of view.

or, more correctly, they will mutually influence one another, so that now one and now the other will predominate. The interest on loans of money in particular, which should theoretically be only a form, a market embodiment of the natural rate of interest on real capital used in production, may diverge from the latter for a longer or shorter period, especially with the assistance of credit institutions. Two consequences then ensue. In the first place, the monetary institutions may, as we have pointed out, exert considerable influence, either *by stimulating or retarding economic life*. In the second place, and more important, a change in the relation between the natural and the market rate of interest cannot fail to exercise a determining influence on the extent to which credit is used, and thus on the factor by which the value of money, or its purchasing power, is finally regulated.

It will be our purpose in the following pages to examine more closely the fundamental nature and functions of money. Our subject will then naturally fall into three divisions: (1) the theory of money itself—currency—by which for the sake of simplicity we mean, unless otherwise expressly stated, metallic money, (2) the theory of the velocity of circulation of money in the widest sense; or, what is the same thing, the theory of credit and banking, in so far as we shall consider the subject, (3) the theory of the value of money or its purchasing power over goods and services, as well as the practical applications of the theory, i.e. the means of preserving the stability of money in space and time, of establishing a medium of exchange which will, as far as possible, function at the same time as a stable store of value payments.

These three divisions of the subject cannot, of course, be kept entirely apart, especially the third from the first two. Indeed, just as we have already expressed some preliminary views on the causes of changes in the value of money, so also in the following pages we shall be obliged to do the same. A consistent presentation of the whole theory of the value of money, unfortunately neglected hitherto by economists, will, however, constitute the final, the most difficult, and at the same time the most important section of our inquiry.

II. CURRENCY

Bibliography.—The above-mentioned works of Nasse-Lexis, and especially Helfferich. The articles on Currency, Currency Unions, the Precious Metals, gold, silver, bimetallic and parallel currency, etc., in the *Handwörterbuch* and the works referred to there. Current accounts of the production of the precious metals in *Statistisk Årsbok*; cf. also, Davidson, *Guldproduktion och Varuprisen* (*Ekonomisk Tidskrift*, 1901, p. 525, and essays by the author in subsequent issues of the same periodical).

In the lively, though nowadays remote, dispute between monometallists and bimetallists we may quote as representatives of the latter the names of Wolowski, Cernuschi, O. Arendt, Laveleye, Ad. Wagner, and others, and as (gold) monometallists Soetbeer, Roscher, Knies, Bamberger, Nasse, and many others, and, more recently, K. Helfferich.

The difficult problems of ancient and early medieval currency are treated in a manner at once intelligible and interesting in Babelon's *Les Origines de la Monnaye*, cf. also Ridgeway, *Metallic Currency and Weight Standards*. Concerning earlier Swedish currency and monetary systems, cf. the respective chapters in H. Hildebrand's *Svenska Medeltiden* and C. E. Ljungberg's essay in Agardh-Ljungberg's *Statsekonomisk statistik över Sverige*. Concerning Sweden's adoption of the Gold Standard, cf. *Kommittébetänkande* of 13th August, 1870, *Handlingar* submitted to the Bank and Law Committee, 1873, and the Report of that Committee, as well as the Riksdag minutes for the same year.

1. *The Precious Metals as Currency.*—Some Historical Notes on Currency in Antiquity and the Middle Ages.

We know nothing definite concerning the beginnings of the use of money. The surmise put forward by Karl Bücher in his *Wirtschaft der Naturvölken* that a commodity which in a certain place, in a certain tribe, is not itself an object of production, but is only acquired by exchange with other tribes, would always acquire the characteristics of money whenever its properties proved suitable for that purpose, seems to have much in its favour. The habit of taking this commodity in exchange and the necessity for keeping stocks of it until the next caravan or shipload arrived would, of itself, have led to the use of the commodity as a more or less accepted medium of exchange in that place; a use which, it must be remembered, would be maintained and developed when once a beginning had been made on a sufficiently large scale. It is known, however, that among the civilized races of the earth the precious metals (gold and silver) have been used as a medium of exchange since the earliest times and have gradually replaced all other media. The qualities which make them especially suitable for this purpose are not difficult to discover. They are their beauty and brilliance, their durability, comparative scarcity, and consequent value (still further increased by their use as money), so that large values can be easily transported, or hoarded. Also their homogeneity, a virtue of the precious metals to which the essential quality of money as a *res fungibilis* applies in a high degree; their malleability, and the unlimited possibility of dividing them into smaller, or combining them into larger, pieces—a quality which, for example, platinum does not possess, and precious stones possess to a much lesser degree. Finally, they possess the quality, at first suspected rather than clearly apprehended, of being *steady in value*, due to the fact that, apart from currency, they are used almost exclusively as ornaments and are therefore exposed to very little wear and tear, and also that the quantity consumed as a rule constitutes only a small portion of the total stock. With the exception of sea-shells,[1] this quality is entirely lacking in the other objects, which have been, and are still used, by primitive peoples as media of exchange, such as furs, salt-cake, tea, cocoa-beans, etc., and

[1] Cowrie shells have in more recent times been used as money in many parts of Southern Asia (the peninsular and the islands) as well as South Africa, etc. According to Laughlin, wampum (another kind of shell) was used in Massachusetts as late as the seventeenth century.

cattle. In these cases we are dealing with goods which are being constantly consumed and the stocks of which cannot easily be very great in proportion to the quantities normally produced and consumed. If production and consumption do not coincide, a surplus or deficiency of the medium of exchange must arise, with a consequent change of values and a rise or fall in the prices of other goods. Among metals the same is true of copper, and even more so of iron—both of which were formerly widely used as media of exchange (the Greek *obolos* originally meant a small iron bar, the *drachme* = 6 *obolos*, i.e. as many iron bars as could be held in the hand. We should remember that, in antiquity, iron was a comparatively rare metal). As regards copper, the original metal of the ancient Roman coinage, we are reminded of its importance in a number of current expressions, aerarium = treasury, estimare = value in copper (aes) ; this metal has also played a fateful role in the history of Sweden, even as late as the eighteenth century ; and the same is true of Russia. But we also know the violent fluctuations in the value of copper plates and copper dollars, which, combined with excessive weight, made them particularly unsuitable for coinage. The fact that copper, or copper alloyed with zinc and tin (bronze), should still be in use in most countries as token money, is quite another matter, for in that case, as we shall soon see, the intrinsic value of the metal is of quite secondary importance. Indeed, in copper coins it constitutes only a fraction of its legal value.

At the height of the classical period, silver and gold both forced themselves into the foreground as media of exchange and standards of value, and in earlier times also "electron", which is supposed to have been a natural alloy of gold and silver. Nowadays we are amazed at the quantities, especially of gold, which existed in Greece under the Macedonian rulers and in Rome under the Cæsars ; quantities which, if the authorities are correct, can even be compared with modern stocks of those metals. Since the population of antiquity was much less than that of modern times, and its turnover of trade, even in proportion to the population, certainly not comparable with that of to-day, it is not easy to understand to what uses such masses of the precious metals were put. We should bear in mind, however, that modern methods of increasing the velocity of circulation of money were then unknown, and especially that hoarding, even for its own sake, as a form of wealth and ostentation, was practised to an extent of which we in modern times have no conception.

During the Middle Ages, the greater part of these hoards were lost and the known mines exhausted; scarcity of the precious metals was general and, to judge by various indications, they seem to have risen considerably in value in the later Middle Ages, until the discovery of the Bohemian, Tyrolese, and especially the South and Central American, deposits brought about a change concerning which we shall have more to say later.

The origin of *coined* or minted money is similarly obscure and still a matter of dispute. Efforts have been made to discover in the peculiar form of early coins the image of the objects, such as fish, cattle, domestic utensils, etc., which had previously served as media of exchange, or at least as measures or stores of value. But probably the purpose of minting money was rather to facilitate exchange by fixing the weight and fineness of the precious metals. Yet, throughout antiquity, the practice persisted, side by side with minting, of valuing the precious metals by weight, as is done in Eastern Asia. Most of the older names like "talents", "*mines*", "shekels", etc., were originally the names of a certain weight of gold or silver. This practice, too, was universal among the Hebrews, as the biblical writings show. The well known mystic words from the Book of Daniel, "Mene, tekel, upharsin," mean, according to one interpretation, nothing more remarkable than three kinds of weights and three names for coins; "mene" was simply the Greek word "mena" or "mina", "tekel" was "shekel", etc. The words could thus be freely translated by pounds, shillings, and pence.

When states developed and their governments took over the minting of money, and when taxes and dues were paid in such coinage, this method of payment probably gained ground side by side with the weighing of metal. In this way, of course, trade was considerably facilitated, though there was a strong temptation to debase the currency, a practice constantly recurring in currency history since Roman antiquity (under Septimus Severus and his successors) until the most modern times. Hence the original designations of weights for money gradually became mere empty names, without a meaning. One cause of this continuous debasement of the currency may be specially emphasized here as it is inherent in the nature of metallic money. The advantage of having as a medium of exchange a quantity of metal easily recognizable by its external form instead of having to bring forth scales and testing stone for every transaction is so great that even considerable inequality in the weight or composition of the currency is generally tolerated before the currency becomes useless as a medium of exchange on account of its diminished value. In earlier times, before the art of making the precious metals more durable by means of alloys, of protecting coins against wrongful clipping and scraping by means of an artistic design, money was much more worn and damaged than it is nowadays. If the coinage of a country comes to consist of such depreciated coins it is futile to attempt to regenerate it by minting new coins of full value. This new money, which can be obtained as cheaply as the old worn money, is collected eagerly by hoarders or is melted down and sent abroad. The bad money, as it is said, drives out the good. This principle has been called Gresham's Law, and was well known to antiquity. A government, therefore, has only two courses open; either to call in, melt down, and remint the whole of the currency, which is very costly, or to mint the new money at a lower value, which is the first step towards currency abasement, and soon followed by others.

Finally, some very difficult problems arise as regards the relation between the values of gold and silver and the exchange value of these metals in terms of goods.

In the old Assyrian Empire, as also in Asia Minor and Persia, the relation between gold and silver is said to have been $13\frac{1}{3}$ to 1 for many centuries. The reason appears to have been that electron, a natural alloy of gold and silver, was reckoned at ten times the value of silver, and pure gold at an additional one-third. The same names were used for the different units of weight of gold and silver (talents, *mines*, *states*, etc.). But the latter were one-third heavier than the former and were calculated at one-tenth of their value. After the discovery of the gold mines in Thrace and Macedonia, and after Alexander the Great had dispersed the gold hoards acquired in the Orient, this ratio could no longer be maintained, and the gold and silver "mine" or "talent" was given the same weight, so that the value ratio became as 10 : 1.

In Rome, where the coinage of gold and silver was of comparatively late date, no fixed value ratio between these two metals appears to have developed. Under the Emperors, gold, which was usually accepted by weight, gradually became the real currency metal, whilst silver, as a result of continuous debasement, fell to mere token money. Ultimately even the State refused to accept it and demanded the payment of taxes in gold. This metal, however, had become scarcer, so that the value ratio, which was 9 : 1 in Julius Cæsar's day, gradually rose, and in Justinian's Code it stands at 14·4 : 1. In the Middle Ages, the movement was in the opposite direction: both gold and silver, but especially the latter, became more and more scarce, so that, at the beginning of the sixteenth century, the value ratio was 10·3 : 1.

It is difficult to say to what extent the attempts to fix a definite legal ratio between these two currency metals were really successful in earlier times. There can scarcely be any question of bimetallism in the strict modern sense, but rather something resembling what we should call a *parallel standard*, which has really existed for long periods in the recent past and in modern times. The two currency metals, and even the different currency forms of the same metal, had their fields of activity and use side by side with each other, and according to circumstances payments were required to be made in one or the other of the metals or kinds of currency. But, on the other hand, one cannot assert that the legal ratio was merely formal and had no influence on the actual exchange ratios or valuations of the two metals in relation to each other. It can be readily seen that Gresham's Law, which in the opinion of many economists would make a fixed value ratio impossible between two metals both used as standards, is chiefly important *as between different countries.* If there is active commercial intercourse across the frontiers of two neighbouring countries and if *different* ratios are established in them between full weight gold and silver coins, it is inevitable that each of the metals will sooner or later find its way to the country in which its value is relatively higher. There are examples of this kind in antiquity. But the greater or the more isolated the territory in which the statutory ratio prevails, the more probable is it that it will really determine exchange relations, even between individuals, though this may in the end become impossible if one or other of the two metals should become too abundant or vice versa.

A similar answer must be given to the extremely obscure question of the purchasing power of money in terms of other goods in earlier times and the causes of its changes. There can be little doubt that, here also, habit and custom played an important part. The determination of the prices of various goods in terms of each other or of money which, under a more advanced economic system, is so easily affected by the influence of the market, is an extremely difficult and complex matter under a primitive system, and it must often have been felt as a great relief, corresponding to a real need, when such prices were fixed, as was often the case until comparatively modern times, by official schedules. Yet the economic forces which in abstract theory alone govern price formation doubtless manifested themselves at all times as a tendency which, when the pressure became strong, enabled them to overcome habit and led to new price formations—which, in their turn, came to acquire the force of habit and custom. Perfectly clear examples of this can, in fact, be adduced from antiquity. Again if we compare antiquity with the later Middle Ages we shall find that the excessive quantities of the precious metals in the former, and the scarcity of them in the latter, period was reflected in a price level which, in the days of the Antonines, for example, is supposed to have been as high as at the present day; whereas in the Middle Ages, at any rate in Scandinavia, the prices of those necessities which it is possible to compare were only a fraction of what they are now.

2. *Currency in Modern Times, especially in the Nineteenth Century.*

Towards the end of the Middle Ages, new silver deposits were discovered in the Tyrol and Bohemia (Joachimsthal in Northern Bohemia, from which the words "thaler" and "dollar" are derived); and after the discovery of America, the Spaniards came into possession both of great accumulated stocks of gold and silver and of the extremely rich silver mines of Potosi in Bolivia. In addition, great progress was made in the eighteenth century in the technique of extracting silver from the ore by means of quicksilver. The consequence was that, during the latter half of the sixteenth and the whole of the seventeenth century, there took place a progressive rise in the prices of all goods and especially a fall in the price of silver in terms of gold from about 1 : 11 in the middle of the sixteenth century to about 1 : 15 at the end of the seventeenth. Silver production then predominated even in value terms and continued to do so until the middle of the nineteenth century; being about two-thirds to three-quarters of the total annual production value, as compared with about three-fifths in the middle of the eighteenth century. During the last centuries of the Middle Ages the reverse was the case. The world supply of currency thus became predominantly silver. In the eighteenth century, England alone, for a reason to which we shall shortly return, retained a certain amount of gold in circulation; and since its silver coinage had become worn out and debased, it effectively went over to the Gold Standard at the end of the eighteenth century (formally in the year 1816). The value ratio between gold and silver from the middle of the seventeenth century and throughout the eighteenth only varied between $13\frac{3}{4} : 1$ and $15\frac{1}{4} : 1$ and during the first half of the nineteenth century between $15\frac{1}{2} : 1$ and $15\frac{3}{4} : 1$.

In the years 1848 and 1851 the goldfields in California and Australia were discovered, followed by similar discoveries in New Zealand, Colorado, etc. The output of gold was thus suddenly increased tenfold; in twenty-five years as much was produced as in the previous 250 years, and the annual production for a couple of decades was as much as three times the value, and one-fifth the weight, of that of silver. That this increase in the stock of precious metal was not without influence on commodity prices can be seen in the statistics, even though the crisis of 1857 caused a set-back in the rising price level. On the other hand, one would have expected the value of silver to rise considerably in relation to gold; but, curiously enough, this did not happen. Despite the complete revolution in the conditions governing the output of gold and silver, their relative values remained for a further twenty years—until the middle of the 'seventies—about the same as had prevailed for 200 years, i.e. $15\frac{1}{2}:1$, or slightly less. This state of affairs undoubtedly constitutes a strong argument in favour of the bimetallists who contend that a stable relation between the two metals can be effectively maintained by law (even though within certain limits) so that both might serve as standards with free coining and be full legal tender. In point of fact, two of the most important commercial countries of Europe at that time had, as early as the beginning of the eighteenth century, set up a statutory ratio between the gold and silver coinage. If this ratio had been the same in both countries it is quite probable that the market value would have related to it and that the circulating medium of both countries would have consisted of a mixture of gold and silver currency. This did not occur, however. The ratio established in England was 15·2 : 1, which was above the contemporary market value of gold in terms of silver. The French ratio was $14\frac{5}{8}:1$, which was lower. It would perhaps be more correct to say that the market value fluctuated between these two limits. The consequence was that gold coins left France for England, whilst the full-weight English currency disappeared from England and only the worn coins remained, in complete accordance with Gresham's Law. This was one of the chief reasons why England, instead of calling in and melting down the debased silver currency in order to replace it by full weight, preferred to go over to a pure gold standard and, to that end, forbade the free minting of silver for private account when, as a result of the fall in price of silver, it had again become profitable to do so. Shortly before, however, France had raised its ratio to 15½ : 1 (subsequently known as the bimetallic parity) and thus succeeded for a time (until about 1820) in retaining a certain amount of gold in circulation with silver. The revolutionary changes in the conditions of production which followed 1848 produced the following results: the market ratio between gold and silver fell below 15½ : 1—the ratio established by French currency law. Hence gold began to flow in and to monopolize the circulation, whilst the superfluous silver was melted down and sold to other countries—a large part of it going to India and the East. The weakening silver served as a parachute for gold and prevented the fall in its value which would otherwise have occurred. It is true that, at that time, there were, besides the bimetallic countries, also pure silver and pure gold countries ready to absorb whichever metal had become superfluous. But the results would probably have been just the same, if not even more favourable, had the majority of countries introduced the bimetallic system with the *same* ratio as France.

These movements in the market for precious metals became the immediate cause, in 1865, of the so-called Latin Currency Union between France, Belgium, Switzerland, and Italy. All these countries had adopted the French currency system and both silver and gold coins circulated quite freely between them, irrespective of the imprint. When silver began to flow away, fears were entertained lest it should disappear altogether, and in order to preserve quantities at least sufficient for smaller payments it was proposed to convert the silver coins of lower denomination (2- and 1-franc pieces and less) into token money and to mint them as such. An agreement was reached whereby the government of each country, under certain conditions, guaranteed to accept the debased silver currency.

Five-franc pieces remained full weight, and might continue to be freely minted; indeed, they still retain within the Latin Union their status as legal tender for the payment of any amount.

At the beginning of the 'seventies, however, something happened which was to disturb completely the 200-year-old stability between gold and silver, and which was to impart to the currency systems of Europe, as well as to several extra-European systems, an entirely new form. Other European countries had, at that time, either a silver currency, as in Germany and Scandinavia (gold ducats and carolinas were also minted in Sweden, but they were accepted at varying rates and scarcely circulated at all) or a depreciated paper currency, as in Austria and Russia. If those countries had gradually attached themselves to the Latin Union, with its free minting of silver and gold at a legally established ratio then the traditional ratio between gold and silver might possibly have been preserved. Adhesion to the Latin Union was, in fact, contemplated by Germany shortly before the outbreak of the war in 1870, but owing to the war the plan never came to fruition. Germany elected instead to adopt the gold standard and to sell all her silver not required for token money; and the Scandinavian countries immediately followed her example in 1873–5. No doubt a contributory factor was a certain fantastic idea that England's economic supremacy was in some way connected with her gold standard. But the step was ominous. Germany did not, indeed, succeed in selling all her silver, some of it remained as late as 1907, and was still to be found in the form of "thaler" pieces which were not regarded as token money but were legal tender to an unlimited extent, like gold. Great quantities of silver, however, were thrown on the market. Thanks to the discovery of new mines and new methods (the furnace and later the electrolytic process replacing the amalgam process), the production of silver increased rapidly; and as the production of gold, though still much greater than before 1850, began to diminish at the same time silver again began to flow into, and gold out of, circulation in the Latin Union. Those countries which did not want to lose their gold had no choice but first of all by common agreement to restrict, and subsequently (Nov., 1878) entirely to suspend, the free minting of silver (5-franc pieces).

The same measures had been taken somewhat earlier by Russia, and soon afterwards by Austria. These two countries still had irredeemable paper money, but this had now risen to par, or even above par, owing to the fall in silver; for which reason minting for private account again became profitable. But, since it was now intended exchange paper not for silver but for gold currency, i.e. to adopt the gold standard, this minting of silver, which would have depressed the value both of the paper and silver currency in terms of gold, came inopportunely.

Thus the old double standard, whether bimetallic in the strict sense, or merely parallel, ceased to exist in Europe. Silver had been degraded to an ordinary article of commerce and its market price fell lower and lower. The United States tried in vain, by the famous Bland and Sherman Bills, to save the value of silver, in the maintenance of which it was now interested as a producer. Before the Civil War, there was statutory bimetallism in the United States, but since the ratio had (since 1834) been fixed as high as 16 : 1 virtually only gold was in circulation. As a result of the war, an irredeemable, and soon much depreciated, government paper currency—the well-known greenbacks—held the field. Not until 1879 did they succeed in bringing these notes up to par and then begin to redeem them. It was felt to be too dangerous to permit the free minting of silver, but shortly before this it had been enacted by the Bland Bill that a certain amount of silver, corresponding approximately to the native production of the U.S.A., should be purchased annually by the State and minted as cover for a special note issue—the so-called silver certificates. This amount was increased by the Sherman Bill, according to which payments were made in inconvertible Treasury notes. Since, however, silver continued to fall in value, the insufficiency of these measures became clear, the more so as gold began to flow out of the country. All attempts to induce the European countries to resume the free minting of silver failed. The only country of major importance with an ordered currency in which free minting still existed was India, which remained on a silver standard until 1893. But the ever-widening gap between the value of British and Indian currency caused numerous inconveniences; and when these became more apparent the Anglo-Indian government resolved (in 1893) to discontinue the free minting of rupees. Thereupon the U.S.A. also abandoned it, with the exception of token money, and henceforth devoted all its energies to the maintenance of the gold exchange.

Of recent years, the production of gold, which showed clear signs of declining at the beginning of the 'eighties, has risen rapidly in consequence of the discovery of new deposits in Colorado, the Transvaal, and Klondyke; so that, at the beginning of this century, it not only equalled the production of the 'fifties and 'sixties, but grew to be three times as great. Simultaneously, the production of silver also increased, despite the tremendous fall in its value, although it looked like becoming stationary from 1893 to 1907. It is now, however, about five times as great as in 1860, though it is nevertheless considerably exceeded, even at its old value, by present gold production. And yet gold is now more than thirty-five times, and has even been forty times, more valuable than silver, whereas before 1873 the ratio had never been known to stand higher than 15½ or 16 : 1, even at times when gold production only constituted a fraction (reckoned in value) of the production of silver.

In England, the value of metallic silver is usually given as so many pence per ounce. Gold of $\frac{11}{12}$ fineness is minted in England at the rate of £3 17*s.* 10½*d.* (= 934·5*d.*) per ounce (about 31 gr.); so that if both metals were of the same fineness it would only be necessary to divide that figure by the price of silver in pence in order to ascertain the value ratio between gold and silver. The so-called English *mint silver*, *standard silver* (not to be confused with the content of the present English silver token money, which is much less) is a little finer than minted gold, i.e. $\frac{111}{120} = \frac{37}{40}$. The above mentioned total must therefore be increased in the proportion of $\frac{111}{120} : \frac{11}{12} = 111 : 110$, or 943*d.*; if the quoted price in pence per ounce is divided into this the correct ratio will be found. A silver price of about 26*d.* thus corresponds to a value ratio between gold and silver of 943 : 26 (= 36·1, approximately) whilst the bimetallic parity of $15\frac{1}{2} : 1$, when it still coincided with the market price, gave a price of $943 : 15\frac{1}{2}$ (= $60\frac{13}{16}$*d.*) per ounce of standard silver.

It can scarcely be doubted that the main cause of the fall in the value of silver is to be found in changes in monetary policy. If silver should again be adopted as a standard in the civilized world, side by side with gold, and be freely minted, then its market value would certainly rise considerably, not improbably to the old ratio of $1 : 15\frac{1}{2}$, if the latter were retained as the statutory ratio. At present, there seems to be no practical reason for attempting this, since the world production of gold appears to be sufficient and the reserves (now obtained mainly by mining operations and not as formerly by washing in old river beds) are probably adequate for the needs of the European states and the U.S.A. and sufficient even to enable extra-European states to adopt the gold standard. This, however, is a question of expediency [1] and does not affect the theoretical foundation of bimetallism, which is essentially unchanged, even if, as we shall point out later, it carries us beyond the conclusions which its advocates draw from it.

For the moment, however, the free minting of silver does not exist in any country with a regulated currency. The currency systems in existence in 1915 may be characterized as (1) those with a pure gold standard, in which silver is only used as token money and is only legal tender up to a limited amount; (2) those with the so-called "limping" standard, in which both metals are legal tender, but only one, gold, is freely minted; and, finally, (3) those with a paper standard in which the currency consists of inconvertible paper money or of metallic (silver) money minted only by the State for its own account. To class (1) belong England and most of its colonies, Portugal, Germany, and the Scandinavian countries (the Scandinavian Currency Union of 1873–5), Finland, the U.S.A., and, for some years past, Russia and Japan. To class (2) belong the countries of the Latin Union and Holland. To class (3) belong South America

[1] A threatened scarcity of gold in the near future has been feared, since the return to the gold standard after the world war.

Production and Value of the Precious Metals in the Nineteenth Century.

10 or 15 years averages.

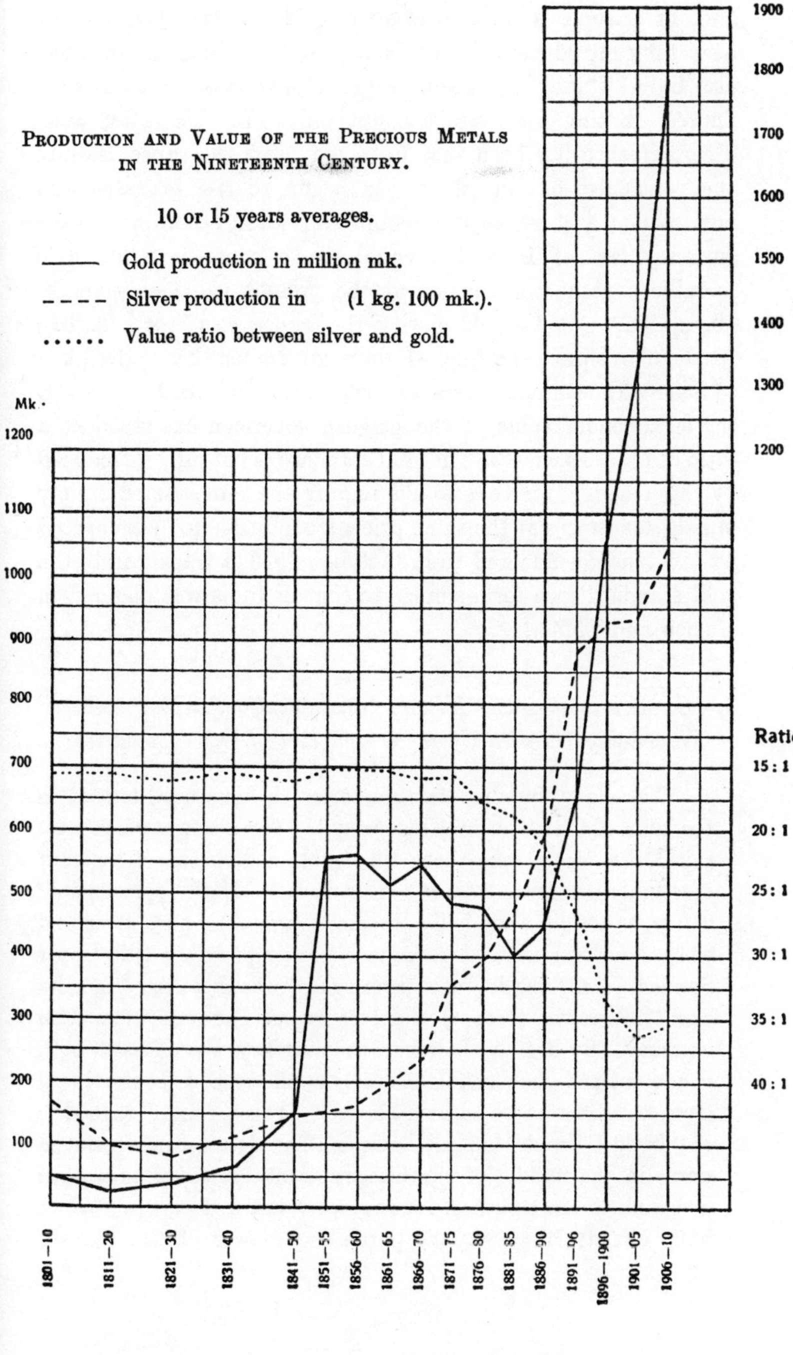

and, in Europe, Austria, where the gold standard has not yet been fully introduced, Spain, Greece, and the Balkan countries, also India, where the rupee (silver) is still the standard but with limited minting for State account only. In this latter case, a consequence has been that in recent years the rupee, despite the continued fall in silver, has begun to rise in value and now stands as high as it possibly can stand according to the currency law of 1893, i.e. equal to 16 pence in gold. (Its metallic content corresponds at the present value of silver to about 10*d.*; at the old parity the rupee was worth 22·6*d.*) At the above price the Anglo-Indian government has undertaken to issue without limit rupees against gold. Since 1899, moreover, the legal tender value of the English sovereign has stood at a ratio of £1 = 15 rupees. The gold standard is not fully introduced by this means; for that would require the unrestricted supply of gold for rupees at the same price, a condition not yet enacted by law, though adhered to in fact. In 1915 a transition to the gold standard in a form similar to that of India was planned in Mexico and China.

3. *Swedish Currency History and a Comparison between Present-day Swedish Currency and that of Other Countries.*

The oldest Swedish coinage seems to have been minted in the time of Olof Sköt or King Anund. These coins, which were called *penningar*, were then still equal subdivisions of the unit of weight, in so far as 8 *öre* at 3 *örtug* made 1 " Mark " (presumably 210 gr. or not quite one-half a Swedish *skålpund*) of pure silver, and every *örtug* was worth 8 *penningar* (earlier probably 4) in Upper Sweden. One " mark " of " penningar " was therefore originally about 32 crowns (kronor) and 1 *öre* about 4 crowns in modern currency. By degrees, however, the currency was debased, both in content and size; so that, as early as the time of the provincial laws, a distinction was drawn between " vägen " and " räknad ", or " karlgell " and " kopgell " marks. This debasement continued until, in the middle of the fifteenth century, the *penningmark* had sunk to one-eighth of its original value, or 4 crowns; as we have already observed, the purchasing power of the *penning* throughout the Middle Ages was considerably greater than now. In this connection, coins of a higher denomination began to be minted—first the *örtug*, then the *öre*, and so on. In the sixteenth century the debasement of the currency continued, so that, towards the end of the reign of Gustavus I, the mark was only worth 1 crown in modern currency. It was thus one-quarter of the large coin, the thaler (Joachimsthal) which was first struck at the beginning of the century in Germany and later in Sweden. The consequence was that, a *daler* (which, from the outset, was the same as a " thaler " or a specie " riksthaler ") was calculated as 4 marks or 32 *öre*, and this equivalent was maintained during all subsequent debasements. Whereas the specie " riksdalar ", which was a kind of international coin, remained practically unchanged in weight and fineness, the originally equivalent " svenska daler " was debased more and more. Our currency history until 1830 is indeed an almost uninterrupted succession of debasements and bankruptcies.

Under Gustavus, Adolphus, and Christina, and even later, with brief interruptions, the currency metal was copper, which was minted not only as token money, but also in large clumsy plates as standard money. A copper thaler was originally supposed to be of the same value as a silver thaler, but this ratio, which from the outset did not correspond to the metallic value of the copper coins, could not be maintained. The copper thaler gradually declined in value—at first to one-half and then to one-third of a silver thaler ; this latter ratio was finally stabilized. Meanwhile, the silver thaler (= 4 silver marks) which sometimes was actually minted and sometimes merely a name for the coined copper plates, sank to two-thirds and then to one-half of its value in 1560, so that towards the close of the reign of Charles XI one specie *riksdaler* was equivalent to 2 silver thalers or 6 thalers or 24 marks in copper coins.

Under Charles XII (apart from the later emergency currencies which were nothing more than substitutes) a new debasement took place, in so far as the 6-thaler plates were restamped to the value of 9 thalers ; as a result, the specie *riksdaler*, soon came to be worth 3 silver thalers, 9 copper thalers, or 36 copper marks, which was the parity in the *Frihetstid*. During the latter period all metallic money disappeared from circulation, and the Riksbank's notes, inconvertible from 1745, became the only means of payment in the country. As a result of an excessive issue, especially during the Pomeranian war, these notes depreciated in terms of silver; or, what amounted to the same thing, the specie *riksdaler*, and the equivalent Hamburg *banco riksdaler*, in which most foreign bills were made out, appreciated in terms of the *daler* or mark banknotes. In 1776 these notes were converted into silver at the rate of 1 *riksdaler* specie = 72 marks of copper coin, i.e. at half their face value. The old ratio, 1 silver thaler = ⅓ *riksdaler* specie, was retained in legal documents and in the valuation of state incomes. The silver *riksdaler* (specie), divided into (3·32 =) 96 *öre* or into 48 shillings was now the currency unit for the whole country.

After the Russian war under Gustavus III the notes issued by the Treasury (originally bearing interest, but subsequently becoming inconvertible paper money) became the chief medium of exchange in the country, driving out of circulation, in accordance with Gresham's Law, both the metallic currency and the inconvertible Riksbank notes. From 1903, the Treasury notes became by decree redeemable at the bank for two-thirds of their value. (A fund had been created for the purpose, partly by means of a general income tax, the so-called "realization contribution", and partly by "pawning" the town of Wismar.) After the Finnish war, however, it became impossible for the bank to redeem either its own notes or those of the Treasury in hard cash, whereupon both, *whilst retaining their value* relatively to each other, gradually depreciated (in other words, the silver value and the value abroad rose) until by the "realization" of 1834 they were redeemed at three-eighths of their nominal value, the Treasury notes being thus redeemed at one-quarter (two-thirds of three-eighths) of their *original* value.

The silver thaler, with its subdivisions the mark and the *öre* were still used in old legal transactions and were calculated at ⅓ *riksdaler banco* = 50 *öre*.

By the currency law of 1830, the silver content of the specie *riksdaler* was reduced by about three-quarters, or from 25·69 to 25·5 gr., whilst the cost of minting, which had formerly been paid separately, was now "thrown in" with the coin. By the law of 1855 no other alteration was made than that a quarter of a specie *riksdaler,* which after the currency realization of 1834 exactly corresponded to a Treasury *riksdaler,* became the unit of calculation under the name *riksdaler riksmynt,* divided into 100 *öre.* The currency changes of 1873 were made on the basis of 1 *krona* (equal in value to 1 *riksdaler riksmynt*) as the unit, the ratio between gold and silver being fixed at 15½ : 1 (15·81 : 1). Thus we may say that the previous silver weight of the unit was evened out, so that 4 *kr.* were regarded as equal to 25 gr.—or 160 *kr.* to 1 kg. pure silver. Against this imaginary silver coinage, gold coins were minted at the ratio of 1 : 15½ in weight.

The result was that 1 kg. of gold was minted into 15½ : 160 = 2480 *kr.*, as is still the case.

In Germany the transition followed the same lines. 1 kg. of pure silver was then worth 180 Reichmarks and consequently 1 kg. of pure gold was minted to 2790 marks; thus 8 *kr.* are worth about 9 marks.

Similarly in France the silver and gold coins stand in a simple relationship to the kilogram, though this applies to their gross weight, and not to their net weight. 1 kg. of silver of $\frac{9}{10}$ fineness is minted into 15½ × 200 = 3100 francs. Thus 8 *kr.* = $\frac{10}{9}$ × 10 francs, or 72 *kr.* = 100 francs. The same applies to the various countries which have adopted the French currency system. Russia's currency also bore a similar relation to the kilogram and therefore to Swedish currency. A silver rouble contained the same amount of silver as 4 francs, but the gold coin, the older imperial of 10 roubles, was minted in the proportion by weight of 1·15 and was therefore worth more than 40 francs. This was equalized in 1886, when the transition to the gold standard was planned, so that the new imperial equalled 40 francs. The intention was gradually to raise the depreciated paper rouble to its old parity of 4 francs. But, as this would have taken too long, it was decided in 1897 to take the existing exchange value of the paper rouble as the basis for redemption, whilst the imperial and half-imperial were fixed at 15 and 7½ francs, or 1·92 *kr.* The Russian gold coins minted were 10 and 5 Tsar roubles. The silver coinage, on the other hand, has remained unchanged, for which reason the Russian value ratio of gold to silver is quite different from that of Western Europe, i.e. 23 : 1, instead of 15½ : 1.

We shall ignore the currencies of the remaining countries

because they do not stand in any simple rational relation to the Swedish, even though in Austria, Hungary, and the Netherlands the same unit of weight, the kilogram of gold, constitutes the basis of the currency. We merely indicate that in practice—

1 pound sterling	=	18·16 *krona*
1 Dutch gulden	=	1·50 ,,
1 Austrian krona	=	0·76 ,,
1 American dollar	=	3·73 ,,
1 Indian rupee	=	1·21 ,,
1 Japanese yen	=	1·86 ,,

4. *The Technique of Currency*

The purpose of minting is, as we have said, to give a state guarantee of the weight and fineness of the metal, for too much inconvenience to trade would be caused if the metal had to be weighed and tested for every transaction. The fineness is now usually nine-tenths for standard coins, both gold and silver (the remainder being copper); but in England eleven-twelfths is the standard fineness for gold. By the expression "standard" we usually mean the net weight of metal in the standard coin, or, what comes to the same thing, the number of units minted from one unit of weight of a precious metal. In modern times the word standard is also frequently used to indicate the metal from which the standard coin is minted: we speak of the gold, silver, or bi-metallic standard, etc.

Even with perfected modern methods of minting it is impossible to achieve absolute accuracy either as regards weight or fineness. In both respects, therefore, a slight latitude is permitted (the "remedium") which, with modern minting methods, is far from being fully utilized. In the Scandinavian countries the margin is ·0015 for 20 *kr*. pieces and ·002 for 10 *kr*. pieces, the margin of fineness being ·0015 for both. But, in addition 10 kg. of newly minted gold coins must not vary more than 5 gr. from the normal weight, i.e. by more than ·0005. The value of coins is, however, reduced by the wear and tear of circulation—although the amount of wear is certainly inconsiderable. It has been estimated at only one-fifth to one-quarter per 1000 per annum for the standard money in regular circulation. The common idea that the purpose of banknotes is to save this wear and tear is incorrect, for the maintenance of paper money actually costs more than that of metallic money. What is saved by uncovered paper money is the interest on the capital invested in the currency. In the course of time the wear may become considerable and, though the form and design of coins nowadays makes this more difficult, the practice of clipping, scraping, and sweating might assume large proportions. For this reason a minimum limit is fixed, below which the coinage ceases to be legal tender as between individuals. In Sweden, as in Germany, the limit is one-half per cent below the normal weight, in England almost one per cent. In France there is no limit within the country, but as between the states of the Latin Union it is only one-half per cent. The establishment of a minimum is, however, not sufficient to prevent the circulation of worn money, because individuals do not trouble to examine the weight and are naturally not disposed to bear the loss themselves if they accidently receive a badly worn coin. The State must therefore redeem its currency even if it has passed the minimum limit. Such is the case in Germany and Scandinavia, where a certain maximum limit of twenty per cent has been placed on the State's liability; this is of no importance in practice. In England, on the other hand, coins cease to be legal tender, even as against the State, when they have passed the minimum. The consequence of this is that the full-weight money is paid to the State or the Bank or England and the underweight money continues in circulation, especially in country places.

Since the minting of money is expensive, the State usually makes a charge for minting on private account. This charge is called "Seigniorage"—a name which is due to the fact that in earlier times the charge was somewhat higher than the actual cost of minting and was therefore a source of income to the State. This fact, and the fact that it was profitable for private persons to have their precious metal coined and pay more or less appreciable charges for so doing, is due again to the fact that the minted metal *qua* legal tender had a higher value within the country than the unminted metal: experience shows that this difference may be enormous and it is in any case very great if the State charges a high seigniorage and does not at the same time contribute to an increase in the supply of money by minting on its own account. This method of procuring revenue for the State should, however, be avoided, for such coinage has very much the same disadvantages as inconvertible paper money. Sooner or late the country may experience an adverse balance of payments—as for example in consequence of a bad harvest; some portion of the money must then be sold abroad in payment for goods. In a foreign country, however, the currency of any country seldom has a higher value than that of its metallic content, since it must usually be melted down and re-minted abroad. The consequence is that the internal coinage loses its artificial value, and the exchange—i.e. its relation to foreign currencies—will depreciate to the same extent. At any rate that is what *should* happen if there do not exist within the country stocks of unminted metal which can be used primarily for export; or else assets or credits abroad against which bills can be drawn. But it will always remain true to some extent. It is therefore advisable to restrict the seigniorage to the actual cost of minting, in which case deviations from the value of the metal and consequent fluctuations in the exchange will be correspondingly slight. In England there is nominally no such charge—coinage being "free and gratuitous". But this is unnecessary and has no practical significance even in England.

The development of modern banking and of the mechanism of international payments have resulted in the almost complete disappearance of direct minting on private account. Instead, the central banks accept the precious metals from individuals in exchange for minted money or notes to the statutory amount. In England, as has been said, anybody possessing bullion can have it minted free of charge at the Mint; but this takes time and involves a loss of interest. Consequently gold importers prefer to deposit gold with the Bank of England, which credits them with the amount at the rate of £3 17*s*. 9*d*. per ounce (about

31 gr.)—or about 1½*d.* less than the Mint would have given (£3 17*s.* 10½*d.*), which is equivalent to a charge of a little over 0·15 per cent. (In Sweden the charge is one-quarter per cent for 20 crowns and one-third per cent for 10 crowns. The position is similar in Germany and elsewhere.) The banks then deal with the gold according to circumstances; they mint it or they keep it in ingots. Similarly, foreign currency is accepted by the banks at a price which usually varies little from par and may even sometimes be above par. Frequently such coin is not melted down, but is used as occasion requires for shipment—i.e. is sold again to importers at a somewhat higher price if the balance of payment is so unfavourable that gold must be exported. Consequently it may be said that, with free minting and a moderate seigniorage or none at all, minted money will have about the same value as the bullion—slightly higher, to be exact.

5. *Standard Money and Token Money*

Money which is unlimited legal tender in a country—so that ordinary debts can be legally discharged by offering payment in that money at its nominal value—is called the standard or current money of that country.

If two or more metals with a statutory value ratio are standard the system is bimetallic or trimetallic. If, on the other hand, only one metal is minted into standard money it is monometallic. If, in the former case, free minting of both metals is permitted there is a double standard in the real and classical sense. If, on the other hand, minting of one metal (silver) for private account has ceased, whilst the money in question is still unlimited legal tender then it is usual to speak of limited double standard, or of bimetallism with limited minting.

Even in a monometallic system the other metals cannot be entirely dispensed with as minting material. Silver money—not to mention copper and nickel—would be too inconvenient to use for larger payments, while gold, on account of its thinness and smallness, would not be handy enough for use in discharging debts of a few shillings. In countries whose standard money is silver, the gold coinage, even where it must be accepted at a varying rate of exchange, is often used as trading money. This was more common in earlier days than now, since banknotes have come into use. Where, on the other hand, gold is the standard money, as it is nowadays in an increasing number of countries, silver must be retained as a means for smaller payments, unless notes of small denomination are used. For the same reason the smallest payments are made in copper, bronze, or (as in Germany) nickel. Such money is called token money and differs from trading money in so far as it is legal tender *to its nominal value*, and not merely according to a varying rate of exchange. In contrast to standard money, its function as legal tender is limited to certain statutory amounts beyond which nobody is required to accept it in payment (in Sweden 20 *kr.* in 2- and 1-crown pieces and smaller sums for the smaller token money). The free minting of token money for private account is also universally forbidden, though this may also apply to the standard money, as was the case not long ago in Austria, Russia, and Holland, and at present in India. To some extent this is also true of the Latin Union, in so far as the 5-franc piece is still regarded as standard money.

If the bimetallic standard is abandoned, and nothing is done by the State to stabilize the relative market value of silver and gold, the situation must necessarily become unstable; hence silver token money and other token money must be minted below its value, i.e. will contain less of the precious metal than corresponds to its nominal value according to the average market price of silver. If it were of full value, its metallic value would sometimes exceed its nominal value; in other words, the weight of silver actually contained in the coin would be worth more in the market than the weight of gold which its nominal and legal value represents. In such case it would be profitable to melt down the token money and sell or export it, and a shortage of token money would arise, however much might be minted at the cost of the State. That is the reason why in England in 1816, and later on in 1865 in the Latin Union, and in 1873 in Germany and Scandinavia, the actual silver token money was minted with a lower content of silver. In Sweden, for example, as has been pointed out, since the bimetallic ratio remained, 1 kg. of pure silver ought to have been worth 2480 : 15½ = 160 *kr*. In reality, however, a 1-*krona* piece contains only 6 gr. pure silver, so that 167 silver kronor would be required to make up 1 kg. of pure silver.

From these figures, however, it appears that more considerable variations as between gold and silver were not expected. But, actually, the fall in silver rendered all precautions ineffective; even the so-called full-weight silver coinage, such as the 5-franc pieces, now have a metallic value of not even half their face value. A 1-*krona* piece, if melted down, is now worth about 40 *öre*. Forged silver money, or, more correctly, illegally minted money containing the usual amount of silver, would therefore be a profitable business. Small-scale forgery is, however, prevented by the form and design of the currency. On a large scale it could scarcely fail to attract attention, for "minting works are rather noisy".

On the other hand, there is no fear that token money may drive out standard money, for the State has power to limit the minting of the former to what is strictly required—which it must do if the whole currency system of the country is not to be endangered. To give token money limited legal tender only, as is done by the English currency laws, although putting a brake on excessive minting, is not in itself of great importance if—in Sweden—the State exchanges token money freely for gold money and the Central Bank is compelled to exchange it for notes.

If, in conclusion, we endeavour to survey the developments outlined above, it becomes clear that great success has been achieved in the solution of that part of the monetary problem which consists in the maintenance of uniformity of currency both in space and time. Instead of the multitude of more or less worn and debased coinages which previously existed—to remedy which it was sometimes necessary to withdraw metallic money altogether—we now have a few types, easily surveyed, with which it is possible—with the help of modern regulations as to minimum weight and the obligation to redeem—to secure a purely automatic replacement of the supplies withdrawn. Thus the earlier irresistible temptation to debasement is removed. By the concession of free minting of the standard coins for a small charge, or no charge at all, an essential parity between the minted and the unminted metal is preserved ; this materially assists international payments. Since, moreover, one metal (gold) has become standard in nearly all countries, the last obstacle has been removed and one may almost say that in modern times all countries possessing a metallic currency have the same money. Whether or not the sacrifice of the free minting of silver was unnecessary and injurious is another question, into which we do not propose to enter here.

But so far we have approached no nearer to the solution of the most difficult problem of currency, namely the preservation of a stable and constant value in terms of goods and services. Even the most careful attention to everything which maintains the full weight of a coinage will not prevent that coinage from falling in value if the production of the precious metals is substantially increased, or the development of credit renders existing supplies unnecessarily great. And, vice versa, if a shortage of precious metals should occur which could not be made good by the increased velocity of circulation occasioned by credit methods, the careful maintenance of a full weight currency would prevent the stabilization of the value of money rather than promote it. Our next duty must therefore be to study carefully the influence on currency of these factors, viz. the increased or diminished velocity of circulation, especially by credit and banking operations. We shall undertake this task, after first glancing at currency from the legal point of view.

6. *Money from the Legal Point of View*

Like most other forms of wealth, money may be the object of legal disputes. Indeed these are of daily occurrence, since most claims to wealth assume the form of money. On the other hand, it is only rarely that money itself—its substance, exchange value, etc.—is the real subject of such legal disputes. Under an ordered currency system, there is practically only one case in which that occurs—i.e. in the transition from one standard to another, in the adoption of new or dissolution of old currency standards, etc. It then becomes a question as to what extent business agreements, forms of indebtedness, and other legal transactions existing before such changes, are influenced by them, and especially to what extent regulations of the above kind are retrospective in action as regards these pre-existing legal obligations.

That states have frequently given such retrospective action to their currency laws is shown by the expression "forced exchange", which usually implies that those who have monetary claims must be content to accept payment in what is perhaps a more or less depreciated paper currency at its nominal value. But it does not follow from this that such procedure is always fair or just; still less is it clear how such questions should be adjudged when explicit regulations on the point are lacking.

An interesting example of this kind occurred in 1873 in connection with Germany's transition from a silver to a gold standard. Certain Austrian railways had issued debenture bonds in Germany payable both in Austrian gulden and German thaler (both silver currencies) the ratio of whose metallic content was 2 : 3. In passing over to the gold standard the German currency law enacted that a gold 10-mark piece should be equivalent to 3½ thaler, and this agreed with the market value of gold and silver at that time. After 1873, however, the value of silver in terms of gold sank rapidly and the difficult question then arose whether the Austrian debtors were obliged to pay their German creditors in gold. The contract had been entered into before the transition to the gold standard was even contemplated in Germany and there was no stipulation as regards eventual payment in any currency metal other than silver, or as to whether the debt should be regarded as consisting only of the quantity of silver which was contained in the specified number of thalers or gulden at the time of the contract. The creditors claimed the former, and the debtors naturally claimed the latter. In the lawsuits which ensued, the Austrian courts all decided in favour of the Austrian claims and the German courts, with one exception, in favour of the claims of their countrymen. Helfferich, himself a German, associated himself with the majority of the German courts on the ground that the legal currency of a country should not be confused with the amount of metal it contains, even if, in consequence of free minting, the two are practically identical in value. He urged that the currency, or unit of currency, of a country is what the authorities decide that it shall be, and those who enter into business contracts without precisely stipulating the kind of money which is to be offered in payment must submit to any chance variations in the standard. They resemble two persons who have entered into a contract in which the determination of certain conditions is left to a third person. The argument seems to me somewhat specious because, among other things, the third person cannot in this case be regarded as fully emancipated. It would undoubtedly be very convenient for a debtor country to effect payment on a standard depreciation of one-half, and also for a country with large claims abroad to demand payment in a currency of double value. On the other hand, the pure metallic theory cannot always be sustained, as for example where the debt is contracted during a period when the currency of the country consists of depreciated paper money. In any case it is certain that this theory, and also the one defended by Helfferich, might give an unfair advantage to either creditor or debtor at the expense of the other. This would be true in the case of Austria and Germany, since it could be shown that silver had depreciated while gold remained constant in value in terms of goods. Inevitably, therefore, we are led back to the postulate which appears to underlie every monetary agreement, namely the presumption of the stability of the value of money. If this is lacking, and if the court is unable (which it almost always is) to ascertain to what extent the exchange value of money has changed during any period, then its decisions in matters of this kind must always appear somewhat arbitrary.

Although the Scandinavian countries went over from silver

to gold at about the same time as Germany, there have not been, so far as I know, any similar conflicts—with the exception of Sweden's differences with Finland before it went over to the gold standard in 1878. This was probably due to the fact that neither had claims against countries on the silver standard and neither considered it advisable to repudiate their debts in a different exchange from the one previously accepted.

Finally, there may arise the question of the obligation of the State in respect of money which has been called in and which has ceased to be legal tender; and especially in respect of the internal obligations of contracting parties to a currency union, when the union is dissolved. It is reasonable to demand that the State should redeem such money as it calls in, although in the case of a depreciated paper money it need not go farther than to redeem it at the value which it actually possessed in circulation at the time of redemption or in the immediately preceding years.[1]

As regards the internal obligations of the State, one must carefully distinguish between the case where the coinage is minted at a depreciated value *ab initio*, i.e. for the account of the State; and the case where free minting is permitted for private account. In the former case it is scarcely possible to evade the liability of each state to redeem its own coinage, and indeed no other procedure, so far as we know, has ever been suggested—even though such a redemption might be the consequence of a fall in the value of the metal involving unforeseen losses. The case

[1] Redemption at the face value would yield the accidental holder of depreciated paper money an unearned profit. In principle, however, all debts including the debts of the State in paper money, should, in my opinion, be redeemed at the value of the date of the contract.

In the "Errata and Additions" appended to the German edition, Wicksell develops the principle, which he defended vigorously and persistently in his speeches and writings during the World War, that the changes in the value of money in Sweden between 1914 and 1923 rendered necessary comprehensive compensation, as between public and private debtors and creditors; so that anybody who, for example, had lent Kr. 1,000 at the beginning of 1914 and had them repaid at the beginning of 1919, when the purchasing power of the krona was greatly reduced, should receive compensation by an amount proportionate to the reduced purchasing power of the krona (i.e. as if the loan had been Kr. 3,000); whereas the person who lent Kr. 1,000 at the beginning of 1919 should have his debt reduced in proportion to the increased value of money (to, for example, Kr. 500).—[Ed. Swedish Edition.]

is different where money has been freely coined *ab initio*; for example, the 5-franc pieces in the Latin Union continued to be freely coined until the fall in the value of silver made a restriction of free minting necessary. Meanwhile, owing to various circumstances, money had been minted in entirely different quantities by the respective states of the Union. Switzerland had not coined any such money, Belgium, on the other hand, had minted a considerably larger quantity than was needed by its population. But since the Belgian State Mint had only benefited the public, and anybody, whether of Belgian nationality or not, could have such coins minted, it seems scarcely reasonable to expect that the Belgian State should redeem at their face value all the 5-franc pieces bearing its imprint. The question has been debated at length within the Latin Union and it has been decided that, in the event of the dissolution of the Union, each State shall be responsible for the currency bearing its imprint—a decision which, with Helfferich, we regard as a solution not in full accord with the principles of currency. For the rest, we refer the reader both on this point and on the legal aspects of currency in general, to Helfferich's exhaustive and, in most respects, correct account.

It is very evident that the cause of all legal disputes concerning money is to be found in the unforeseen changes in its exchange value. We see therefore more clearly than ever the sovereign importance of the stability of money through time, though all efforts to secure such stability would appear vain so long as metals are used as standards of value and free minting of the standard money on private account is permitted.

III

THE VELOCITY OF CIRCULATION OF MONEY. BANKING AND CREDIT.

BIBLIOGRAPHY.—Since the following exposition will be primarily theoretical in character, we must necessarily refer to the works which describe more or less exhaustively the actual working of the money market, especially in our own day. Among them, in the Scandinavian languages, we must note W. Scharling's extremely well-written *Bankpolitik* ; Aschehoug's already cited work, ch. 62 et seq. ; J. Leffler, " Krediten och Bankväsendet " (in *Ekonomiska Samhällslivet*) ; Davidson, *Europas Centralbanker* and essays in *Ekonomisk Tidskrift* ; Goschen, *Foreign Exchanges.* Among the many foreign works on the subject, the English are especially remarkable for richness of content and concise treatment. The English money market remains the model for other countries. We will only mention here the smaller textbooks by Clare, *A Key to the Money Market*, *Money Market Primer* and *The ABC of the Foreign Exchanges* ; Withers, *The Meaning of Money*, *Stocks, Shares and Debentures*, and *Money Changing*, and particularly Bagehot's *Lombard Street*—a work which, although not up to date, is unsurpassed from the point of view of exposition.

For a deeper study of practical banking and stock exchange questions there are numerous relevant articles in Conrad's *Handwörterbuch*, in which guidance is given to the literature of the subject.

1. *On Velocity of Circulation in General. Cash Balances and Credit*

Unlike goods, which, with every purchase and sale, advance one step further on the road from producer to consumer, and which usually leave the market when a transaction is completed, money (to use the common expression) *remains* in the market. As we have already pointed out, however, this is not entirely true, unless the seller who has received the money remains there also, and in turn becomes a purchaser. If he withdraws from the market or remains there only as a seller, then the purchasing power and the exchange function of the money will be latent; it will, for the moment, cease to function as a medium of exchange, but will remain in his safe as a store of value. The period during which any piece of money is on an average retained in the safe, between a sale and a subsequent purchase, may be called the average period of idleness; and the inverted value of this period of time, expressed as a unit (say a year) will be the average velocity of circulation. In other words, if a piece of money on an average lies untouched for a month at a time, then it will circulate (change owners) twelve times a year. This velocity of circulation is twelve (times per annum) when its period of idleness is one-twelfth (year). Included in the circulation of money is, of course, the transfer of money from one person to another by means of loans or advances. In dealing with certain questions, however, it is necessary to treat exchange and loan transactions separately and to consider the circulation of money in the narrower sense as relating only to the former. Which usage is meant will, as a rule, be clear from the context without special reference.

Theoretically, therefore, the concept of velocity of circulation is a very simple one. But in practice its investigation is one of the most difficult problems in economics, because, among other things, the velocity of circulation varies so enormously with each portion of the monetary stock of a country; and even with every single coin. Unfortunately, a number of economists, including the otherwise admirable James Mill and John Stuart Mill, have tended to obscure the problem by the assertion that time has nothing to do with the velocity of circulation of money: it consists rather of the number of times a certain quantity of money must change hands in order to effect the turnover of a certain quantity of goods. But with this thesis the whole concept vanishes: in order to determine the velocity of circulation in this sense we must know the actual prices of the goods (or, what comes to the same thing, the exchange value of money);

and the average velocity of circulation would only be another name for that. On the other hand, if we regard velocity of circulation in the sense we have described above, it really becomes an important independent factor in the regulation of the prices of goods. That the velocity of circulation really has, or at least can have, entirely independent significance it is not difficult to show. If, for technical reasons, purchase and sale could only be effected every half-year by the same person—e.g. if rural products were offered only in the autumn, urban products and colonial products only in the spring, and credit were unknown—then money would evidently lie idle every time for half a year. It would therefore have to be sufficient in quantity to equal one-half of the total value of the goods offered in a year, and either commodity prices or the quantity of money available and necessary, or the extent of money transactions relative to transactions in kind—or all three simultaneously—would have to be regulated in accordance with this fact. That the velocity of circulation of money, under present conditions, is somewhat variable is a separate matter. But of course it does not destroy the conception, even though it affects the influence of velocity of circulation as a factor in the determination of value.

The longer the average period during which a piece of money lies idle before it is used, the greater, obviously, will be the cash holdings relative to the annual turnover. It might even be said that the magnitude of the cash holdings relative to the total annual turnover is in inverse proportion to the average velocity of circulation of money. On the other hand, the absolute amount of cash necessary for each individual will clearly depend on the magnitude of his individual turnover. For the economy as a whole, the absolute total of cash holdings will be the same as the quantity of money in the country, and therefore constant if the latter quantity undergoes no change.

Example.—A wholesaler in a northern seaport purchases his stocks of coffee, spices, grain, herrings, American bacon, etc., annually, and sells them again in small parcels to retailers. On the average throughout the year, his cash holdings will then be—or rather should be in a cash business—about half as great as his turnover. The retail trader, again, who perhaps replenishes his stocks once a month, only requires a maximum cash holding of one-twelfth of his turnover—if sales are gradual, on an average only one-twenty-fourth of it. In the same way, the owner of a sawmill who ships the whole of his annual output at once and then pays his workmen week by week would require (assuming cash transactions) an average cash holding of about half his annual turnover; whilst the workmen would, as a rule, use up their wages in a few days and would therefore, on the average, have very small cash holdings in relation to their total annual expenditure. If we assume for the sake of simplicity that these two businesses balance each other—the wholesaler buys up the timber exporter's foreign bills of exchange and the workmen make their purchases from the retailer—then it is easy to see that, during the course of the year, every piece of money will change hands four times—and has consequently been idle, on the average, a quarter of a year between each transaction. The whole of the money in circulation, which we will call a, corresponds partly to the value of all the timber exports, partly to total wages and partly to imported goods, but when this is bought and sold twice the total turnover will be $4a$. With more exact calculation, it will be easy to see that, under our assumptions, the cash holdings of the wholesaler during the twelve business months will be successively, $0, \frac{1}{12}a, \frac{2}{12}a, \frac{3}{12}a$ and for the last month $\frac{11}{12}a$, or on the average $\frac{11}{24}a$; the retailer's $\frac{1}{24}a$, the sawmill owner's similarly $\frac{51}{104}a$, and the workmen's combined, $\frac{1}{104}a$; corresponding to an average period of idleness of the money they hold of $(11 + 10 + 9 \ldots + 2 + 1) \div 12 = 5\frac{1}{2}$ months ($\frac{11}{12}$ of a year) for the wholesaler, $\frac{1}{2}$ a month for the retailer, $25\frac{1}{2}$ weeks for the sawmill owner, and $\frac{1}{2}$ a week for the workmen. The total of the cash holdings will be unchanged ($= a$) and the total period of idleness 1 year, thus on an average for the four groups $\frac{1}{4}$ year.

An increase in the velocity of circulation might occur if, for example, the timber exporter lent the importer his bills of exchange against weekly payments, according as the latter received payment from the retailer, who in his turn would repay as and when he received payment from the workmen. In that case the necessary volume of money might be reduced to $\frac{1}{52}a$, and since the total turnover remains the same ($4a$) the velocity of circulation would be 208 (times per annum). The average period of idleness would therefore now be one-quarter of a week. And this is correct, for, under these conditions, the money would pass in one week from the timber manufacturer to his workmen, from them to the retailer, from him (by payments for goods delivered) to the wholesaler, and back again to the timber manufacturer in repayment of his loan.

Other things being equal, therefore, the more the individual succeeds in reducing the volume of his necessary cash holdings, the more he has contributed to increasing the velocity of circulation of money, and the less will be the part of the existing stocks of money which he will require for his own turnover. If his example is followed by many others, the monetary needs of the whole country will be reduced in a corresponding degree. From the individual's point of view, each step involves a saving both of capital and interest, and the same is true of a particular country as against other countries. For the world as a whole, the principal advantage of such a saving of money is that the production of the precious metals, which now absorbs a not insignificant part of the labour and capital of the human race, may be restricted, and the productive power thus set free employed for more useful purposes.

In the above example, the timber manufacturer was compelled to advance the value of the whole of his annual production, a, in goods or money, and the importer was forced to engage capital in his business in the form of goods or money to the amount of a. By the credit operation referred to above the amount of both of these capital sums is reduced to about a half. The manufacturer now requires for his business only the minimum and indispensable amount of capital $= \frac{1}{2}a$ (corresponding to the average time between each employment of labour and the sale of the completed goods). The remainder of the capital he transfers, at interest, to the importer, whose minimum requirements for capital are in fact also only $\frac{1}{2}a$ (corresponding to the average time between the harvest or the importing of goods and their sale) and who need not now provide his own capital. The gain to both is the interest on the whole of the money, *a*, which can now (except for an insignificant part) be employed abroad, and which was at one time imported into the country against a final sacrifice of capital goods to the value of *a*.

To a certain extent, changes in the velocity of circulation are undoubtedly purely automatic, as a result of superfluity or shortage of money, by which the existing stocks adapt themselves to the changing needs of trade. Everybody who happens to be short of money will, as far as possible, postpone his purchases until the time when he has money—and must do so unless he can procure credit—or he may, perhaps, be driven to forced sales of his goods or other assets in order to procure money. He may call upon a customer where otherwise he would have waited for the customer to call on him, etc. In the latter case, there will be an immediate increase in the velocity of circulation. In the former case, owing to his postponement, the owners of the goods which he would otherwise have bought will also become short of money and must postpone their own purchases. If, finally, the first in this chain of interdependent persons obtains some money, then in quick succession *A* will buy from *B*, *B* from *C*, *C* from *D*, and so on. The circulation of money has obviously been quickened. The opposite would be the case if money became too plentiful and tended to lie longer than usual in the form of cash holdings. But evidently this automatic regulation of the velocity of circulation of money has a definite, though elastic, limit. Every postponement of an essential or desirable purchase occasions some discomfort or loss; every premature or untimely sale occasions a pressure on prices corresponding to the purchaser's less pressing need for the goods—a pressure which the seller of course tries to avoid.

A partial remedy for a shortage of money—using the term in its real sense and not as synonymous with a general absence of means—has been sought from earliest times in arrangements by which buyers and sellers must meet in larger numbers, especially at fairs and markets, where the circulation of money is automatically stimulated; and in the use of credit. A person who wants to buy, but has no money for the moment, asks for postponement of payment—buys, as the expression is, on credit. Or else he borrows money for his purchases in order to avoid postponement, and, not least, in order to be able to retain his own goods until a suitable purchaser is found. In this manner there is constantly being formed, on a larger or smaller scale at various points in the community, a credit nexus : *A* has bought on credit from *B*, *B* from *C*, *C* from *D*, and so on. If, by selling his goods for cash or by an advance from a third person, *A* obtains money, the nexus is rapidly dissolved. *A* pays *B*, *B C*, *C D* and so on, all with the same result—an increase in the velocity of circulation. Thus, as we have several times remarked, credit is a very powerful, indeed the most powerful, means of quickening the circulation of money. This fact has perhaps not been sufficiently emphasized by economists. As a rule, they take into consideration only the extreme cases in which credit renders money superfluous by making a transfer of receipts for payments and debts do service as a medium of payment. In the numerous cases, again, in which a credit obligation is discharged by a cash payment, it is often said that credit does not reduce the need for money, but only postpones its use to a later date. Yet, as a rule, that is the same thing as diminishing the need for money. So long as the credit obligation lasts, the need for money is actually less than it would have been because, if the purchase had been made for cash, the seller, other things being equal, would have had the money lying in his safe until he himself wished to make a purchase; whereas now the same amount of money can circulate elsewhere. We shall shortly return to those cases in which the use of credit makes hard cash quite superfluous.

If we now suppose that the various forms of credit were used only as a corrective to an occasional shortage of the medium of exchange, even then changes in the velocity of circulation would be in effect automatic, self-regulating, and would tend to cancel out fluctuations in the amount of money (either absolutely or relatively to the turnover requirements) which might arise for one reason or another in a country. The available money, in the widest sense--i.e. the quantity multiplied by the velocity of circulation—would be constant; or, more correctly, would vary in proportion to the volume of transactions, so that prices would not, on this account, undergo any change. But, as everybody knows, this does not happen. *The gain, individual and social, obtained from every saving in the medium of exchange or of future payment constitutes a spur to invention and habitual use of a number of forms of credit which finally become an integral part of the mechanism of trade.* At every stage in commercial progress, therefore, we note a new, and generally higher, average velocity of circulation of the medium of exchange, which does not subsequently decrease, and which cannot be increased without inconvenience. The practical consequences, as regards the need for money and the exchange value of money, are counteracted partly by the fact that economic progress is accompanied by an increase in the total turnover, partly by increasing population and prosperity, and particularly because trade *in natura* is more and more replaced by trade based on exchange and the division of labour.

We need not discuss the truth of the contention that the use of credit in its various forms is more pronounced in times of monetary shortage than at other times, and that, therefore, it is more active in maintaining an already existing price-level than in raising it. The difference need not in the end be great, since periods of shortage and superfluity usually alternate, and if here, as elsewhere, necessity is the mother of invention, it is scarcely probable that when once the credit system has been expanded during a period of shortage of money, a subsequent superfluity would lead to a return to the more primitive system of cash payment. Whether a higher standard of living would itself create a tendency to maintain larger cash reserves is quite another matter. This Helfferich maintains to be true of France —whose stocks of money are notoriously enormous, and where money bags and bundles of notes (for which full metallic cover is kept at the banks) play the same role as bills of exchange, letters of credit, cheque books and notes with ordinary banking cover in other countries. To a certain extent this may be the case, but it is probable that we are here concerned with some national peculiarity, probably strengthened by the unfortunate experiences in the field of banking and credit which that country has so frequently had in the past.

Apart from the steady underlying progress in the direction of a more rapid circulation of money, there have occurred periodic fluctuations arising out of the exaggerated use of credit and followed by a reaction known as a credit or money crisis, which arises from a lack of confidence between individuals, rendering difficult or impossible the use of even ordinary credit instruments. But these occasional disturbances, however serious they may sometimes be, must not be allowed to distract our attention from the progressive development in the use of credit and the economizing of metallic currency.

2. *Virtual Velocity of Circulation*

We have already remarked by way of introduction that the influence of credit on currency may, *under all circumstances*, be regarded as accelerating the circulation of money. This point of view should be kept clearly in mind, for it imparts to an otherwise somewhat complicated subject a high degree of simplicity. The occasions on which credit actually replaces money and thereby renders it superfluous may, quite simply, be regarded as special cases of the general acceleration of circulation; for instead of a purely physical transfer of money we have a *virtual*, i.e. a merely imaginary or possible transfer, but of the same effectiveness. We shall illustrate this point by some examples.

Suppose a person buys goods to the value of 10*s.* and pays with a ten shilling note. It is said here (and quite correctly) that the note functions as a means of payment instead of money, by which we mean only hard cash. This, however, is not the only, or even the most important, function of the note in this case. The actual payment might very well have been made in hard cash and the notes might still have found useful employment if, for example, both parties had gone to the issuing bank and the buyer had exchanged his note for a half-sovereign and paid the seller with this. The seller would then pay in the gold piece over the counter and receive the same note in exchange. However inconvenient and unnecessary this procedure may appear, it was in fact the earliest method of using banknotes. And, what is more important, it is precisely in this way that banknotes perform essentially the same service as they now do in economizing cash; in both cases, *in the interval between purchase and sale* they lie in pocket-books or safes *as cash reserves or as a store of value* in place of hard cash. The half-sovereign, which only left the bank's till for a moment, might immediately have circulated to and fro across the counter again. It would thus have had an extremely rapid actual circulation, consisting of: (1) the discharge of the bank's obligation to pay, as expressed on the note; (2) the discharge of a payment for goods between buyer and seller; (3) a new deposit in the bank against the obligation to repay on demand, etc. The circulation of the notes outside the bank may thus be regarded as a *virtual*, i.e. imaginary, but in any case physically, or at least logically, possible circulation of one or more coins lying in the bank's keeping.

A current account at the bank is equally important, payments being effected by transferring deposits at the bank. The transfer in the bank's books, which is the only visible record of the transaction, might equally well have been accompanied by the actual circulation of money, i.e. by a withdrawal of hard cash from the bank, a subsequent discharge of a debt in cash, and a further deposit in the bank. That this does not actually happen is of secondary importance. The real saving of currency lies in the circulation of business at the bank, so that, as we shall soon see, its cash may be considerably less than the amount of its obligations.

Or let us look at an ordinary three-months trade bill, which instead of being discounted at a bank circulates as a medium of payment among merchants; this practice was much more common in the past than it is now. If the bill of exchange, or some corresponding credit instrument, had not existed, then clearly the amount of money which it represents would have lain in the safes of the successive holders for a total length of three months. That is now unnecessary. In other words, the quantity of money which now suffices for the total circulation during these three months would have been insufficient but for the existence of the bill of exchange. Actual payments might, however, still have been made with ready money and the bill would have served the same uses as now. We can conceive, for example, that the drawing and endorsing of the bill (which, before payment was madé, did not absolve absolutely from liability) constituted not the transfer of a claim but a promise of cash payment on the date of maturity. The result would have been that, on this date, the acceptor would have paid the drawer, the latter the first endorser, he the second endorser, and so on, so that the money would remain with the last holder—just as does in fact happen. The saving of money during the three months, and the importance of the bill as a security and as a cash reserve, would have been equally great in both cases

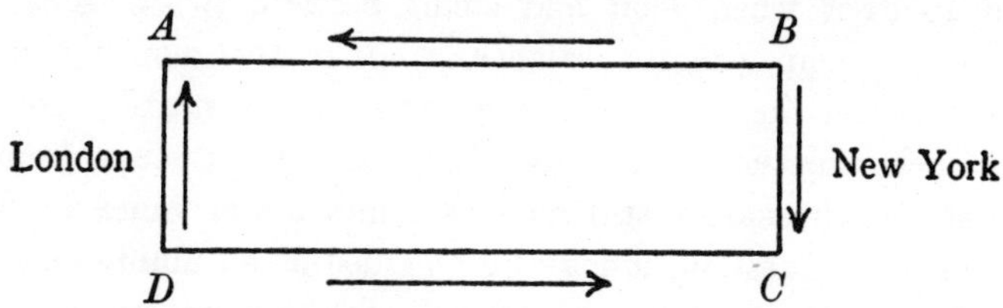

Finally, we may take the case mentioned above, in which buyer and seller are in different places, or different countries. Here payment (in ready money) requires a considerable time and, apart from the risk and trouble of actual transport, demands the withdrawal of a sum of money from circulation for a corresponding period. The real function of credit here is to create claims which, being immaterial, can be transferred from place to place unimpeded by limitations of space. For example *A* in London has a claim for £1,000 against *B* in New York, and *C* in New York has a claim for an equal amount against *D* in London. Instead of allowing two payments of the same amount to cross each other in mid-Atlantic, *A* and *C*, with the consent of *B* and *D*, exchange their claims, so that the money in question only needs to traverse the shorter distance between two business houses in London; and similarly in New York. In actual life this is accomplished, as we know, by a bill of exchange. B buys a bill which C has drawn on D—by which C is paid—and sends this bill in payment to A, who on the due date recovers payment from D. Here also it may be said that the velocity of circulation has been virtually accelerated since two payments at a shorter distance have been substituted for two at a longer distance.

All these cases relate to a series of obligations to pay which can be *surveyed* by the interested parties themselves and which can be replaced by one or more simpler transactions, just as in mechanics a polygon of forces or a corresponding series of transfers in space is replaced by the diagonal of the polygon. Thus in mechanics also it is usual to speak of virtual transfers; and just as mechanical equilibrium is achieved when the virtual transfers yield a resultant of nil, so economic equilibrium can be said to exist when debit and credit between two persons or within a group exactly balance, so that the money which would cancel these claims would revert to its starting point. If in such cases the use of ready money becomes quite superfluous, whilst metallic money still remains a measure of value for the payments in question, it may be regarded as an infinitesimally small amount of money circulated with infinite velocity in accordance with the formula $0 \times \infty$ (nil multiplied by infinity), which according to circumstances may signify any quantity whatever.

3. *Forms of Credit*

We shall now consider the various forms of credit and their importance for money. It is clear that simple *credit*, as between individuals, has only a very limited influence as a substitute for money tending to accelerate the velocity of circulation. Here the discharge of claims or debts as well as the exchange or transfer of claims is only the exception. Credit for goods is certainly very common between individuals, but it is combined, especially over longer periods, with difficulties and risks. Finally, loans of money between individuals, as we shall show, can never occur to such an extent that they make cash holdings superfluous. The functions of cash holdings, as has been pointed out, are twofold; or, more correctly, every cash holding consists of two parts, (1) cash in the literal sense, ready cash, for meeting foreseen but not immediate expenses, and (2) reserves for unforeseen expenses. In the latter may also be included money saved and awaiting profitable investment. Obviously I can only lend the former if I am certain of getting my money back at the right time, when my anticipated need for the money arises. But this period is usually too short to be of any advantage to the borrower. Still less, of course, can I lend my reserve unless I am confident of my ability to borrow at the same or even better terms in case of need. In addition there is the risk that I may not recover my money at all, a risk which cannot be measured by the mathematical law of probability; a loss of Kr. 1,000 for a person of small means is undoubtedly more than one hundred times as great as a loss of Kr. 10. The former might bring him into great distress, indeed ruin his economic position. Compensation by way of interest, even if, objectively, it fully covers the risk he runs, or thinks he runs, can therefore not cover it subjectively. For these reasons then, in countries where organized credit, banking, and stock exchange facilities are comparatively undeveloped, the necessary cash holdings will be many times greater and the turnover will require large quantities of money.

In civilized countries this is especially the case. In France P. Leroy-Beaulieu estimated some years ago the whole metallic currency of France at 8½ milliard francs, whilst the whole national income, corresponding to the total value of the goods and services annually consumed, were estimated at 25 milliard francs. Even if we assumed, with Leroy-Beaulieu, that these values, i.e. of the necessaries represented by income, including raw materials and depreciation were turned over three or four times, which seems to me excessive, then the average velocity of circulation of money would scarcely exceed one purchase and one sale per month for each coin. In Great Britain the volume of money is much less, certainly not half as great—even though the English banks have recently kept much larger gold reserves than was formerly customary—and the total amount of business considerably greater, so that the velocity of circulation is much higher owing to the highly developed organization of credit.

Organized credit tends to reduce risks by spreading them over a wider area; the subjective element of risk disappears in proportion as the wealth which affords the guarantee is great in relation to the amount at stake, so that only the mathematical risk remains. In this way, and also through the centralization of credit facilities, it helps to make loan transactions safe and convenient. The very documentation of credit transactions in the form of credit instruments, their transfer to others and eventual conversion into claims for payment, valid in the hands of each holder, creates a powerful organization which it has required thousands of years to develop. Every recipient of such a credit instrument usually takes over at the same time the risk of non-payment, though perhaps only for a shorter period, since he counts on passing on his claim at an early date to another. In ordinary business transactions security, and therefore its range of application as a means of credit, is increased partly by quicker execution, partly by the fact that each new endorsement, each new name on the bill, is as a rule a new guarantee for the regular honouring of the bill. In this way not only is the risk of the recipient of the bill reduced, but he is enabled at any moment to dispose of or to obtain money for it. In other words, the bill of exchange, if it bears good names, serves almost as well as a cash reserve as actual ready money. In this manner, especially in earlier times, bills of exchange drawn for business transactions between the great trading houses were used during the period before maturity in ever widening circles as a common medium of payment, whilst being successively covered with a mass of names, for which there was often not enough room on the back of the bill, and which were guarantees that the last holder, whoever he might be and whatever happened to the acceptor, would certainly get his money.

4. *Banking. Some historical notes on the origin of banking*

The highest forms of credit organization, however, are the stock exchange and banking system, especially the latter. Here we shall make no more than occasional reference to stock exchange activities. The real concern of the Stock Exchange is with long term credit, fixed capital investments, government stocks, shares, etc., whereas the credit directly associated with money as a medium of exchange is short term credit, and is the immediate concern of the banks. Yet it should be noted that the boundary line between the two is fluctuating. Just as it is the function of the banks to consolidate short credit, in other words, to create as it were one long credit out of a number of short credits, so, on the other hand, it is the function of Stock Exchange speculations, which are so often misunderstood, to mobilize fixed capital by creating a permanent market for long term capital investments, and, like every other credit organization, in the dual form of centralization and insurance against risk. In our days banking and stock exchange activities merge into one another more and more as a medium of exchange and payment, especially in international settlements.

We must, therefore, devote all the more attention to the banks, which are in fact the heart and centre of modern currency systems.

The origin of banks is not known with certainty. We may take it for granted that banking operations, i.e. the combining of the borrowing and lending of money, have been conducted by wealthy persons since the earliest times. A speech of Demosthenes (Phormio) is often quoted, from which it appears that such banking operations were conducted by wealthy people in Athens. Similarly, in *The Captive* of Plautus we read,

> " subducam ratiunculam
> quantillum argenti mihi apud trapezitam siet."

A " trapezita " (trapeza = table) was a person who received money on deposit, though it does not appear from the passage whether he paid interest on it. In the Middle Ages such movements of money were frequently associated with the functions of the *money-changers*, of which the name (bill of) exchange is a survival. In London the goldsmiths were the first bankers and dealt extensively in money at the time of the foundation of the Bank of England. On the other hand, the large banks which arose in the Middle Ages in Italy and in Northern Europe at the beginning of the seventeenth century (in Venice, Genoa, Amsterdam and Hamburg) had, initially at any rate, quite different functions from those of modern banks. Their chief task was to provide for a full-weight currency of guaranteed metallic content, or in other words a medium of exchange. Thus as regards the Hamburg Bank (1609–1873), the Hamburg mark banco was an ideal coin, of a certain weight of fine silver, which did not circulate, and which individuals deposited in the bank, and which the latter undertook to repay in the same weight of fineness. The great Hamburg merchants made it a condition of their sales that all payments to them should be made in this currency, and they discharged their debts to each other by means of drafts on their deposits at the bank. Such a bank was called a giro bank (giro = circle, in their case a circle of customers), but as it did not (in its original form, at least) lend out its deposits, it could therefore not pay interest, but on the other hand made a small charge on the deposits. These operations, therefore, did not lead to any economy in the use of hard cash. The sole function of the banks was, as has been said, to maintain the value of the currency; and this was difficult enough in times of incessant currency debasement, especially in the case of such a conglomeration of States as existed in Germany, where each one claimed the right to mint its own money. The other older giro banks had operated in the same manner. But one of the results of this system was that masses of money lay idle and useless. It frequently happened, therefore, that Governments utilized these assets in times of monetary difficulty by borrowing them from the banks, thus causing the money to return into circulation, either *in corpore* or in the form of deposit certificates which did not correspond to actual deposits in the banks. In effect, and contrary to the original plan, the banks became credit institutions, instruments for increasing the supplies of a medium of exchange, or for imparting to the total stock of money, an increased velocity of circulation, physical or virtual. Giro banking continued as before, though no actual stock of money existed to correspond with the total of deposit certificates. So long, however, as people continued to believe that the existence of money in the banks was a necessary condition of the convertibility of the deposit certificates, these loans had to remain a profound secret. If they were discovered the bank lost the confidence of the public and was ruined, especially if the discovery was made at a time when the Government was not in a position to repay the advances.

The history of the Amsterdam bank is remarkable in this respect. It was founded in 1609 and was intended from the beginning to be a pure giro bank, without the right to lend any of its deposits. Gradually, however, the curious custom mentioned by Adam Smith arose, by which the bank issued against deposits of metallic money or bullion receipts on the production of which the money could be recovered, and documents which certified a credit at the bank, *bank money* so-called, which could be used in all payments to the bank and consequently circulated between individuals as a means of payment throughout the country. The receipts, again, had to be renewed every six months and the prescribed commission paid, otherwise they lapsed and the money deposited became the property of the bank. The " bank money ", on the other hand, retained its character as a bank liability and therefore continued to circulate throughout the country. Consequently many merchants sold their deposit receipts or let them lapse and carried on equally well with "bank money" alone. Only when payment in metal became necessary, e.g. to foreign countries, were they obliged to procure valid deposit receipts, which could usually be obtained on the market at prices varying with demand and supply. The bank, again, regarded the lapsed money as its own property and considered itself free to lend it without any restriction. But in this way a corresponding amount of " bank money " was converted into mere credit notes without any metallic cover. It appears to have been the obscurity in this arrangement—

especially uncertainty as to the bank's obligation to redeem in regard to the amount of "bank money" in excess of the deposit receipts still valid—rather than real insolvency which brought about its downfall in 1795, when in consequence of political events its status became known for the first time.

The discovery that money deposited on a guarantee to repay on demand could be partially loaned without endangering the liquidity of the institution in question constituted, however, an important advance in banking technique, which in its turn led to the discovery of the credit note. For just as simply as deposits of money were accepted against a certificate of deposit and were then lent out to others, whilst the certificate of deposit might continue to be used by the owner as a medium of payment and be transferred to others, so also such certificates of deposit might be issued against ample security to persons who had *not* deposited any money in the bank. The result remained the same, both to the public and to the bank, provided that the solvency of the borrower and his credit status were the same in both cases. And yet in reality the latter method constitutes a further advance. If, for example, experience has shown that an amount corresponding to one-half the deposits or other credit certificates payable on demand and issued by the bank, is sufficient cover for them, then by the first method out of (say) Kr. 10 millions deposited in the bank, Kr. 5 millions might be lent and the virtual velocity of circulation would thereby be increased in the proportion of 1 : 1½. By the second method, again, the bank might issue credit notes for Kr. 10 millions for the whole cash reserve, Kr. 10 millions would remain in the bank, and would on our assumption be sufficient cover for payments of both the Kr. 10 millions deposit certificates and the Kr. 10 millions credit notes; in other words the velocity of circulation would be increased in the proportion of 1 : 2. Indeed, the gain would be still greater, for, other things being equal, the requirements of the banks grow relatively less in proportion as their business and their circle of clients increase.

The first use of the credit note is sometimes attributed (though its use is probably older) to the Palmstruch bank in

Stockholm in 1656, which later became the Swedish *Riksbank*.[1] What created the bank here was a need for some substitute for the clumsy copper which, except for an interval at the end of the reign of Charles XI and the beginning of the reign of Charles XII, remained the standard money of the country. The copper plates were deposited in the bank in exchange for certificates of deposit, which from the beginning were only valid against the bank when presented by the depositor, but which might subsequently be transferred to another person with the endorsement of the possessor—the so-called transfer notes. The difficulty in lending the copper itself probably directly led to the bank's issuing credit notes instead, i.e. deposit certificates without any corresponding deposit. If this had only been done to substantial individuals under an obligation to repay, no inconvenience might have arisen, but since the State constantly borrowed from the bank without repaying, difficulties arose which even if not responsible for the insolvency of the bank a few years after its formation, subsequently in the "Age of Liberty" led to the necessity of absolving the bank from its obligation to redeem its notes, a suspension which lasted until 1776, when they were redeemed at one-half of their face value.

It was only some years later that the Bank of England was founded. It began its career in 1694 by lending to the State the whole of its wealth, £1,200,000. In exchange for this it obtained a privilege, which at first consisted in the right to deal in money as a joint stock company with limited liability. After repeated loans to the State it was in 1708 granted the right, as a company with more than six members, to issue notes. Smaller companies and private persons had already possessed this right in England. The loans to the State have never been repaid, and the Bank's claims in this respect still constitute a considerable portion of its capital. In the strict sense of the word this bank has never been insolvent, but its metallic reserves fell so low at the beginning of the Anglo-French war that the Government saw fit in 1779 to forbid the redemption of its

[1] On this point and on what follows, cf. Sveriges Riksbank, i–ii (1918).—EDITOR.

notes in cash. This was the beginning of the restriction period, which continued until 1821, when redemption of the notes at the full value was resumed by the bank.

On the other hand the banking institution which was founded on such fantastic principles by the famous Scot, John Law, under the regency of the Duke of Orleans in France in 1716, and which for a long time brought every kind of banking enterprise into discredit in that country, came to a quick end.

As in the case of the English bank, Law obtained this privilege by making loans on a large scale to the French Government, but when the bank's means were insufficient, he endeavoured to obtain further capital by founding, at the same time, large business houses, of which the first was a trading company for the colonization of the Mississippi area. State bonds were accepted in payment of shares in this company at par, or 6 per cent above the actual rate at which they were then dealt in. The bonds were then handed over to the Treasury for cancellation. In this way the Company was almost entirely without working capital and was compelled to resort to a further issue of shares, for which payment was obtained by the bank lending money on the shares and issuing new notes to the amount of the loans. It is obvious that such procedure must soon come to a terrible end, for though the circulating metallic money of a country can be replaced by paper money, yet for the conduct of real business enterprise it is necessary to have real capital, acquired by real saving. The chief cause of the crash was, however, as in other countries at the same time (and not least in Sweden), the immoderate appetite of Governments for money and the contempt with which they placed themselves above ordinary business morals.

The only bank which carried on without severe misfortune was the Hamburg giro bank. Leroy-Beaulieu praises it in high terms and blames Bismarck for suppressing it in 1873. This praise does not, however, seem to us entirely in place. A bank conducted on such principles would be quite impossible as a modern central bank, as it is devoid of all elasticity. This proved to be the case in a fateful manner in the world crisis of

1857, which affected Hamburg severely. During the crisis the bank was bursting with metal, for everybody who possessed money or succeeded in acquiring it hastened to deposit it there, as all were afraid, under the prevailing general lack of confidence, to lend it out. Yet under its own statutes the bank was unable to assist the depressed business world by lending it.[1]

In a word, the early history of banks is the history of vague liberal principles, sometimes too narrow, sometimes absurdly exaggerated, but the bitter lessons which their history teaches us have not been in vain. Nowadays we are agreed on at least a number of points, though not on all, and we understand the real functions of these important, though sometimes dangerous, institutions.

5. *Modern Banking*

It is not my intention to give a detailed account of the technique and special forms of modern banking in different countries, but to refer the reader to the bibliography on those points. My purpose is rather to attempt to describe the theory of money, still so greatly neglected by political economists, and the great principles underlying the variable complex of monetary phenomena. We are also concerned here with banking and the system of credit, but only in so far as they influence monetary phenomena, velocity of circulation, the demand for money, the level of prices, and so on. The great part which, in addition to this, the banks play as promoters of credit, a function which may influence the whole of industrial life to a very high degree, will only be touched upon in passing.

We have already said that the old giro banks in Hamburg and Amsterdam did not originally provide credit. Lending operations were conducted by private capitalists or smaller companies, who received the capital of others for profit. In the course of development, the deposit or giro banks began to lend out deposits, and the private bankers combined

[1] The bank did, it is true, make some loans, but, so far as I know, these were restricted to loans against the security of precious metal and were in fact a kind of disguised giro transaction.

in larger groups, so far as the law permitted. In both cases there developed the modern type of bank, whose most characteristic feature is that it accepts deposits both for repayment on demand (money at call, account, current, etc.) and on notice, whilst lending as large a part of these deposits as is consistent with safety, sometimes with, and sometimes without, the concurrent issue of their own banknotes.

Another important feature is that bank deposits and bank loans are almost always short dated, e.g. three to six months. Loans for a longer period are not supposed to be part of a bank's activity—" a bank should only give the same kind of credit as it accepts " says Wagner; frequently it is forbidden by law to make long-term investments. This, however, is still a much disputed question, but without entering into the practical questions involved, it may be said that one of the most important functions of the banks is precisely to *prolong* credit, i.e. to assemble the credit which in the nature of things can only be given for a short or uncertain period of time and then because of the Law of Large Numbers, which we shall shortly consider, to convert them into more stable credit in the interests of borrowers and producers. The banks borrow sums of money repayable on demand, but they do not as a rule lend on such terms, or if they do, as in the case of the English joint stock banks, they do so only to a special class of credit middlemen, i.e. bill brokers, who themselves carry on a sort of banking business, and who in case of need can turn to the central bank, the Bank of England, to have their bills rediscounted. And even if the greater part of the loans is normally for a short period, the discounting of bills, for instance, yet in reality credit relations are made more stable by the prolongation of the bills or by the discounting of new bills for the same persons. After all, it is the rule that the bank turns away a customer whom it considers deserving of credit only if it is compelled to do so. If, on the other hand, a lender is in a position to lend his capital for a longer period, he does not require the assistance of a bank in the same degree, if at all. The borrower and the lender then have a better opportunity of getting to know each other, and the lender especially is able to inform himself concerning the nature of the business of the borrower, so that the risk is diminished or at any rate easier to estimate. Even longer dated loans, especially if they are very large, may require intermediaries, as when a State loan is floated—although it may be, and often is, effected by direct subscription—or when landowners over a larger or smaller area combine mutually to guarantee each other's loans and thereby obtain better terms (mortgage associations and mortgage banks), or when large amounts of capital, especially from abroad, must be acquired for some branch of industry, such as town building plans, etc. But all these do not enter into banking in the narrower sense. Frequently enough, however, short date borrowing and lending by banks leads to stable credit relations between individuals which are subsequently maintained without the banks' assistance. A builder, for example, with the assistance of a bank credit, may build a house which he later sells or mortgages in order to repay the loan. The persons who buy the house or grant a mortgage may perhaps previously have had money on short deposit at the same bank. In such a case they might be regarded as lenders or part owners, with the bank as an intermediary, in this transaction. The credit relation is then dissociated from the bank and becomes an independent one. In connection with bank investments the savings bank movement should be mentioned. The savings bank book, it is true, serves to some extent as a current account, but its chief purpose is to accumulate small savings which cannot be suitably invested separately in profitable enterprises, State loans (post office savings banks), mortgages on land or buildings, etc.

However important these various forms of credit may be, more important perhaps than the actual banking system, they are nevertheless far from having the same influence on currency. Credit will be created with or even without the intervention of a credit institution and will then remain possibly for decades. The money which has once effected a transaction, if indeed the latter was effected with ready money, has long since returned into circulation. But not so with short-dated loans. A person who can only dispense with his money for a few months cannot usually find a suitable borrower during that time and can still less investigate his reliability. The risk, especially the subjective risk, becomes too great, and the terms of the loan would therefore be too onerous. Without an organized regulation of credit such sums of money would therefore lie idle. A central organization where money can be borrowed at any time with the best security and at the same time where deposits are accepted at any time, then becomes of the utmost advantage. All money which can be dispensed with for however short a time ceases to be idle and credit relations (more or less indirect through the mediation of the banks) are introduced instead. For example, A, a merchant, requires goods but does not expect money for three months, when the retailer will pay him. B, a manufacturer, possesses goods, but requires money immediately for the payment of his workmen. A third person, C, possesses money but has no use for it for three months. Then A will buy goods on credit from B against a three-months bill; simultaneously C has deposited his money in the bank for three months. B discounts his bill at the bank and then obtains the money deposited by C, whom he has probably never seen or heard of before. He distributes this money among his workmen in wages and they gradually make their purchases from the retailer, who pays A in three months. A then pays the bank and the bank pays C. If, on the other hand, the bank had not existed, then either A or B would have been compelled to retain the amount in his safe and a corresponding amount would have lain idle with C. The saving in the circulating medium is, if possible, even greater when those parts of the cash reserves retained for unforeseen or current expenditure are confined to the bank. B in our example probably did not withdraw the whole sum derived from his bill of exchange, but left some standing on current account, so that one part of his money, lent by the banks at three months, also served its purpose in circulation.

At first sight it might appear that the borrowing of money which may be, and is often, reclaimed at any moment would be somewhat pointless. What can the banks do with it? it is asked. Experience shows, however,—although it has taken centuries to acquire and interpret this experience—that if the ready money of a number of individuals is aggregated in the vaults of a bank, it will lie there unused to a large extent unless the bank lends it out or makes some other use of it. The explanation of this apparent paradox is twofold. In the first place there is the Law of Large Numbers. Even if the bank's customers were entirely independent of each other, the simultaneous withdrawals of their funds by all of them, or by the majority of them, would be one of the rarest of occurrences. The rule is that, apart from certain seasonal fluctuations, withdrawals and deposits roughly balance each other from day to day, and still in accordance with the same law, the difference becomes, in proportion to the volume of the turnover, relatively less and less, even if absolutely greater, the more extensive are the bank's activities.

Starting from a simple hypothesis, incapable of proof, but confirmed by experience in the most varied fields, it has been possible to embrace all these phenomena in a mathematical law, the Law of Large Numbers, which lays it down that purely accidental variations from a certain highly probable average—e.g. an equal number of odd and even numbers in a continuous guessing of "odds and evens"—certainly increase absolutely the more often the experiment is made, but diminish relatively in proportion to the number of experiments, so that the variations increase only in the progression, 1, 2, 3, 4, 5, etc., when the number of experiments is increased in the progression 1, 4, 9, 16, 25, etc.; i.e. they increase as the square root of the number of experiments. Even with 100 such experiments the betting is even that the number of even figures will not exceed 53 or be less than 47. With 1,000 experiments there is the same probability that they will not exceed or be less than 500 ± 34.

Thus if experience shows that a business man must have a certain amount of money in hand in order to be reasonably sure that his reserves will not be exhausted within a year, then if 100 independent merchants had an account at the bank, the latter need only retain $\frac{1}{10}$ of its total deposits in hand to be insured with the same degree of probability against the exhaustion of its reserves during one year. If again the bank, for greater security, retains two, three, or four times this amount, i.e. $\frac{1}{5} - \frac{2}{5}$ of the total deposits, then the calculation shows, and experience fully confirms it, that the probabilities against exhaustion rise quickly in an enormous degree. If, for example, the betting is even that cash holdings to a certain amount will not be exhausted in a year, one can bet more than $4\frac{1}{2}$ to 1 against a holding twice as large, and 142 to 1 against a holding four times as large, being exhausted under similar conditions. In the latter case, therefore, it would not occur once in a century.

In the second place, and if possible to an even greater extent, there is the operation of the fact that the customers of a bank frequently have direct or indirect business with each other, so that a withdrawal by one of them for the purchase of goods necessarily leads within a short time to a deposit by another after the sale. If the customers are in direct business contact the money need never leave the bank at all, but payment can be made by a simple transfer from one banking account to another. If we suppose for the sake of simplicity that all such business is concentrated in a single bank with branches in all business centres throughout the country and that the keeping of a bank account has become universal, a situation rapidly being realized in Scotland, for instance, where for many years at least a fifth of the adult population possessed banking accounts, then the position in the money market will be as follows. The whole monetary stock of the country will be collected in the vaults of the bank and will be, so far as internal turnover and business activity are considered, absolutely idle. All payments will be made by cheques drawn on the payer's banking account, but these cheques will never lead to any withdrawals of money from the bank, but only to a transfer to the payee's account in the books of the bank. On the other hand, the bank cannot lend *in concreto* a farthing of the money deposited with it, because it would flow back to the bank in the form of deposits as soon as it had been used. The lending operations of the bank will consist rather in its entering in its books a fictitious deposit equal to the amount of the loan, on which the borrower may draw, whilst the actual documents, e.g. a discounted bill, will be added to the bank's securities; this is the so-called English system. Or it might open against real security or sureties a direct credit on which the borrower may draw cheques at will up to a maximum amount (the Scotch system, common also in Sweden). Thus in both cases payments will be made by successive drawings by the borrower upon his credit in the bank, and every such cheque must naturally lead to a credit with another person's (seller's) account, either in the form of a deposit paid in or of a repayment of a debt. The obligation of the bank to the public will thus still exceed its claims by the whole amount of these cash holdings, less the bank's own capital. It is true that the banks need pay little or no interest on a large part of its debts to the public, as otherwise the money would have lain idle, yet nevertheless in its own interest it will be driven to seek a useful and profitable employment for the money lying idle year after year. This cannot be done within the country, however, except possibly for the gold industry, to which we shall return later, but we may assume that the bank succeeds in lending its surplus at interest abroad. This interest, which, if the bank were a Government institution, would naturally benefit the public, will of course be the only real economic gain on the whole transaction. If subsequently, in consequence of growing population and production, or the more extended use of money, more of the medium of exchange were required, this would be obtained quite simply by the bank increasing its discounting of bills or its lending in general, by which a corresponding amount of deposits would automatically flow in. The virtual velocity of circulation would thus tend to increase to infinity. A very small quantity of money would suffice for a very large business turnover.

To avoid misunderstanding it must be observed here that the above remarks only apply to a bank or a co-ordinated system of banks which has absorbed all the monetary transactions of the country. And even so it only applies to the internal turnover. If, on the other hand, the banks are more or less isolated from each other, as is actually the case, then each bank must be very careful not to extend its credit too far. Even if every payment in the country were made by drawing on bank accounts, customers of one bank would, as a rule, have business with customers in other banks. The cheques drawn by them would thus soon pass into the hands of those other banks and would be presented by them for payment in gold, or at best the bank would obtain on its current account with the other banks the same, or a higher, rate of interest than it had itself obtained on its loans. But simultaneously the other banks would thereby have an excess of demand and might with impunity expand their credit to the public further than before. Very much the same applies to the banking system in a country taken as a whole, as against the foreign money market, as we shall soon see.

E. Jaffé in his work, *Das Englische Bankwesen* (2nd edition) makes a sharp attack on the statement of the English writer Withers that the great majority of deposits in the banks arises from the loans granted by the banks, an opinion which in Jaffé's view shows a confusion between " money as a medium of turnover " and " money as capital ". Yet formally Wither's opinion can be easily defended. Even so-called fictitious deposits are real deposits ; the borrower has acquired the right to withdraw the whole amount of the loan, and if he allows a part of it to remain in the bank, then clearly that part is obviously just as much a deposit in the bank as if it had been made by a third person. If the borrower had withdrawn the whole amount in order, for example, to purchase goods, and the seller of the goods had paid the money into his current account, everybody would have regarded this deposit as " real ", though in reality there is no difference between the two sums of money. Moreover, on the whole, bank deposits and bank loans must always march together. Which of them occurs first in time is of no importance, since the difference in time is only a few hours, or at most a few days.

On the other hand, the difference is great between deposits which are based on money saved, and are therefore intended for long date capitalization, and those deposits which consist of occasional surpluses of bank credits. Even if in the former case the savings are deposited in the bank for a shorter time only in order to be more permanently invested later, they reduce in a corresponding degree the current demand for loans, i.e. a corresponding portion of bank claims is thereby finally paid in—as in the case of the builder above, who can now sell his house or obtain a mortgage on it—so that the money would lie in the bank as though withdrawn from circulation and therefore would not influence prices unless the bank itself resolves to make this increase of its cash the foundation of further lending. In the two other cases, again, the occasional deposits will stimulate a much quicker turnover, the virtual circulation of money will be accelerated, and prices within the country will rise to a height which will affect unfavourably the balance of trade and the foreign exchanges, so that the banks may find themselves compelled to raise their interest rates to prevent gold from leaving the country.

This process will be made clear in the following pages.

6. *The "Ideal Bank" and the Obstacles to its Realization*

The ideal banking system sketched above has in recent times engaged the attention of many writers under the name of "universal comptabilism", and various proposals for its realization have been made. That developments tend in this direction is clear. We need only look at the English, German, and American banks with their "clearing houses" and the extensive cheque business of the Austrian post office savings banks throughout the country, etc. Theoretically this imaginary system is of extraordinary interest, in so far as it provides a very important means of appraising the factors influencing the value of money, with which we shall be concerned in the following main section of our work. What prevents its realization in practice, and must continue to do so, under existing conditions, is not so much the difficulties of effecting a centralization, for these might be progressively overcome, but rather the following three circumstances: (1) the special requirements of *small payments* for wages, retail trade, etc.; (2) international payments; and (3) the circumstance, with which we have so far concerned ourselves very little, that the precious metals, in addition to their use for currency, are also the raw materials of certain industries. This function, which is at present of subordinate importance, might, in proportion as the metals ceased to be used for currency, become of primary importance and dominate the situation, with the result that the precious metals, and especially gold, would become unsuitable as measures of value. We shall consider these points separately in the following pages.

A. Small Payments. Banknotes.

Not all payments can. be made by cheque. Some are too small for the purpose, though for them token money usually suffices, so that they do not affect the question of standard money. More important is the fact that the majority of purchasers have not sufficient credit or are not sufficiently known to the sellers for the latter to accept their cheques without inquiry, even if we assume the system to be so highly developed that even the poorest have a banking account. This difficulty might be overcome if cheques were in such a form that they themselves carried a guarantee that the sum in question was actually deposited in the bank. For this purpose they should be issued for round sums by the banks themselves and should be so designed that they could not easily be imitated or forged. Such cheques have, in fact, been in existence for more than two hundred and fifty years. They are called banknotes. In reality a banknote is nothing else but a cheque, a certificate of deposit of a certain amount in the bank. Whether it is a question of an actual deposit or a fictitious one, in other words, whether the banknote was originally exchanged for hard cash or was issued in the form of an advance to a customer is here, as in the case of cheques, of no importance, since in both cases the bank is responsible for payment or redemption of the note, which as a rule is sufficient for the receiver. Indeed, it is as a rule more than sufficient, for the certainty that other people will accept the note in payment is good enough. That banknotes are not made out to order is also of no importance, for the guarantee lies in the note itself. In some countries, England for example, it is quite customary for the person tendering a note to give a further guarantee to the receiver by endorsing his name. When the note is accepted in payment and remains in the possession of the recipient its significance is, as we have said already, *virtual*, i.e. it has the same force and effect as it would have had if he had himself deposited the amount in question in the bank against the receipt of the note, or rather had allowed the sum to remain there on his account instead of immediately withdrawing it.

The fact that a cheque and a banknote are in essence the same has recently been noted by several writers on money who, not without reason, have pointed out the inconsistency of the numerous restrictions recently imposed on their note issues by States who have, on the other hand, taken no special steps to secure the prompt payment of cheques in currency.

It must be admitted, it is true, that there is a not unimportant difference between cheques and notes. Notes, especially those of lower denomination, remain in circulation for indefinite periods and are largely in the hands of persons not in a position to inquire into the solvency or liquidity of the bank in question; and to that extent it is natural that the public should watch more carefully over the convertibility of notes than of cheques. But the principal explanation of the differences in legislation in the two cases is historical. Severity as regards the issue of notes is to be regarded as a reaction against the fatal abuses of earlier times, for which abuses the State itself was nearly always chiefly responsible, not least in our own country. On the other hand it should be said that cheques, or, more correctly, those deposits ("repayable on demand") which give rise to cheques, are more dangerous than banknotes, at any rate if the latter are guaranteed by the State. For if a bank fails the owners of deposits in the bank will find themselves in difficulty, and will at least be unable to make immediate use of their deposits. Banknotes, on the other hand, may be given a forced currency, i.e. may be declared legal tender instead of money—our own Riksbank notes are legal currency whether or not they are redeemable by the bank—and retain, as experience shows, at least a part, and frequently the whole, of their value. This happened, for example, in France in the years 1870–4, when the French notes were made legal tender. Moreover the use of cheques presupposes a certain amount of confidence between individuals, for which reason it has been shown that in times when confidence is lacking, as in crises, the demand for a medium of payment turns more than otherwise towards hard cash and banknotes.

Without entering any further into the questions of banking technique to which we have here referred, it may be asserted that in a country such as ours, where notes of lower denomination may be issued, and where in consequence the standard money, gold, scarcely circulates at all in ordinary business, the metallic stocks of the bank are used exclusively as a reserve for eventual payments abroad and, so far as the normal demand for a medium of exchange is concerned, might with impunity be restricted to as small an amount as desired.

The position is quite different where the lower denominations of notes are expressly forbidden by law, as in England and France and Germany (with the exception of a limited amount of State Reichskassenscheine).[1] Not only does this compel the employment in ordinary business of quantities of hard cash (gold), but also bank reserves are drawn upon to satisfy the internal demand (cf. p. 14). If commodity prices rise, or the turnover of money is increased, then internal settlements require more hard cash, which must in the first instance be met by the withdrawal of deposits, without any corresponding payments into the bank from other sources. And since private stocks of cash, though small, amount in the aggregate to many times the amount lying in the banks, it follows that even a small percentage increase in the public demand for hard cash must lead to a relatively much greater strengthening of the metallic reserves of the banks. In addition, however, not only is more hard cash required in such periods, but also more notes and more of the media of exchange in general. However strict the regulations for the redemption of notes may be, therefore, they will be of

[1] The German Reichsbank has, however, acquired the right to issue 20-mark notes. [It will be remembered that Wicksell is writing of pre-War conditions.—Ed.]

little use. What is really of importance is that the banks should possess sufficient *reserves* of the medium of exchange for use when required, as we shall demonstrate later on. In expert circles the view is becoming more and more widely held that the various systems of note convertibility are only of value in so far as they compel the maintenance of such a reserve. If notes of lower denominations were permissible, then for all internal requirements this reserve might without any risk be composed only of notes, i.e. of unused bank credit, whereas in the countries mentioned it must necessarily and essentially consist of hard cash. The note reserve of the "banking department" of the Bank of England can at any time be converted into gold in the "issue department". In writings on money from the middle of last century we not infrequently find it laid down as a condition of a sound currency that large amounts of hard cash must be in circulation, yet it is difficult to understand the foundations of this reasoning. It would perhaps be truer to say that under present conditions this would be a source of weakness and disquiet, and there can scarcely be any doubt that if a country has at its disposal a certain quantity of gold currency, its currency will be much more sound if that gold is collected in the vaults of the bank than if it were distributed among individuals; for in the former case it is incomparably more accessible, for example, in case of necessity for payment abroad.[1]

We shall now pass on to the second of the above-mentioned obstacles to a currency without metallic money, i.e. the need for the precious metals in international settlements and the maintenance of a standard of value common to all countries.

B. *International Payments. Balance of Trade and Balance of Payments.*

There are in a country at any given time a number of persons who have claims abroad and who have debts abroad.

[1] It was the realization of this fact, no doubt, which induced the German Reichsbank to issue notes of lower denominations, as mentioned in the previous note.

Although these as a rule represent personal business transactions and consequently do not affect that country as a whole any more than do internal business transactions of the same amount, yet they nevertheless sometimes affect the currency of the country and have to some extent the same effect as if the country as a whole had these claims or debts abroad. The relation between the total of payments claimed and the total of debts due, at a certain moment or within a certain period, is called the *balance of payment*. It is said to be favourable if the claims exceed the debts, and unfavourable in the contrary case. Most of these claims or debts arise, of course, from trade, from the import or export of goods. For that reason it has long been customary to regard the total of a country's foreign relations arising from current trading as a unit by itself under the name of *balance of trade*, and this is said to be favourable or unfavourable according as the value of exports exceeds that of imports or vice versa. In considering practical questions involved, however, we must remember that the balance of trade only constitutes one part, though usually the most important, of the balance of payments. Indeed, as it is usually drawn up it does not even include certain obligations arising directly from that trade, in particular the earnings of shipping. Imported goods become more expensive because of freight costs, but exports are usually taken up in a country's statistics at their value at the port of shipment, or f.o.b., though the foreign country must, of course, also pay the freight on them. Thus, if a country has carried about one-half of its imports and exports in its own vessels, whilst the other was carried in foreign bottoms, then its total debts abroad on merchandise account fall short of the declared value of its imports by one-half the cost of their freight [1]; and conversely, its total claims on foreign countries for goods exported exceed the declared value of those exports by one-half their cost of freightage. From this arises the

[1] In American trade statistics, however, exports are usually reckoned c.i.f., i.e. the cost of insurance and freight is added to the cost of the cargo. In American trade statistics imports are taken as f.o.b. value, i.e. at the prices at foreign ports of shipment. The difference makes the American balance of trade seem more favourable than others.

apparent paradox, frequently commented upon, that the combined imports of all countries considerably exceed the combined exports in value; for even if a country's claims and debts abroad on merchandise account actually balance, they will nominally exceed the debts by about the total gross profit of the country's *outward* shipping.

In the year 1912 this amounted in Sweden to Kr. 106 millions, of which Kr. 40 millions were from freights between foreign ports. Imports and exports in the same year were Kr. 783 and 760 millions respectively. We should therefore in that year have had a real export surplus in the balance of trade. Moreover, we must not forget that the statistics of trade are themselves still very imperfect, despite all improvements. In particular, export statistics, for obvious reasons, leave much to be desired and are as a rule probably underestimated in value.

It was, in fact, a gross misunderstanding of this kind with regard to our trade turnover with Norway which lay behind the argument of those who zealously advocated and finally achieved the annulment of the so-called inter-State law, thus contributing more than anything else to the dissolution of the Union.

But in addition there are a number of other items necessary for drawing up a complete balance of payment, some of them on the debit side and some on the credit, which can here be mentioned only in passing. If a country has large capital investments abroad, e.g. in foreign Government securities, bonds, shares, or other direct capital investments, then naturally the annual interest accruing is an item of credit from abroad, and that country can for years continue to import far more than it exports without injuring its position relative to foreign countries. It may even improve it—Great Britain is, or at any rate has been, a conspicuous example—in so far as a debtor country may have an apparently very favourable balance of trade and yet become year by year more heavily indebted. If, as is usually the case, shipments of the precious metals, or of coin, are not included in the balance of trade, the latter must of necessity be somewhat misleading. A gold-producing and gold-exporting country habitually has an apparently unfavourable balance of trade, for as a rule it exports less of other goods than it imports. Most countries, on the other hand, which normally import gold *always* have on that account a relatively favourable balance of trade *on an average* since the gold must be paid for year by year with goods, so that a surplus of goods flows out and gold flows in. Finally we should include the sums which travellers take with them or have remitted abroad and spend there—and vice versa. A special category is the money taken out or sent home by emigrants —a not inconsiderable sum in the case of Sweden—also inheritances and testamentary bequests, as well as loans, to and from foreign countries.

> The inclusion of the Nobel estate had the same effect on our balance of trade as if we had in that year borrowed some thirty millions from abroad. The prizes therefore which are now annually distributed, mostly to foreigners, from this fund are similar to the annual interest on such a loan.

All these items combined constitute the foreign balance of payments. If it is unfavourable, then either (1) the excess claims of foreign countries must be *prolonged* for a shorter or longer period, which is tatamount to the contraction of a debt to a foreign country, or (2) a corresponding amount must immediately be shipped, for which purpose the accumulated stocks of precious metal can be used. Banknotes can also be used as a means of payment and in fact are so used on a large scale by countries with an inconvertible paper currency—an example was the well-known rouble exchange in Berlin, now extinct—but, whether convertible or not, they cannot be accepted at their full face value, since as they are not legal tender there, they must be taken by the foreign receiver as a speculation until they can be employed in payment of goods imported from the issuing country; and meanwhile they carry no interest.

This protraction or consolidation of outstanding trade debts occurs daily in various forms, usually with the assistance of the banks. The banks nowadays take the lead in all international business, and they are doing so more and more. If there is a shortage of suitable bills, some bank will sell to the importer of goods a draft or cheque on its account with some foreign bank, and when its account there is exhausted it will replenish it by borrowing or by the sale abroad of securities, all of which, from the point of view of the country as a whole, is the same as a new debt abroad, an increase in the difference between the outstanding debts and current claims on foreign countries. Or a direct foreign loan may be negotiated, often with bodies not engaged in international trade, such as the State, mortgage banks, etc., and ultimately for quite different purposes, but with the immediate result that a breathing space is gained in respect of the payments falling due, until exports are increased or imports decreased. For example, Swedish coffee importers accumulate large stocks of coffee, but in consequence of bad times, low prices for timber and so on, less coffee is consumed than usual. At the same time, perhaps, the State raises a railway loan abroad; the railway workers, paid by the State, buy milk, bread, potatoes, etc., as well as coffee, in the neighbouring villages. The rural population thus acquires money for the purchase of coffee, and the coffee importers can now, with the assistance of the banks, obtain drafts on the amounts which, in consequence of the loan, the State has to its credit in foreign countries, i.e. on the portion of the loan not yet called up. The real result will be that foreign countries have given us credit in the form of coffee, and we have used this coffee for productive purposes, i.e. for the direct (or indirect) payment of railway workers. When the railway is finished the population of the interior may be enabled to sell butter to foreign countries, exports will increase, and in the meantime coffee dealers may perhaps have prudently reduced their imports, so that all will be well again.

It is only when such a protraction of external debts cannot suitably or rapidly be effected that shipments of metallic money come into question. In order to appreciate the conditions, as well as the process and effects of such action, it is important to bear the following in mind. *Vis-à-vis* the goods imported from abroad there is always alternatively a *consumer* who, in order to obtain possession of the goods, offers an equivalent value, i.e. goods of the same exchange value saleable directly or indirectly to the foreign country. To pursue our example further: the coffee importer sells to the rural trader, the latter to the farmers, who in order to obtain money for the purchase of coffee sell cream to the dairies, whereupon the latter sell butter to a butter agent or exporter.

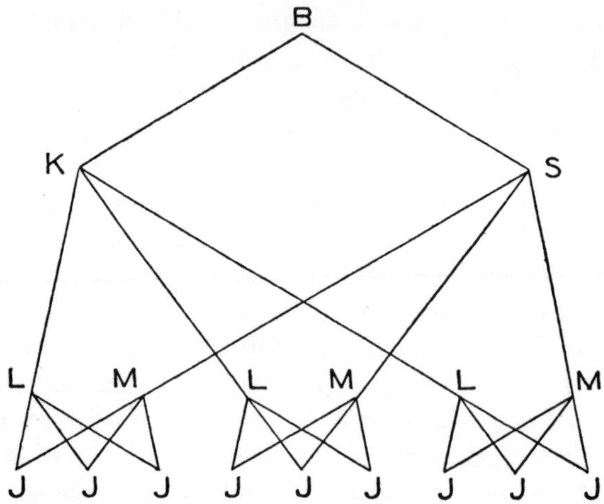

B—a bank.
K—coffee importer.
S—Butter exporter.
L, L, L—dealers in agricultural produce.
M, M, M—dairy farmers.
J, J, J—agriculturists.

The money which facilitates all these exchanges circulates incessantly within the country. For the coffee importers regularly hand over the money they receive from the rural traders to one or more banks in exchange for the drafts or bills; and similarly the banks obtain foreign bills from the butter exporters, who receive in exchange the money equivalent with which the latter pay the dairies. The coffee indebtedness to Hamburg is paid all the time by butter bills drawn on London or Newcastle and these bills are subsequently used for payments as between Germany and England.

Therefore, since people as a rule endeavour to improve, or at any rate to maintain, their economic position, a surplus of debts or of claims outstanding can really only be conceived on one of the following assumptions. A public calamity or an adverse crisis may occur as a result of which the goods saleable abroad are available in smaller quantities or at lower prices than usual, or else the customary imports rise in price considerably, as recently happened in the case of coal, or finally, consumption goods such as grain, usually produced within the country, must be imported to a larger extent than usual owing to a bad harvest or other circumstances. The simplest and most obvious result would then be, in the first two cases, that the consumption of foreign goods, and consequently their importation, would be correspondingly reduced, or, in the last case, that the extra imports of grain now necessary would be counterbalanced by a decreased importation of other articles. In consequence of persistent drought, for example, the production of milk is less than usual, the dairies reduce their output of butter, and the farmers therefore receive less money with which to buy coffee; or the price of timber falls, and with it the wages of the timber workmen who are forced to consume less of the agricultural products of other parts of the country than usual and possibly obtain them at a lower price, all with the same result to the farmers: reduced capacity to buy their usual articles of consumption, including coffee. If the rural traders and the importers of coffee had been able to foresee these results, their imports of coffee would have been counterbalanced by a diminished demand for remittances for coffee imports. But it so happens that they already have their stocks for the immediate future; the result is a demand for additional means of payment abroad, which must be found in one way or another. But by the following year the disparity will already have corrected itself automatically, in so far as the inflated stocks will lead to diminished imports, whilst the export of butter, under favourable circumstances, resumes normal proportions, or timber fetches normal prices. With a normal supply of bills, therefore, there will be a decreased demand for remittances in the following year, the position relative to foreign countries will improve, shipments of precious metal abroad, if they have been made, will cease, and give way to the import of metallic money, and everything will resume its normal course. It may indeed happen that the demand for foreign goods, such as grain, is so great during a famine year that a restriction in the use of other imported goods cannot fully make up the difference. In such a contingency, of course, individuals must obtain credit for consumption purposes, which in this case has the same effect as if they had consumed their own capital. Directly or indirectly the increased demand for credit is satisfied by the great credit institutions, and since the money thus lent is soon returned to the banks, to be exchanged for foreign currencies, the position in relation to foreign countries will be the same, i.e. unfavourable. But even a credit for purposes of consumption will in the nature of things be of short duration. The worsening of the individual's business position must be remedied, and is remedied, partly by diminished consumption and partly also, no doubt, by greater intensity of work in the immediate future, the more so if the State or other great corporations are able to employ their foreign credits for the future benefit of industry, whilst at the same time assisting in the correction of the increased requirements of consumption and the balance of payment.

Our purpose here is merely to point out the fact which is often forgotten that an unfavourable balance of trade or payments undoubtedly *corrects itself automatically* in most cases by the steps taken by individual consumers and producers and this, too, without any serious disturbance of the price or credit structure, or, indeed, any influence on the currency other than, at most, a temporary shipment of a part of the gold reserves. A raising of the bank rate would only tend to hasten a process which would occur automatically in any case, even though more slowly.

But an unfavourable balance of payments may also develop under conditions which will render necessary the direct influence of the banks on the money market in order to restore equilibrium, because *disturbances have been occasioned by abnormal conditions in the money market.* This may occur especially during periods of exaggerated speculation and large capital investments for productive purposes, and it is connected with the peculiar circmstance that productive capital is nowadays almost always transferred in the form of money through the monetary institutions. As was shown in the first volume, practically all production requires, in addition to labour and land, capital, which is really so much saved up labour and natural resources. If capitalistic production is increased or the capitalistic character of production is intensified, in the last analysis it means that an additional amount of labour and land is withdrawn from the current production of immediate necessities in order to be employed instead in production intended for consumption in a more or less remote period. But if the accumulation of *real capital,* i.e. actual saving and the restriction of present consumption, accompanies the increased demand for labour and land intended for future consumption, then no immediate disturbance of the relation between the supply of, and demand for, the means of production and especially no occasion for an unfavourable foreign balance of payment will arise. In the contrary case the capital which cannot be obtained in sufficient quantities within the country must be obtained abroad. This is often done directly. The person desiring to start a *capitalistic* enterprise first borrows money from abroad, which means that in reality he obtains from abroad partly tools, machinery, and raw materials on credit and partly certain necessities which directly or indirectly pass to the workmen employed in the enterprise and to the owners of the necessary land. For example, the State raises a foreign loan for railway construction, or a private railway company does the same thing, or such a company obtains a loan from the State, which itself isues its bonds abroad, or neighbouring landowners subscribe for shares in the enterprise and obtain the necessary means by a mortgage, which we will assume ultimately to come from abroad. If this is done there will be no immediate debt due abroad and consequently no disturbance of the equilibrium of the balance of payments until the enterprise is complete. If it does not come up to expectations, the consequence will be either bankruptcy, in which case the foreign country will have to write off its claims, or else private persons within the country, for example taxpayers as against the State, will have to economize in order to procure the necessary means for the interest and amortization of the loan. Even in that case, therefore, there need not necessarily be an unfavourable balance of trade or payments.

But it may also happen that the enterprise was started with *no means other than a bank loan* ; the entrepreneur perhaps submitted a debenture loan, which the home banks took up at a certain price with the object of issuing it themselves, though they have not yet succeeded in doing so. Or, what amounts to the same thing, the shareholders have obtained the money for their subscriptions by a loan from the bank, or else deposits have been withdrawn from the banks in order to be converted into shares or debentures in the new enterprise, these deposits being deposits on the retention of which the banks had counted and with which they had granted loans to other persons. In other words, the money or credit to be used in effecting the transfer of the necessary capital comes into circulation and exercises its purchasing power without any corresponding accumulation of real capital. A larger portion of the available land and labour than usual is employed for future production, and a lesser part than usual remains for supplying the present demand for necessaries, though the demand for them has increased rather than diminished, since the increased demand of the entrepreneur for land and labour has presumably led to an increase of wages and rent. If the country had been isolated, then, as we shall show later on, economic equilibrium would finally have been achieved notwithstanding a more or less pronounced rise in the prices of all necessaries. Entrepreneurs would have had to pay more for their raw materials, machinery and tools, etc., and future creation of the means of production they contemplated would be kept within narrower limits than the purchasing power of the money they had obtained might at first lead them to believe ; but at the same time the price of all consumption-goods would also rise considerably, all incomes would buy less than usual and everybody irrespective of his income, would be compelled to restrict his consumption, and this enforced restriction would in fact constitute the real accumulation of capital which must under all circumstances be achieved if the total means of production for future consumption are to be increased. In reality, however, this is not exactly the process, but the superfluous money purchasing power goes abroad instead, whither it is directed by a relatively slight rise in prices in the home market. Raw materials, machinery, and some necessaries of daily consumption are drawn from abroad ; but since no simultaneous decline has occurred in the otherwise normal imports from abroad and no increase in the exports to foreign countries, but if anything the reverse, the balance of trade will necessarily soon turn to the disadvantage of the home country.

Even so, serious inconvenience need not arise. The banks may possibly be able to borrow capital abroad on favourable terms or induce foreigners to deposit their capital here. If the foreign rate of interest is considerably lower than at home, then the procuring of foreign credit is indicated and is nearly always effected automatically. In that way the balance of payments reaches equilibrium for the time being, in spite of the " unfavourable " balance of trade. The effects, good or bad, only appear in the future, according as the enterprises requiring increased capital prove profitable or not.

But if the home banks have lent money at *about the same, or even a lower, rate of interest* than they themselves can borrow abroad, so that in consequence a prolongation of the surplus of trade debts becomes economically impossible or disadvantageous, then by means of the mechanism which we shall now proceed to examine, money, bullion, will necessarily begin to flow out of the country, and in *that* case it will not return of itself, for there exists no direct reason for the public to restrict its consumption. The reversal of the flow of gold requires special measures on the part of those who control the currency of the country and who have brought about what has happened through their own imprudent credit policy.

C. The Foreign Exchanges.[1]

The first symptom of an outward flow of gold is a rise in the rate of exchange on foreign countries. The great majority of international purchases and sales are made on long or short term credit, and so long as the claims arising from them balance each other international payment is made, directly or indirectly, by a cancelling out of claims. Considered in greater detail payments abroad may be made in one of two ways. Either the debtor allows the creditor to draw a bill on him, which the latter can subsequently use to effect payments in our market, though he usually sells it to persons in the foreign market who have debts to pay in Sweden, and obtains money for it. Or the buyer can undertake to send to the seller abroad a corresponding value, either in gold or bills of exchange payable in the country of the creditor, and which consequently have a fixed value there, at any rate up to the time on which they fall due. The former is called payment by acceptance and the latter by remittance. There is also a third method, which is really a combination of the two and which is much employed for payments at a great distance, namely *reimbursement* or indirect acceptance. A person in Sweden desiring to purchase goods from the Argentine arranges with a bank or a large business house in London for the Argentine merchant to draw on it for the amount of his claim; before the bill falls due the Swedish purchaser must reimburse the acceptor, e.g. by bills payable in England which he purchases in Sweden. Such bankers' intervention also occurs, and to a steadily increasing extent, in the exchange of goods between neighbouring countries. If, for example, a person who enjoys no credit abroad has ordered goods there, payment is usually made by sending invoice and bill of lading to a bank here for payment, and after the purchaser has deposited the agreed amount the banker sends the seller a draft drawn on its credits abroad.

[1] On foreign exchanges between countries with a paper currency, cf. *Ekon. Tidskr.*, 21, 87 et seq., 1919.

The essential difference between acceptance and remittance is obviously that in the former the purchaser has only bound himself to pay at home in the currency of his own country, whilst the seller accepts the risk and the trouble of transporting the money. With remittances, on the other hand, the purchaser undertakes to pay abroad in the currency of the seller, and the cost and risk of transport now fall on him. Sometimes, of course, a bill may be drawn in the currency of a country other than that in which it is drawn, but in that case it is usually to be regarded from the acceptor's point of view as a promise to remit. According to the Swedish Exchange Law, Section 35, he must pay in Swedish currency according to the current rate of exchange, which is the same as saying that he must purchase bills of exchange on the foreign country to the agreed amount.

If there is equilibrium between the claims and obligations of a country abroad, this difference between acceptance and remittance is of no importance. If, for example, the merchants in one country are accustomed to make all their debts abroad payable by acceptance, and all their claims by remittance —as is very largely the case in England—then creditors abroad simply sell their acceptances to those who have to make payments to the country in question; this is the procedure in international bill of exchange transactions usually laid down in the textbooks. The procedure is the same if on both sides some claims have given rise to bills of exchange and some to promises of remittance. If, on the other hand, all, or the major portion, of the debts in both countries is payable by bills of exchange, then in both countries there will consequently be a number of sellers of bills, but no, or at most a few, buyers, for most buyers have undertaken to pay their own acceptances at home in their own offices, or at a home bank, on the date they fall due; and they therefore have no need to buy bills. This, however, does not cause a fall in the rate of exchange, but the matter is so arranged that some sellers in order to obtain their money, send their bills abroad for payment, or, if they are not due, have them discounted at the bank. In this way the supply and demand for bills soon reach equilibrium.

If, on the other hand, all or most of the debtors in both countries undertake to pay by remittance, which might easily happen in countries which have only just entered into business relations with each other, and in which mutual knowledge and credit as between merchants is not extensive, then the immediate effect will be that a number of buyers of bills will exist on both sides; the sellers, on the other hand, will then have no bills to offer, for they have instead the promise of payment at home in their own currency. But in such a case a debtor here (an importer) can find a friend abroad to draw a bill (so-called accommodation bill) on him or on a bank here, which he will reimburse. This bill will then be in demand abroad, and will be sold at a profit. The original creditor abroad will receive payment of the sale price, and when the debtor at home pays his accommodation bill or reimburses the bank he will have definitely discharged his debt.

If there should be an excess or shortage of bills in our market, this will not affect the rate of exchange if at the same time there is an excess or shortage abroad of the bills drawn on us, for the remedy is very simple. If there is an excess we can cash the bills abroad and purchase bills drawn on Sweden. If there is a shortage, we can draw accommodation bills or reimbursements. If, on the other hand, there exists a shortage in one place, say Sweden, and an excess in foreign countries, the matter becomes more serious; no merely formal credit operations can be of use, because there is a real deficit, and if this is not met immediately by securing a loan abroad for a longer period, i.e. a prolongation of the debt, the necessary consequence will be that the demand for bills at home will begin to exceed the supply and, conversely, abroad the supply of bills drawn on one country will exceed the demand; the rate of exchange for foreign bills will rise here and the rate of exchange for our bills abroad will fall simultaneously and, when this has gone far enough, it will be more to the advantage of a debtor in Sweden to obtain gold and send it abroad then to buy bills at the high rate of exchange; and our creditors abroad rather than sell their bills below face value will send them here to be cashed or discounted and have the proceeds sent in *gold*, since the purchase of foreign bills in our market would also be too costly. Thus gold will begin to flow out of the country. Frequently gold shipments are made to persons who make it their profession and who draw bills on foreign countries for the amount sent and sell these bills in the home market.

A country threatened with this fate is said to have an unfavourable balance of payments. Before we proceed further we shall consider for a moment the meaning of this term, which is often misunderstood. It is clear that a high rate of exchange is in reality only unfavourable to those who have debts to pay abroad, and that only when they have contracted to pay by remittance. If, on the other hand, they have allowed themselves to be drawn upon abroad, they are more or less unaffected by fluctuations in the exchange. Similarly the rate of exchange is unfavourable to those who presently intend to purchase from abroad, since the seller, in view of the difficulty abroad of disposing of his bills drawn in our country, must demand payment by remittance or demand a higher price for his goods. On the other hand, the same rate of exchange is clearly favourable to sellers, especially if they themselves have drawn on foreign countries bills which they can now advantageously dispose of in the home market. If, on the other hand, they have stipulated for payment by remittance they will also be unaffected by fluctuations in the exchange. So also the exchange is favourable for the person who presently proposes selling his goods to a foreign country, as he will receive more for the bills which he draws on foreign buyers. In former days, when exchange rates fluctuated much more than they do now, and even to-day as between countries with a different standard (bullion or paper), the above circumstance constitutes an important corrective tending to restore the balance of payments. Between countries with the same metallic standard, on the other hand, the fluctuations of the exchange can nowadays amount only to a fraction of one per cent and therefore play a very unimportant role ; but in any case the gain or loss falls only on the individual contracting parties, whilst the country as a whole is not affected.

This is at any rate the position if, as often happens, payments by acceptance and remittance are so distributed that takers of bills drawn on foreign countries are present in sufficient numbers in the country itself. If, on the other hand, as in one of the two cases mentioned above, all sellers have drawn on foreign countries and at the same time all buyers have allowed foreign sellers to draw on them, it is clear that the latter cannot lose anything by a rise in the exchange, since they are only bound to pay in their own currency in their own country. The former, again, who sold abroad, can under such circumstances advantageously send their bills abroad to be cashed in order to buy up bills drawn on the home country, which have simultaneously fallen in exchange. They therefore make a profit which does not correspond to any loss within the country, so that the latter as a whole has profited by the supposed unfavourable rate of exchange and has thereby reduced its ultimate foreign debt. In the exactly opposite case where all sellers have stipulated for payment by remittance and all buyers have undertaken to pay by remittance, then in the event of an unfavourable balance of payments and of rate of exchange the buyers will clearly suffer. The accommodation bills which, as we have shown, they must get their friends to draw on them for effecting payment will be sold at a loss abroad. The sellers, on the other hand, will neither gain nor lose, for they will simply await payment at the due date at home in their own currency. The country as a whole, therefore, will suffer a total loss, so that the deficit on the balance of payments will be increased further. Cournot took the former case as the foundation of a whole theory of foreign exchanges, which he thought would be regulated in such a way that credit and debit would cancel each other out if the difference between them was not too great from the start. This hypothesis is, however, entirely without foundation and assumes a combination of conditions of payment which probably does not occur in reality.

As regards the consequences of a higher rate of exchange, i.e. the outflow of metallic money, this need not necessarily be regarded as disadvantageous to the country in question. In a gold-producing country, as we have seen, the balance of trade, and consequently the rate of exchange, is normally unfavourable, since a country which exports precious metals will naturally import more of other goods than it exports and therefore always has a relative shortage of bills of exchange payable abroad. The shortage is made good by exports of metal, but even here this cannot be effected until the rate of exchange has risen so far that the export of metal is commercially profitable. But even in countries which do not themselves produce gold, but import it, there always exist accumulated stocks of gold intended when necessary for the discharge of debts abroad. These stocks must at some time be drawn upon and when this happens it need no more, in itself, be regarded as a misfortune than when a private person spends his money in order to procure necessary goods for himself. The expressions " unfavourable balance of trade " and " balance of payment " are in fact an inheritance from the mercantile school with its well-known over-estimation of money, *qua* money, in comparison with goods. Nevertheless, a high rate of exchange with its consequent outflow of gold is always a serious matter for a country, for if it goes too far the banks will be compelled, as we shall shortly see, to restrict the granting of credit, which may lead to disturbances in the whole economic life of the country.

D. *Exchange Parity and Gold-points.*

Under normal conditions, when foreign debits and credits are approximately equal, the price of a foreign bill falling due for payment will be roughly such as to correspond to the relation between the gold content of home and foreign currency. In Sweden the price of a 900-Rm. bill payable at sight or otherwise falling due will be Kr. 8,000, of a 1,000-franc bill Kr. 720, and of a £100-bill Kr. 1,816.

The rate of exchange will, and does, oscillate round the parity either in one direction or the other, according to supply and demand, but nowadays it does so only within narrow limits. Whoever buys a bill in order to settle a debt abroad saves in the first place the cost of transmitting money, which may be an expense over great distances, though never a heavy one, for it is really no more than the cost of insurance or payment for special care in transport. And if the gold is to be converted into a currency acceptable abroad there are added the costs of melting down and reminting or the corresponding deduction which the central banks make when exchanging bullion for coin and notes. But there is the additional circumstance that the home currency may be, and often is, worn down to the legal minimum. Whoever presents notes to the bank for payment, or withdraws a deposit in gold, will therefore not obtain the full value of gold corresponding to the nominal gold content of the coin. For all these reasons the remitter of money will be inclined to pay a price higher than the par value of the bill —for the bill can be sent by post, either registered or ordinary —and he may even go so far as the limit set by the three charges mentioned above.

An exchange rate for foreign bills which would make it as cheap to ship gold as to buy the bill is called the gold-point, or, more exactly, the upper gold-point.

On the other hand the person in possession of a foreign bill who wishes to receive the amount in gold here must also submit to the same deductions; he will therefore prefer to sell his bill here, if necessary below par, to the limit at which it will pay him to send the bill abroad for payment and receive the gold here after deduction of the costs. This rate of exchange, which is below par and which is the lowest possible, is called the 'lower' gold-point. When it is passed, gold flows into the country.

These are the main factors: minor considerations which also influence rates of exchange and gold-points cannot be taken into consideration here. We refer the reader in this connection to the special literature, such as Goschen's work. One of these considerations is that the banks frequently accept foreign coin at a higher value than their metallic content (after deducting minting costs), as they can use it sooner or later for payments to the country in question, so that the limits of the rates of exchange are somewhat reduced in both directions. It may also be observed that gold shipments to and from a country are not entirely excluded even when, in theory, the prevailing rate of exchange does not require them to be made. If, for example, the currency of one country becomes very worn and must be reminted, or if a country is about to adopt the gold standard, then in one way or another it must procure the necessary gold and is sometimes obliged to procure it from abroad, even when commercially speaking it might be profitable to export gold. As a rule, of course, such operations are postponed to a time when the rate of exchange is favourable and gold flows in of itself or can be obtained at as low a cost as possible.

E. *The Central Banks' Discount Policy, when there is an Efflux of Gold.*

If a country's rate of exchange reaches the upper gold-point, or, what is the same thing, and in fact usually occurs at the same time, the exchange on that country falls in foreign countries to the lower gold-point, so that shipments of gold abroad begin, what should the country do ? The simplest thing would be to let matters right themselves and permit coin, whether melted down or not, to flow out in the expectation that sooner or later it will return by itself, unless the actual quantity is superfluous for the turnover of the country and the necessary reserves, in which case there is no desire to see it return. We have already attempted to show that in many, indeed in most, cases such a return occurs automatically, simply because excessive imports for one or two years necessarily lead to relatively diminished imports during the following years. According to the classical school this would occur in any case, owing to the fact that the diminished supplies of hard cash within the country would lead to a fall in all internal prices, tending to check imports and stimulate exports. In my view the abstract truth of this thesis cannot be denied, but its practical importance, especially under modern commercial conditions, is not so great. A fall of the commodity price level in one country is not in itself desirable unless the level was previously abnormally high, which may possibly, though not necessarily, be the case with an unfavourable balance of trade. It is not impossible that as a result of a heavy fall in our export prices, total money receipts, in spite of larger sales, might be less than before and therefore counterbalance these effects. The function of the bullion reserves may therefore be said to consist in the prevention, as far as possible, of disturbances in the commodity price level; for this purpose, however, either the reserves must be enormously great or else measures must be taken to replace them as soon as they begin to be exhausted. Our own annual imports amount to about eight times the total reserves in minted and unminted gold in the Riksbank. Consequently only a very inconsiderable percentage increase of the value of imports would be necessary to affect our gold reserves very sensibly, if the difference had to be met by hard cash.

Since, in addition, it is difficult to determine beforehand to what extent the change in the balance of trade will be of a kind to correct itself quickly by diminished consumption, or will, on the contrary, continue and cause a continued outflow of gold, it is not strange that at the first indication of gold shipments the banks should seek for means to prevent it and reverse the movement.

The simplest and, as is generally recognized, the most efficacious method is for the banks to raise their discount and other loan rates simultaneously with their rates of interest on deposits, when such exist. Every reduction in the gold stocks creates a more unfavourable relation between the banks' metallic reserves and their obligations to pay on demand, and, if the reduction occurs by the presentation of notes (for the shipment of gold), it also diminishes the amount of the medium of exchange in the hands of the public, thereby increasing the demand for loans: in consequence, a tightening of loan conditions in these circumstances occurs almost spontaneously as long as the banks are under an obligation to redeem notes on demand and to pay out deposits in gold. If, in addition, the unfavourable balance of trade is actually due to excessively cheap credit, i.e. to excessively low rates of interest on loans, then a raising of this rate is immediately indicated, and the higher rate must be maintained until the conditions of production and the state of the capital market have changed. But even if the unfavourable balance of trade is of a transitory nature, an occasional raising of the interest rates may be the means to a much desired respite and may avoid the causes of unrest and lack of confidence in business which in any case exist with a falling cash reserve under the existing banking law.

The ways in which a higher loan rate tends to improve the balance of trade and the rate of exchange and to reverse the direction of the flow of gold are numerous, but have all the same origin, namely that they postpone the payment of our outstanding debts to foreign countries or stimulate the recall of our deposits abroad for a longer or shorter period. With higher rates of interest at home foreigners are more willing to lend us money (unless the sharp rise in interest rates has itself undermined confidence, as happened in the crisis of 1866 in England), and whether the form it takes be the opening of credits, the deposit of money in our banks, or the purchase of domestic securities which owing to higher interest rates have sunk in value at home—though not abroad—the first result for us will always be larger volume of foreign deposits on which bills may be and are drawn, so that the rate of exchange will fall and gold shipments will become unnecessary or even imports of gold may become profitable. The same effect will attend the recall from abroad of domestic capital invested in foreign securities, which must also follow the higher loan rates in the home market. A special method of extending a country's outstanding debt is connected with the difference between long- and short-term bills of exchange. Most commercial bills are drawn for a comparatively long period, two, three, or even six months. Other bills, especially bankers' drafts, run only for a few days, short-term, or are payable on demand (*à vista*). As a rule, of course, a bill which is only due for payment after a period of time is less valuable than a bill of the same amount payable at sight by the discount rate which determines the difference in value in the first place and which the holder of the bill has to pay if he wants to obtain money at a bank; in this way it becomes the rate of interest in the country on which the bill is drawn. There are, however, certain important qualifications to this rule. If, for example, the discount rate is 4 per cent per annum, then a £100-bill drawn abroad and maturing in three months will be worth £99 at par (or its equivalent in foreign currency). If England's balance of trade becomes unfavourable then the exchange rate both for bills payable at sight and long-term bills will fall but the difference between the two remains about the same, i.e. £1. If, however, the English market raises its discount rate to, say, 6 per cent then the long-term bills, if they should *now* be used for payments to England, would be worth 10*s.* less. The direct effect of the higher rate, therefore, is that the long-term bills fall still more on the exchanges. For the holder of such a bill who does not immediately require his money, this will be a reason for keeping the bill in his portfolio until the date when it falls due instead of selling it immediately, for it will later be worth its full face value, at any rate in England. For the same reason the banks and other monetary institutions find it profitable to buy up such bills in the market, since in this way they obtain better interest on their money than they could obtain elsewhere. Therefore the long-term bill rate rises more or less above its minimum, i.e. it does not fall quite as much as it would do, if the factor mentioned above alone were operating, and, since such bills obviously become useless for remittances, the whole of the demand for them is directed towards short-term bills or bills payable at sight, the exchange rate on which will also begin to rise, possibly as high as the upper gold-point, so that gold exports to England will become profitable instead of the reverse. On the other hand in England, in consequence of the rise in the foreign exchange, the long-term bills on foreign countries, which may be held by banks or individuals as means of capital investment, and which would otherwise be retained until the date of maturity, will immediately be thrown onto the bill market, so that England's stocks of means of payment abroad will increase whilst those of other countries on England will diminish.

At the same time it is clear that all these measures are by themselves only palliatives. As soon as interest rates in

England revert to the old level, foreign capital will again be withdrawn and to the normal supply of English bills on foreign markets will now be added those which, for reasons mentioned above, are retained until maturity, so that the position will again grow worse. But meanwhile the balance of trade may itself have taken a turn more favourable to England, so that no steps need be taken to prevent gold shipments.

A high discount rate, however, especially if it has persisted for some time, so that it has begun to affect interest rates on long-term loans, has also other effects of a more serious nature, though they are more difficult to establish and are therefore very controversial. A high rate of interest encourages saving, and saving is, be it remembered, equivalent to diminished present consumption. On the other hand a high rate of interest discourages new enterprises and the expansion of old ones requiring new capital, so that the productive forces in the country are employed to a greater extent than before in the production of commodities for immediate consumption. In addition the difficulty of borrowing money leads to forced sales of stocks in hand, etc. In other words, the demand for goods and services decreases whilst the supply increases; prices fall, imports are checked, and exports are stimulated. But a fall in prices is not an unmixed blessing for a country and should not be resorted to unnecessarily. As a rule, such a fall does not occur, for a brief raising of the discount rate should suffice to reverse the flow of gold before the increased rate has had time to influence commodity prices. If for one reason or another they have risen too high in comparison with foreign prices, their lowering is indispensable to the restoration of equilibrium; in other words, the *higher rate must continue somewhat longer* than would otherwise be desirable. Here an important factor is that whilst normally the increased foreign credit will be withdrawn as soon as the special inducement of a high rate of interest is removed, the fall in prices caused by the higher rate will remain, even when the interest rate has returned to its previous level, as we shall show in the next section. But if the interest rate had previously been abnormally low, so that it was itself the cause of a progressive increase in prices in the country, this would not, of course, apply. There would be no occasion for a return to lower rates in the immediate future, and the new higher rate would then be just the correct normal rate. We shall examine later what is meant by the normal rate of interest.

The foregoing applies directly only to the great trading countries which only occasionally use foreign capital and in which, consequently, interest is usually as low as in neighbouring countries, or even lower. In a country such as Sweden, where capital is relatively scarce, and must be borrowed in large quantities from abroad, and where interest rates are generally higher than in larger countries, the situation is perhaps not quite the same. In order to induce foreigners to lend us their money when we need it, it is perhaps not so much a question of raising the rate of interest as of overcoming the reluctance to invest, despite the already high rate of interest. If this can be achieved by substituting the better credit of the State, the mortgage banks, etc., for individual credit, then the flow of foreign capital, with the consequent improvement in the balance of trade and rate of exchange, may be possible without any further raising of the interest rate. This would be all to the good, assuming always that the borrowed money found productive employment. If it only served a momentary need and added to future burdens which ought to be borne by the present generation, then it should be rejected. Moreover, it is questionable whether a high rate of interest, by stimulating new saving in the country, would not in the long run have been better.

In the appendix to the Swedish translation of Goschen's *Theory of the Foreign Exchanges*, I. Heckscher raises the question whether a raising of the rate of interest by the Swedish banks would not to some extent *drive out* foreign capital. He assumes that at a time when the rate of exchange in England stands unusually high, we might succeed in inducing English capitalists to deposit capital in Swedish banks by raising our discount rate. Since such capital would be transferred by bills drawn *on* England, the immediate consequence would be that the exchange rate on

England would fall. But, says Heckscher, "as soon as the sterling exchange falls below the limit which for the moment corresponds to the value of sterling bills in German currency, the Hamburg banks will appear as buyers of sterling; in that way the demand for sterling will increase on the one hand and possibly part of the German capital in this country will leave it in the form of English bills on Germany. These factors will again cause the sterling exchange to rise and will deprive the country of a certain amount of foreign currency, thus counteracting the effects of the higher interest rates."

It is natural that Hamburg financiers should avail themselves of a low rate of exchange here for profitable arbitrage business, so long as the exchange in German bills does not sink at the same time. But the position in our market is not made worse, since for every English bill leaving the market there is created a corresponding credit for us in Germany. On the other hand it appears paradoxical that German *capitalists* who had left their money here at the lower rate of interest should withdraw it when the rate is raised. It is certainly true that a low rate of exchange here may in itself facilitate and accelerate the withdrawal of foreign capital, in just the same way as it checks foreign investments here; but if the lowering of the rate of exchange is itself caused by a raising of the discount rate, this may create a certain reaction against, though it cannot completely offset, the natural attraction of foreign capital which a high rate of interest causes.

Heckscher himself admits that an unusually low rate may disadvantageously affect the balance of trade and the bill rate, in so far as long-term bills drawn abroad on Sweden which are usually retained until maturity, will often be presented before they fall due. But this is perhaps of lesser importance, since our rate is lower than, or is as low as, rates abroad.

F. *Coins of Small Denomination. Gold Premiums. The Loan Policy of the Central Banks.*

If raising the loan rate is an almost indispensable means of improving a country's balance of payments and of lowering the rate of exchange, it is not on that account a particularly pleasant one. The high rate of interest creates difficulties for the business world, not so much in itself as in the fact that securities and forms of wealth which gave a definite yield will tend to fall in value when the loan interest in the country is high. In particular securities which are pledged against a bank loan frequently become insufficient cover in consequence, and if the borrower is unable to offer further security, he is refused credit and may perhaps have to stop payment. A persistently high discount rate in the banks is therefore a signal that businesses which have with difficulty kept their heads above water will go bankrupt. If the rise in the rate of interest is caused by radically changed economic conditions such as too high a commodity price level or a relative shortage of real circulating capital, then such catastrophes are inevitable. A form of wealth which under given circumstances possesses a certain capital value cannot retain that value unchanged in different conditions, but if the outflow from the banks' gold reserves has been of a more casual nature, then the higher rate will, on the contrary, produce difficulties that could have been avoided. Consequently in recent times attention has been directed to certain other measures, such as the use of coins of small denomination, which are employed by some central banks when an outflow of gold is threatened, and especially to the gold premium policy of the French and English banks. In France the silver currency (the 5-franc piece) is legal tender to any amount—though it is no longer freely coined—and the French banks are not obliged to redeem their notes in gold unconditionally, but may equally well do so in silver. The bank avails itself of this privilege when large withdrawals of gold, especially for foreign account, are imminent ; it refuses to deliver its own gold coin but demands a larger or smaller premium over and above par value for bullion and foreign gold coin in its reserves (it is legally forbidden by law to demand such a premium for its own gold coins). Since as a rule only gold, and not debased silver currency, can be used for foreign payments, the consequence will be, so far as the necessary amount of gold is not available in ordinary circulation, that the French upper gold-point, which is the highest point for foreign exchange in France, will change its position; for the cost of shipping gold will rise—in terms of French gold—by the amount of the premium imposed. This additional rise in the exchange rate will now have the same effect as a rise in interest rates would otherwise have had; it will make imports more difficult, stimulate exports, and lead to a demand for foreign credit, all of which will improve the balance of payments. But at the same time, so it is said, it will leave internal business untouched; the inconvenience of the higher exchange-rate will only affect those who have brought the gold reserves of the country into danger by excessive imports. The gain from this step will, however, be somewhat doubtful from the national point of view. The import of goods from abroad is in itself a praiseworthy and useful business; if it has been carried too far, the importers will inevitably suffer by having to sell their goods at a lower price. To make them suffer still more by preventing them from obtaining on the usual terms a means of payment acceptable abroad seems ill-advised and must in the long run necessarily restrict our export trade. As regards the stimulation of exports, this will certainly benefit exporters, but for the country as a whole such forced sale of goods to foreign countries is not always advantageous, indeed, it is often the exact reverse. That imports and exports must in the long run balance each other is true, but this would also happen if the banks did not demand a premium on gold. It is the possibility of shipping gold or other means of payment abroad in case of need, instead of goods, which is just what prevents forced exports or an excessive restriction on imports at times when such measures would be disadvantageous to the country as a whole.

The Bank of England also occasionally makes use of the gold premium in two ways. In the first place with a strong demand for gold on foreign account it takes a higher price than usual for bullion and foreign gold coin, though within narrow limits, for the price is limited by the legal minimum weight of English coins, or their permissible degree of wear and tear.

For the Bank, unlike the French Bank, cannot refuse to redeem its notes or pay out deposits in gold. In the second place the Bank of England, when in need of gold, pays a premium on unminted gold. Its legal purchasing price is £3 17*s.* 9*d.* per ounce mint gold, but sometimes it pays the full mint price of £3 17*s.* 10½*d.* and even £3 18*s.* or more. In this case also, the limit is obviously determined by the degree of wear of the English gold currency.

Of these two measures the latter is a natural consequence of the former, but it operates as though it were a deposit rate paid by the Bank of England itself. The stocks of bullion continually flowing into Europe from the producing countries are directed, under the influence of the high price of gold, to the Bank of England where they remain until the removal of the premium makes it profitable to withdraw them and send them elsewhere. The premium acts therefore as a small rate of interest. This leads us to another question which deserves attention, though it has not been much discussed in the literature of money, namely the advantage which the central banks themselves have in allowing interest on deposits under certain circumstances. As we know, this is usually done, though frequently in a disguised form. When, for example, the Bank of England is compelled to raise its discount rate, but cannot induce the other banks and the discounting houses—the so-called open market—to do likewise, it endeavours to diminish the supply of loan money in the open market by selling some of its large holdings of English government bonds and consols. This is usually done in the so-called terminal market. The Bank sells securities for cash but repurchases them at the same time for delivery in, say, a month's time at a somewhat higher price. This operation is in effect merely the lending of its consols at a rate of interest corresponding to the difference between the selling and repurchasing price. But it seems to me that the same, or a better, result would be achieved if the Bank of England and other central banks gave direct interest on deposits when they wished to attract money.[1] The reasons advanced against this seem

[1] Compare on this point Emil Sommarin, " Om rätt for Riksbanken att

to me to be unconvincing: that a central bank should not compete with other banks may or may not be true, for the essense of all banking activity is really concentration,[1] and all the banks in a country do in virtue of their clearing house system constitute a much more unified system than exists in most other branches of business. But if in addition the central banks restricted themselves to allowing interest on deposits at times when they raise the discount rate above the normal and when it is a matter of inducing the other banks to restrict, in the public interest, their lending operations, it is scarcely possible to speak of unsound or improper competition. It seems to me that in this way the present violent fluctuations in discount rates might to some extent be avoided just as a closer approximation of the deposit to the loan rate would prove the banks' best means of concentrating and controlling the whole currency system of the country, even though it might not be as profitable to them as the existing system.

G. The Regulation of International Payments without Bullion.

The foregoing observations relate in large part to well-known matters. I have nevertheless not felt justified in omitting them because they are a necessary preparation for an answer to the question which really concerns us here, namely, to what extent can the maintenance of large gold reserves for payments abroad be regarded as inevitable from the point of view of modern banking developments? It would seem that the answer to this question should be in the negative. Already attempts are being made, with growing success, to render as superfluous as possible international trans-shipments of gold, and the manner of avoiding them is fundamentally the same; the mutual credits of the great monetary institutions and of States themselves—for the export of government securities as a means of payment is nothing else but a use of

gottgöra ränta å depositioner," in *Ekon. Tidskr.*, 20, 97–121 (1918), and the Report of the Bank Committee No. 7 (1919). In the 1920 Riksdag the Riksbank obtained permission to allow interest on deposits.

[1] This view is further developed by K. Wicksell in an essay in *Ekon. Tidskr.*, 21, ii (1919).

State credit—are called in whenever the ordinary merchant bill credit is insufficient. It is true that every year even larger sums of gold pass from one country to another, but they consist largely of the necessary movement of newly produced gold from the producing countries to all other countries, according to their need for, or capacity to absorb, gold. Or it may be due to the fact that certain countries are about to pass over from an inconvertible paper or a silver standard to a gold standard and therefore desire to attract larger amounts of gold. Since the actual costs of transport of gold are very low, they are of little importance, whether the necessary stocks are derived from the countries of production or not. Frequently trade relations and the position of the foreign exchanges may make it cheaper to procure gold direct from a neighbouring country, which will recoup itself again from other countries or directly from the gold-producing areas. These gold movements are therefore an effect and not a cause of the maintenance of large gold reserves. Again, as far as the regulation of the balance of trade by means of gold is concerned, presumably only a slight further advance on the developments already achieved in international banking is required in order to render entirely superfluous the meaningless shipments of cases of gold to and from the central banks. All that is required is an agreement between these banks to sell to the public bills payable at sight on each other, disregarding any difference in the rate of exchange, i.e. at par. A more radical step would be for the central banks to agree to redeem each other's notes—and also the gold currencies of their various countries, though this would not often be necessary—in the notes and currency of their own country, also at par. If this were done there would, of course, still exist a difference in value between long- and short-term bills (or bills payable at sight) of the same nominal amount, but the rate for the latter would always remain at par or very near it, as otherwise it would be possible to purchase bank drafts or to send notes by registered post. Gold shipments under such conditions would never be profitable unless the receiver desired gold for some reason and was willing to pay transport costs, i.e. for industrial purposes or for the banks' own use if they were compelled to strengthen their gold reserves. It would be difficult to maintain that such an agreement is impossible even at the present moment. It existed between the Scandinavian central banks until 1905. In 1885 they agreed to sell bills payable at sight on each other without any difference in exchange rate, a step which according to the view of Heckscher mentioned above "contributed greatly to a greater general stability of the exchange rate on foreign bills between the three countries; was of advantage to wholesale trade in so far as the market for the purchase and sale of bills was extended, and indirectly to consumers, though possibly not to the bankers, who lost the opportunity for profitable arbitrage transactions". After a number of years this agreement was supplemented by another, by which the three northern central banks expressly bound themselves to redeem each other's notes free of charge, so that remittances of gold on private account between the Scandinavian countries need never be necessary. If such an agreement became universal, then, of course, the exchange of these notes and the balancing of the amounts drawn upon each other would be the banks' affair and could be facilitated by such a common "world clearing house" as has often been projected.

It is clear that the sums which the banks of the different countries, and especially the central banks, would under such circumstances have to keep on account with each other would be considerably larger than now, although in any case they would be a trifle compared with the colossal sums of various kinds of credits which now exist between countries. Settlement of such current accounts in *gold* would certainly be very seldom necessary. But since as soon as they reached a certain magnitude they would, of course, yield interest, then clearly there would be just the same need as now for each country's banks to provide, by raising the internal rate of interest, for the restoration of equilibrium in the balance of payments as soon as it became unfavourable; though the rise in the rate of interest would be effected with far less disturbance and excitement than is now often the case. It should, however, be mentioned that the violent fluctuations in interest rates nowadays, as K. Helfferich points out in his *Zur Erneuerung des deutschen Bankgesetzes*, are perhaps more often occasioned by the fluctuating demands of the internal market for means of payment and especially for gold, where it is in circulation, than by a demand for gold for foreign account.

H. *The Final Obstacles to a Pure Credit System and the Possibility of their being Surmounted.*

If we summarize the conclusions to which we have come in the preceding section, the result will be, at least theoretically, that gold could easily be replaced by credit, both for internal needs and for international payments of any amount, and that the great and ever-increasing stocks of gold in minted form, accumulated with so much toil and trouble, are useless and superfluous. And this applies not only to the state of affairs in ordinary normal conditions; even as a safety reserve for unforeseen circumstances, these reserves of gold would be entirely unnecessary. The distrust of banknotes, even of those of central banks, which so often appeared in former days in times of unrest, has now completely vanished, especially since the secrecy surrounding banking operations has given way to periodic public reports on their position, and the unfortunate mixing up of State finances with currency policy has become a thing of the past. What the business world is afraid of nowadays in times of crisis is that the banks' credit facilities will be exhausted and credit thereby become stringent, and not that their instruments of credit will lose their value and their purchasing power. Nowadays we never hear of a "run" on gold by the public, but frequently of a run by business men and bill brokers to get their bills discounted at the Central Bank, in case the bank reserves or the unused portion of the statutory note issue falls unusually low and the private banks begin to restrict credit in consequence. The famous panic in the U.S.A. in 1907 was clearly connected with the peculiar banking conditions in that country, and no repetition of the occurrence is likely since the American banking system has been reorganized on a more rational basis. The conditions might perhaps be somewhat different in a political upheaval such as the outbreak of war. But even there real capital plays a most important part directly in the supply of subsistence goods, horses, weapons, etc., and to a greater extent, indirectly, through the general wealth and the Government credit which is based on it. The idea that a modern State without credit could successfully wage a war because it possessed a few hundred millions in gold is too naïve. The well-known German war-hoard of 120 million marks in the Julius Museum at Spandau was largely a curiosity, even after it was increased in 1913. For the purpose of a German mobilization nowadays it is a mere drop in the ocean.

Are we then justified in the conclusion that gold as a means of payment and a standard of value could be entirely or largely dispensed with and that the currency as a whole could be based on credit alone ? If this were the case, there would undoubtedly be a very great national saving. The whole of the stocks of minted gold, amounting to over forty million kronor, could be placed at the disposal of industry and in future the production of gold, of which at present only about one quarter can be used for industrial purposes, would be entirely available for that purpose, or rather, three-quarters of the immense amount of capital and labour employed in its production, or even more, would be available for other and more useful purposes. Some authors, both earlier and more recent, have leaned to this view, among others no less than Wagner, who in his famous work *Geld und Kredittheorie der Peelschen Bankacte* expresses the opinion that mere " bank cover ", i.e. the holding of bills and securities in the portfolios of the banks as the sole basis of note issues and cheques would be the ideal, from the point of view not only of cheapness but also of *maintaining the stability of the value of money*.[1]

But it is just this conclusion that is premature and even incorrect under present conditions. So long as gold remains

[1] Wagner appears in his later writings to have abandoned this view and to lay what seems to me an exaggerated emphasis on gold as the basis of note issues and banking credit.

a standard of value, i.e. so long as the free minting of gold for private account is the foundation of the currency system, the holding of large stocks of gold, however sterile it may be from other points of view, is an unpleasant necessity. This ought to be obvious, and becomes even more so if we try to imagine how the transition to a pure credit system would be effected under existing conditions. By the issue of notes of smaller denominations, down to that of the smallest gold coin possible in ordinary use, and even lower—as in Sweden—or by a corresponding development of the use of cheques and current accounts the gold coinage would no doubt be entirely forced out of use, but only, in the first instance, to be deposited in the banks, whose stocks would thereby become swollen. With the same price level it would have become physically impossible for the banks to dispose of this new gold or to prevent the steady increase of stocks which would result from the continuous production of gold. For if they attempted to sell their gold at the current mint price, e.g. against securities or other forms of wealth, where would they find purchasers? It would be equally impossible to sell bullion below mint price, so long as the banks are themselves obliged to purchase at that price, or slightly below it, all gold offered to them; in fact, so long as free minting on private account is allowed. Not even if the banks wanted to *give away* their gold would they finally succeed in getting rid of it, for most of it would soon return to them in exchange for banknotes or in the form of deposits.

Only by using the power, which we shall assume them to possess and which we shall discuss in the next section, of considerably raising prices by lowering interest rates and at the same time lowering the exchange value or purchasing power of both minted and unminted gold, as against goods and services, could the banks succeed in their object. This raising of prices would act as a brake on gold production, the cost of which would thus be increased and would stimulate the industrial uses of gold, and when this industrial consumption equalled, or began to exceed, production, the bank reserves would gradually become exhausted by withdrawals for industrial use. But simultaneously the seeds would be sown of severe future fluctuations in the value of money, because as the banks' supplies continually depleted by the industrial demand they must sooner or later consider how to replenish them—for they still remain under the compulsion to supply gold for their convertible notes or to depositors who withdrew their deposits in gold—and this they could only do by forcing prices down again in order to check the industrial uses of gold and at the same time make the production of gold more profitable. The more the gold reserves shrank the more violent and the more frequent these price fluctuations would be. In a word, the exchange value of money would be subject to fluctuations similar to, though perhaps not as great as, those which prevailed when copper or iron was the standard.

On the other hand the existence of large stocks of coin is no guarantee of the stability of monetary values. They do indeed tend to act as shock absorbers to the changes which occasional disturbances in the volume of production or of industrial consumption would otherwise cause; but accumulated stocks are quite powerless against persistent and radical changes in those spheres, such as the discovery of great new goldfields, or the exhaustion of existing ones. If the experience of the last seventy years does not seem to confirm this to the degree that one might expect, it is due entirely to the fact that the great discoveries of gold and silver in the latter part of the nineteenth century occurred simultaneously with a great increase in population in most countries and a transition from trade in kind to trade in money, whereby the demand for gold was considerably increased, in spite of rapid developments in the credit system; and, more important still, these discoveries were accompanied by the almost universal adoption of the gold or some cognate standard, whilst silver became a mere commodity. These factors, however, are of a more or less accidental nature and their combination in the desired direction cannot always be counted upon, as the much higher price level during the decade 1893–1913 clearly shows. The excellence of our present monetary system is therefore largely an illusion, and the danger of basing the whole of our economic system on something so capricious as the occurrence of a certain precious metal must sooner or later come to light. Indeed, our modern monetary system is afflicted by an imperfection, an inherent contradiction. The development of credit aims at rendering the holding of cash reserves unnecessary, and yet these cash reserves are a necessary, though far from sufficient, guarantee of the stability of money values. Moreover, we must reckon with frequently considerable variations of the general price level, the immediate cause of which is the expansion and contraction of credit in good and bad times.

Only by completely divorcing the value of money from metal, or at any rate from its commodity function, by abolishing all free minting, and by making the minted coin or banknotes proper, or more generally the unit employed in the accounts of the credit institutions, both the medium of exchange and the measure of value—only in this way can the contradiction be overcome and the imperfection be remedied. It is only in this way that a logically coherent credit system, combining both economy of monetary media and stability in the standard of value, becomes in any way conceivable.

At this point we are directly confronted with the question: on what, in the last analysis, does the exchange value of money depend? How can this value be regulated in time and space, assuming an ideal banking system and pure capitalism, and how is it in fact regulated under the present system of mixed cash and credit operations? We shall now concern ourselves with these questions. It should be clear from what has been said that they are of the utmost importance not only in theory, but also in practice.

IV

THE EXCHANGE VALUE OF MONEY

BIBLIOGRAPHY.—In view of its central importance in a rational theory of money, the problem of the exchange value of money and its fluctuations may well be said to have received scanty treatment in the literature of the subject. The most important writings on the subject date from the first half of the nineteenth century, especially Ricardo's famous pamphlet, *High Price of Bullion, Reply to Mr. Bosanquet*, etc., to some extent also Senior's *Lectures on the Cost of Obtaining Money* and *On the Value of Money*, as well as the polemics occasioned by Peel's second Bank Act of 1844, especially Tooke's *Enquiry into the Currency Principle* (also Newmarch's *History of Prices*) and Fullarton's *On the Regulation of Currencies*, both directed against Peel. The writings of Peel himself and of his followers are of less scientific interest. A very good account of the whole of this dispute is given in Wagner's most readable work *Geld und Kredittheorie der Peelschen Bankacte*. In more recent times the problem has scarcely advanced towards a solution. On the contrary, its known difficulties have led most writers to ignore the problem as far as possible and have occasioned the most fantastic and nugatory attempts at explanation. Perhaps the most interesting work of recent times on this problem is the Report of the Gold and Silver Commission, 1887 (3 vols.).

On the other hand the statistical aspect of the problem of measuring changes in the value of money by a general index number has occasioned innumerable writings of varying quality, C. M. Walsh's exhaustive work *The Measurement of General Exchange-Value* (New York 1901, 580 pp.) contains an account of all the proposed methods of measurement as well as a complete bibliography.

The history of inconvertible money, which is so important for a proper appraisal of the various theories of the value of money, is presented in a fascinating and exhaustive manner by

Subercaseaux in his *El papel moneda* (Santiago de Chile, 1912). Finally we may refer to Irving Fisher's *The Purchasing Power of Money* (1912) and " A Compensated Dollar " (*Quarterly Journal of Economics*, 1913). The former is an interesting attempt to confirm the quantity theory statistically. The latter contains an account of the author's much discussed proposals for the regulation of the value of money, which in my opinion are built on insufficient grounds.

1. *What is understood by the exchange value of Money? The Value of Money and Commodity Prices*

So soon as money becomes a general measure of value and is made legal tender, the avoidance of all violent and unexpected fluctuations in its value is of the utmost importance. In essence this desideratum is expressed in the very term " measure of value ", for if this definition is to have any real meaning or to bear any analogy to other physical units of measurement, then we must assume that that which is to measure all other things must itself remain constant. But this is not the same as saying that the measurement of value must be such a simple mechanical process as that of length, area, or cubic content. Even in the physical world we are often forced to content ourselves with purely hypothetical measurements, until more precise ones have been discovered. For example, when heat is measured by degrees of the thermometer, it does not follow that every rise in the column of mercury means a proportionate rise in the volume of heat itself, but the latter must be made the object of special exhaustive research. Yet we require of a good thermometer that under given conditions it will always register a certain temperature, e.g. 0° when water freezes and 100° when it boils.

All practical proposals for the improvement of currency systems actually proceed, though more or less consciously, from the desire to guarantee this stability of value. When it is said that Governments or banks should seek to provide enough money of full value, or a monetary system at once *sound and flexible*, all that is really meant is that the value of money should be protected against violent fluctuations, either downwards in the form of the depreciation of money or upwards in the form of a fall in commodity prices: this includes a demand for the preservation of the stability of value of money in space, i.e. the maintenance of the currency unit of one country at the same level as that of another.

Sometimes, it is true, we hear it said that certain changes in the value of money, especially a gradual decline or a progressive rise in commodity prices, might be preferred under certain circumstances to complete stability. Rising prices would act as a stimulus to enterprise and a falling value of money would free debtors from the burden of obligations thoughtlessly incurred. This view is, however, evidently naïve. It need only be said that if this fall in the value of money is the result of our own deliberate policy, or indeed can be anticipated and foreseen, then these supposed beneficial effects will never occur, since the approaching rise in prices will be taken into account in all transactions by reasonably intelligent people. What is contemplated is, therefore, unforeseen rises in price. The result of this would seem to be that we should cross our arms and wait in order not to frustrate the beneficial workings of nature. But nature does not always guarantee rising prices; falling prices also occur.

The first step towards a rational regulation of the value of money must obviously be a thorough study of the laws and causes of the fluctuations in the value of money. In this study, however, we encounter serious difficulties both of a theoretical and a practical nature. The first and not the least difficulty is in determining *what exactly we mean by a constant value of money.* For ourselves we mean by the value of money exactly the same thing as the exchange value of money, its purchasing power as against goods and services. To us, therefore, the value of money and the price level are synonymous, or, more correctly, correlative ideas. Where we have spoken of the intrinsic value of money we have meant only the exchange value of the unminted metal when, as in the case of token money or the limited minting of standard money, it is essentially different from the nominal value of the minted money. In the real sense there does not exist any intrinsic value of money with which, as is sometimes supposed, the inherent value of commodities can be compared and measured. The subjective value of money, its marginal utility, is, as we have already pointed out in the introduction, mainly dependent on its objective value, its purchasing power. Of course, like any other object of consumption, the metal itself, employed for industrial purposes, has its use and its marginal utility, but under present conditions this only plays a secondary part and, being in its nature variable and of too little economic importance, should not determine the value of money.

In recent times, attempts have been made to make a certain aspect of the exchange value of money the criterion of stability, i.e. its purchasing power in terms of *Labour*. In such a case the value of money would be regulated in such a way as to maintain wages of ordinary simple labour constant in terms of money. This is in reality a survival of the Adam Smith-Ricardo conception, subsequently adopted by Karl Marx, that labour alone is the measure of all exchange values. According to Ricardo, a quantity of goods which is the product of a constant amount of labour should always have the same value, even if it increases physically in consequence of the increased productivity of labour. If the wages of labour, the price of labour in money, remains unchanged, then we may say that the real intrinsic element of value, which in itself is essentially always the same and which has the same personal significance to us, has remained unchanged. That this view is one-sided scarcely needs proof: labour is only *one* factor of production among others, and therefore only one source of value among many. But even if it were correct, what practical conclusion are we to draw from it? Can it be maintained that a person who has borrowed a certain quantity of goods *in natura* should at the time of repayment, say in ten years, be legally bound to procure twice as much because his labour during the intervening ten years has become twice as productive? To put it another way, if commodity prices remain unchanged, whilst the wages of labour are doubled, ought he to be obliged to pay, in addition to interest, double the amount in money ? There may be some element of justice in this, but scarcely full justice, for it will be the creditor who will harvest the whole profit from the change, whilst at present it is the debtor.

Moreover, such a system would scarcely be feasible in practice. Not only do the various kinds of labour stand in perpetually changing relation to each other, but both real and money wages for the same kind of work, are in fact different in different countries and even in different places in the same country. If, despite this, we were to endeavour to enforce equal money wages everywhere it would only make commodity prices more variable and could not be realized without customs duties, for it is absurd that one and the same commodity should have different prices on both sides of a duty free frontier. That wages should exercise a certain influence on the average level of prices is, on the other hand, indisputable, for directly consumable services, such as domestic labour, play the same part in consumption as other necessaries. But this is quite a different story. At bottom, all this talk of the desirability of a stable value of money as against labour is only the argument by which in default of better reasons the gold monometallists sought to turn aside the objection of the bimetallists that the limited minting of silver would cause—till the middle of the nineteenth century, when increased output of gold began to have its effects, it did in fact cause—a fall in commodity prices, i.e. a lack of stability in money in the usual sense; whereas wages had certainly not fallen, but rather risen.

The special, and from the present point of view independent, circumstance that in this period real wages rose, while money wages remained more or less unchanged despite falling commodity prices, was also advanced as a counter argument. For, it was said, the value of money in the sense of its purchasing power as against human labour, which was the major consideration, remained constant.

The only really scientific measure of monetary value would, as Edgworth emphasized, be its indirect marginal utility, i.e.

the increase in welfare we could obtain if our income is conceived as being increased by one unit of money, say a shilling, for a certain period of time, e.g. by an increase of weekly or daily wages. Unfortunately this amount is never the same for two persons and still less so for persons of different classes of income. Such a measure therefore is of no use for the regulation of the value of money in practice. But there is no doubt that it is what most people have in mind when they consider whether the exchange value of money has risen or fallen.

2. *The Average Level of Prices and its Measurement*

Let us abandon these speculations and consider only the conditions for a stable purchasing power of money in the ordinary sense, i.e. as against goods and services. In the solution of this problem we shall encounter equally great difficulties, some of them insurmountable. If everything has risen (or fallen) in price by the same percentage, then we may assert that the purchasing power of money has fallen (or risen) by the same percentage. This would be the case, at least approximately, if, for example, the whole production of society remained otherwise unchanged, but the discovery of rich goldfields enabled the owners to ship year after year greater quantities of gold than usual—always on the assumption that the change in the value of money did not occasion any change in the relative prices of other goods which would to some extent be the case. In actual fact, however, the internal exchange values of goods will repeatedly undergo changes which will find direct expression in fluctuations in their money prices. Thus if we compare two points of time, the prices of various goods may perhaps have risen in quite different degrees, or the prices of some may have risen and of others fallen. How shall we decide under such circumstances whether or to what extent the purchasing power of money has in reality fallen or risen? This is one of the most important problems underlying price statistics. Attempts have been made to solve it by calculating an average price level by means of so-called index numbers. Of course it is not possible simply to take the average of the commodity prices quoted at any moment, for these prices relate to purely arbitrary quantities, 1 kg. for one commodity, 1 ton for another, and probably 1 grain for another. Sometimes the quantity is measured by the weight, sometimes by the piece. For this reason it is usual to take the average of the percentage changes in these prices from one date to another. The price of one unit at a given time is represented by the same figure, e.g. 100, and the corresponding prices at all other times, which are usually somewhat above or below 100, are called the index numbers of the various commodities and represent the percentage rise or fall in their prices in the intervening period. The average (usually the arithmetic mean) of all these index numbers is called the general index number. The divergence from 100 is then supposed to represent the changes in the general price level. If this figure is the same as 100, or near it, no change will have taken place in the general price level and money will have retained its average purchasing power as against goods, however the prices of individual commodities may have varied during the period.

It need scarcely be observed that this method is also very imperfect; it does not take into account the fact that some goods have a very large, and others an extremely small, significance in general economic activity. A 10 per cent increase in the price of a commodity consumed in large quantities, such as grain, meal, cotton, leather, coal, timber, iron, etc., is not counterbalanced by a price decrease in some dyestuff or spice. This weakness is also shown by the fact that under certain circumstances the method may lead to positively contradictory results. Assume, for example, that we are only dealing with two articles, coffee and sugar, and that one has doubled in price during a certain period whilst the other has fallen to half its former price in the same period. Let us, further, take the first year of the period as our starting point, when the price of both commodities for the year is represented by 100, and the average, the arithmetic mean, is, of course, also 100. In the last year of the period again, coffee, of which the price is assumed to have doubled, will have an index number of 200, whilst the corresponding index for sugar will be 50. The arithmetic mean of these two figures is 125 and should indicate that the price of coffee and sugar, taken together, has risen by 25 per cent or, what is the same, the average purchasing power of money in terms of these goods has fallen by 20 per cent.

But we might equally have taken the last year of the period as our starting point. In that case we should have had to represent the price of the commodities for that year by 100 and for the first year of the period the index number for coffee would have been 50 and for sugar 200, and their general index number, the arithmetic between the two numbers, would have been 125. This figure would clearly indicate that both commodities taken together had fallen in price by 20 per cent, so that the purchasing power of money in terms of these two commodities would have risen by 25 per cent.

The Englishman, Stanley Jevons, who was, I believe, the first to point out this contradiction, suggested, in order to avoid it, that instead of the arithmetic mean the geometric mean of the index numbers should be used, in which case the result would be the same, whether the base-year was an earlier or a later year. In the present case the geometrical mean would be the square root of the product of the index numbers, 100, indicating however, one calculates, that the average price of the two commodities had undergone no change at all. But this is scarcely an improvement of method : the error indeed lies not in the selection of the arithmetic mean as such but in the fact that any average calculation must be meaningless if the actual quantities of goods consumed are not taken into consideration. If we substitute concrete terms in the above example it will indicate that in the first year of the period, say 1900, a certain amount, say 1 kg. of coffee cost 100 öre, and a certain amount, say 1 kg. of sugar, also cost 100 öre, or both together 200 öre. At the later date, say 1910, 1 kg. of coffee cost 200 öre, whilst the price of sugar fell to 50 öre. Thus 1 kg. of coffee and 1 kg. of sugar combined cost 250 öre, and if we assume that the total consumption of the country at both points of time was, say, 10 million times that amount, then undoubtedly at the latter date the country would have to spend 25 per cent more than at the former date on coffee and sugar. If, on the other hand, we wish at the latter date to set the price of coffee or of sugar at 100 öre, there is nothing to prevent us, but the unit of quantity would in that case be $\frac{1}{2}$ kg. of coffee and 2 kg. of sugar, and there is no contradiction whatever in the fact that the combination of $\frac{1}{2}$ kg. coffee + 2 kg. of sugar (or some million times those quantities) has fallen in price, whilst the combination 1 kg. coffee + 1 kg. sugar has risen in price. The choice of the geometrical mean, again, excludes the possibility of giving a concrete meaning to the calculations and therefore in reality yields a result which is meaningless though formally free from contradiction.

Doubtless the only right thing to do is to include in the calculation the quantities consumed or, in technical terms, to adhere to the *weighed* average of the prices. This procedure has also been attempted with some success (by Palgrave and others) although it involves various difficulties in the present state of commercial statistics. In the usual published index numbers, such as those of *The Economist* and the English statistician Sauerbeck, and those begun by Soetbeer in Germany and continued in Conrad's *Jahrbücher*, some attempt is made to satisfy this requirement by including various qualities or grades of the most important goods, so that they are in fact counted several times in the calculation.

The method goes astray, however, even in its most satisfactory theoretical form, as soon as the consumption of the various commodities at the times which are compared have undergone appreciable *relative* changes—i.e. have not merely increased or decreased in the same proportion. This is in reality nearly always the case, being itself a consequence of the changes in the relative price or exchange value of the commodities. Various attempts have been made to remedy this defect. In particular there is the much discussed, apparently very complicated, but actually quite simple, method proposed by the German economist, J. Lehr (the calculation of so-called units of consumption).[1]

[1] Cf. my work, *Geldzins und Güterpreise*, p. 10 *et seq.*

But both his and all other similar attempts merit no special consideration, for a real solution of the problem is and will remain an impossibility, as can most easily be seen if we make the extreme assumption that a certain commodity has been entirely supplanted by another, e.g. rye and oats for bread by wheat, wood as fuel by coal, and as a building material by bricks and iron, oil by paraffin or gas, etc. In such a case in order to institute any comparison whatever we must first know to what extent two such substitute commodities are able to satisfy one and the same human demand, i.e. their respective nutritive value, calorific effect, tensile power and durability, illuminating power, etc., and also the more subsidiary qualities, better taste, greater convenience in use, etc.,[1] which are yet of importance in consumption.

The simplest way in practice, and one which would be entirely satisfactory if it were attainable, would be the following. If at two different points of time we know the amounts of all kinds of goods produced and consumed in a country or in the whole world then we can note the amounts at one of these two points and multiply them, each separately, in the first place by the price prevailing at the same point of time, and in the second place by the prices ruling at the other point of time. The totals thus obtained clearly represent on the one hand the amount of money spent on, or at least corresponding in value to, these goods at the two points of time *if* the same quantities of goods had been produced and consumed. The relation between these two sums of money undoubtedly constitutes a sort of measure of the rise and fall of prices during the period in question, and it would constitute an exact measure if consumption had in fact remained unchanged or had only undergone a purely proportional increase or decrease. If we indicate the quantities of goods consumed by m_1, m_2, m_3, etc., we shall obtain the equation :

$$m_1p_1 + m_2p_2 + m_3p_3 + \ldots : (m_1p_{11} + m_2p_{22} + m_2p_{33} + \ldots) = 100 : (100 + x)$$

in which the value of x indicates the average percentage increase or, if x is negative, decrease between the two points of time.

[1] Cf. the conclusion of the preceding section, p. 132.

One would then follow the same procedure for the quantities of goods involved at the later date. If we call these quantities m_{11}, m_{22}, m_{33}, etc., we shall obtain the following equation:

$$(m_{11}p_1 + m_{22}p_2 + m_{33}p_3 + \ldots) : m_{11}p_{11} + m_{22}p_{22} + m_{33}p_{33} + \ldots = 100 : (100 + y)$$

and the value of y thus obtained evidently constitutes as correct and as in itself reliable a measure of past rises and falls in prices. If, then, these two calculations lead to the same or approximately the same result, which often happens if the two selected points of time are not too remote, x will equal y and we can properly regard this identical result as definitely correct. If, on the other hand, the values of x and y are different, then we must be satisfied with the fact that the general price level has risen in *one* sense and fallen in another, or risen more in one respect than another. For practical purposes we might take a mean between the two different values, but it would have a purely conventional significance. It is not possible, in the nature of things, to advance further.

Neither need this occasion any surprise if only we clearly understand the nature of the question to which the general index number is expected to give an answer. What is aimed at is in fact such an average of prices as will, if it remains stable, have an unchanging economic significance for society however much the relative in prices of commodities may change. But such an average does not exist, or, more correctly, the calculation of such a figure would require a knowledge of altogether different, more fundamental data than the mere quantities consumed at various dates and their prices. It is obvious that its meaning cannot be the same for different individuals and classes of society; this is a defect which attaches to all averages and cannot be avoided.

Another difficulty inherent in all such statistics is the question as to which goods or utilities should generally be included in a calculation of this kind: whether only finished consumption goods or also raw materials: whether only goods in the strict sense or also the services of durable goods, such as rent of houses: and in particular whether the wage level should play a part in such a calculation. A complete answer can scarcely be given to this question. If one only wants to know to what extent the "cost of living" has become dearer or cheaper, the most obvious thing to do is to include all commodities, both material and immaterial, which can be directly consumed, and these only: and therefore wages would enter only in so far as they directly affect the price of those personal services which can be directly consumed. The problem is quite different if considered from other angles. In a country whose main products consist of raw materials which are shipped abroad in exchange for manufactured commodities, the price of the former plays as important a part as the combined prices of all the manufactured goods. Or again, it seems somewhat onesided to take into consideration as some writers do, only the great staple commodities of world trade, because only these prices are of major importance in business life: it is not only business men in the narrower sense who are interested in the level of prices.

The commonest index numbers, such as those of *The Economist*, suffer from yet another defect; they only take the prices in bond at the ports, i.e. the price of goods without the duty or tax, whereas the consumer must pay for the goods with the addition of customs and other duties and taxes, as well as the cost of transport within the country. But if, for example, high import duties are imposed, other things being equal, in a number of countries, then, at least from the point of view of the Quantity Theory, this would effect no difference in the average price of the goods finally consumed, duty free or not, for the quantity of money as well as the volume of transactions would still be the same. The result would then appear as a fall in the price of the goods still in bond, though in reality they would not have become cheaper. It must be asked whether precisely this considerable increase in protective duties in most European countries since the end of the 'seventies has not been one of the causes of the well-known fall in prices of staple commodities in the world market since. Yet it should be observed that such a change in prices is only of a formal nature and leaves the relative exchange value of the commodities apart from duties unchanged. It should therefore not be confused with the real pressure on prices which a great country can sometimes exercise on imported goods by imposing import duties.

Similarly, an increase in the international exchange of commodities would have the same effect if customs duties remained unchanged. Let us assume for the sake of simplicity that two countries impose duties on each other's products equal to the original value of the products, and that after this step has been taken one country (or both) imports *one-tenth* of its consumption goods from the other. If the value of money has not changed, then—always assuming that the particular producers of the goods which are now dutiable do not content themselves with a smaller profit than the producers of those goods which are produced and consumed in the country itself and are therefore duty-free—the results will be that the prices of all goods produced within the country and of those which are in bond and on which a duty has not been paid in the country will fall 10 per cent and those *subject to duty* will rise 90 per cent; for only in this way can the internal price level remain unchanged. If, with unchanged import duties, imports are increased to *two-tenths* of the total consumption of the country, then the result must be a further fall of 10 per cent in the price of all internal goods and foreign goods not subject to duty, and consequently in the index number calculated as above.

Although the example is highly artificial and leaves out of account many factors of importance, it nevertheless shows that the much discussed fall in prices between 1878–1893 (or 1873–1895) was *in part* only apparent, whereas the subsequent rise was in all probability *greater* than the changes in the index number indicate. It also explains why calculations using index numbers based on *market prices* actually paid show a greater rise for Protectionist countries than for Free Trade countries. So far as I can see, any great increase in the international exchange of commodities would necessarily have the consequences indicated above.

But from the recognition of all these imperfections it is a big step to the rejection of all attempts to measure changes in the purchasing power of money, for it would involve even more decisively the rejection as impossible of all efforts to stabilize this purchasing power. Certain changes such as those which arise from a continuous large production of precious metals under otherwise unchanged economic conditions, are on the contrary too obvious to escape anybody's attention or to be generally in dispute. Nor must it be forgotten that the present method of compiling price statistics as a basis for an index number is certainly capable of great improvements which would surely be of benefit in any practical attempt to regulate the value of money; at present these calculations have in the main only a theoretical interest. The price statistics already published in England and elsewhere are certainly far from valueless; their mutual agreement is great, much greater than one would expect, as they comprise different groups of commodities. And the attempts made by Palgrave and others to revise existing index numbers by basing them on the amounts of goods produced and consumed have shown that thereby only a modification in detail would be involved, and not a radical reconstruction of the general course of the price level previously calculated. That some artificiality must always attach to calculations of average is inevitable, especially if they are to apply to all countries simultaneously. But in so far as price statistics are to be made the foundation for the regulation of the value of money, it is necessary, unless we wish to sacrifice the most important advantage of the present system, to have a common measure of value for the whole world. There is, moreover, nothing to prevent each country compiling its own price statistics and suitably expressing its general price level in a general index number which would be extremely useful for a number of internal problems, such as wages, taxation, etc. In order to assess the general fluctuations in the value of money and to establish the primary conditions for its eventual regulation, it would then become necessary to compile year by year from the general index numbers of the various countries a world-wide or universal index number based on an accepted norm.

But even with such a perfected measurement of the value of money and its fluctuations only one-half of the problem, and that theoretically the easier, has been solved. There remains the difficult question of the causes of these changes and the means of preventing them.

3. *The Different Theories of the Value of Money. The Quantity Theory*

The only specific theory of the value of money which has been propounded, and perhaps the only one which can make any claim to real scientific importance, is the Quantity Theory, according to which the value or purchasing power of money varies in inverse proportion to its quantity, so that an increase or decrease in the quantity of money, other things being equal, will cause a proportionate decrease or increase in its purchasing power in terms of other goods, and thus a corresponding increase or decrease in all commodity prices. All other theories—and there are not many—are in reality no more than generalizations of the general theory of value applied to money; to that extent, therefore, even if they were otherwise tenable, they cannot be called *specific.*

Since, however, it is true of all commodities than an increase in supply in itself tends to lower their exchange value, there is nothing unusual in the quantity theory nor anything peculiar in money as such. The special peculiarity of the Quantity Theory consists in the proportionality required between the quantity of money and commodity prices. Whereas with other goods a diminished supply may now produce a violent, now a slight and hardly perceptible fluctuation in their exchange value, according to the different elasticities of demand, yet only in the case of money do these two factors always stand in this simple relation to one another. Let the abscissa of our curve be the supply, and the ordinates the exchange value as against all other goods in their mean. Then on the assumption of stable demand, this curve will, in the case of ordinary commodities, fall sometimes slowly, sometimes rapidly, towards the x axis, and the rest of the curve can as a rule only be indicated hypothetically. For money, on the other hand, we should obtain a determinate mathematical curve, in the form of a rectangular hyperbola asymptotic to the two axes.

It is here that we find the purely formal character of money, its quality of performing a single social function, that of a medium of exchange and store of value: for we may regard these two concepts as different aspects of one and the same function. Money evidently only performs this function to the extent that it possesses exchange value, and since the general economic principle undoubtedly tends to the utmost possible employment and efficiency of every economic factor, we must assume—at any rate, for the purpose of the Quantity Theory—

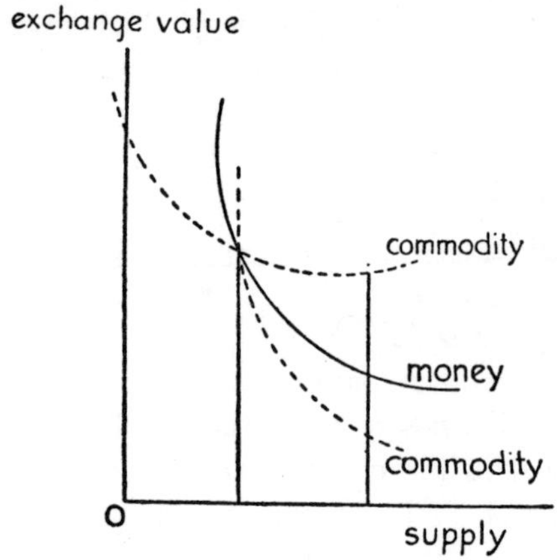

that the inconveniences of too small a quantity of money will be gradually and as it were automatically corrected by money acquiring a correspondingly higher purchasing power, and the inconveniences of too large an amount of money will be neutralized in the same way by a corresponding fall in the value of money, since some part of the money will lie idle in individual hands.

Naturally we must not suppose that a sudden increase or decrease in the quantity of money immediately produces an equally large rise or fall in commodity prices. In the first place the latter would presumably remain as high or as low as before, and the whole change would be noticeable as a retardation or acceleration in the circulation of money, or, the same thing, an increase or decrease of average individual cash holdings. Only gradually would the excess or deficiency in the holdings lead to increased demand (and diminished supply) for goods, or vice versa (cf. p. 157).

It is also clear that the theory in its pure form can only apply to money as such, and therefore—if only metallic coin is used or is regarded as money—to *minted* metal alone. With free minting, however, the limits between minted and unminted metal are very indefinite and variable. It is therefore tempting to apply the theory to the whole of the existing stocks of gold. But in that case it must be somewhat modified, since gold fulfils two functions, that of money and that of an industrial raw material: even if all the assumptions for the correctness of the quantity theory were satisfied, our curve would more or less deviate from the simple form of a hyperbola because of the hitherto little studied laws concerning the dependence of the industrial demand for gold upon the value of gold and its influence upon the amount of gold available for minting purposes.

In reality, of course, it is very rarely possible to establish such precise mathematical relations as theory demands. Both the advocates and the opponents of the quantity theory therefore content themselves with asserting or denying that an increase or reduction in the relative quantity of money will cause a corresponding change in the commodity price level and a reverse change in the value of money. It may seem strange that even in this modified form the theory can be in dispute, for it states nothing more, after all, than what is true of all other goods, namely that an increase or reduction of supply *in itself* leads to a consequent fall or rise in price. However, the conceptions of supply and demand have no direct application to money, and those who consider that the velocity of circulation, or the use of credit instruments as a substitute for money, is automatically regulated according to the need for a means of turnover, must naturally and logically reject the conclusions of the quantity theory *a limine*. It will readily be seen that the whole dispute turns ultimately on this last point: whether the velocity of circulation of money is of autonomous or merely subordinate significance for the currency system; for that the quantity of money, multiplied by the velocity of circulation—the latter in the widest sense of the term used here—must always coincide with the total value of the goods and services turned over against money in a given period of time, is not a theory at all; it is an axiom.

The originator of the Quantity Theory is usually held to be the Italian writer Davanzatti, who lived in the sixteenth century. The theory, however, became widely known through the writings of Locke and Hume. From the latter it was taken over by the classical economists. It is possible, however, to discover traces of it as far back as in the ancient world; at any rate the seed would appear to have been sown so soon as people observed—as they must often have done during the Roman Empire—that money struck exclusively for the State might for long periods maintain a value considerably higher than that of its metallic content, but sank in value when it was minted in too large quantities. In more recent times the Quantity Theory has arisen rather as a reaction against the mercantile theory, which regarded money itself as the essence of wealth and not merely its external expression, and which consequently had to attribute to it an inherent value independent of its exchange functions. Diametrically opposed to this is the view that money as such has no value; it acquires full value only by serving as a medium of exchange, and it acquires just that value which is necessary for its satisfactory performance of this function. In this way the Quantity Theory arose in its fully developed form.

The difficulty of testing the theory empirically lies, as with all economic doctrines, in isolating from concrete reality just those elements of which it consists. In fact, an increase—or when it occurs, a decrease—in the volume of money always coincides with a number of other economic changes which tend to cancel out or to conceal its effects on the price level and the value of money. Population increases and production expands as a result of technical improvements, so that the amount of goods annually consumed increases not only to the same, but to an even greater extent than the increase in population. The turnover may increase to an even higher degree than production owing to the national and international division of labour and to the resulting transition from barter and payment in kind to business based on exchange and money wages. All these factors bring it about that an absolute increase in the volume of money may very well be accompanied by no change or even by a reduction in its quantity *relatively* to the needs of turnover and thus be followed by a fall instead of a rise in the level of prices.

In an article in *Ekonomisk Tidskrift* (1904, p. 113) Professor Cassel, bearing this circumstance in mind, makes an interesting attempt to compare changes in the supply of gold and commodity prices in the nineteenth century. The attempt suffers greatly, however, as F. Brock has rightly pointed out, from the fact that he has not extended his remarks to the changes in quantity of silver also, even at a time when the commercial currencies of the world consisted mainly of silver.

On the other hand, commercial progress also acts in a contrary direction, increasing the physical or virtual velocity of circulation, effecting, by the use of credit, a more intensive use of existing money with the consequence that the maximum efficiency in the medium of exchange which the Quantity Theory requires and presupposes is raised to a higher level. A relatively smaller quantity of money need not necessarily involve a proportionately increased exchange value in order to perform the same services as media of exchange and as cash holdings as a larger one, if the same purpose can be achieved by a more intensive use or an increased velocity of circulation of the smaller quantity.

It is very common, though of course entirely illogical, to find these circumstances, or their actual effects adduced as a conclusive argument against the Quantity Theory, almost as illogical as it would be in the case of the upward movement of a balloon to say that it disproved the general validity of the law of gravity. If we merely wish to assert that the Quantity Theory, owing to all these disturbing factors, cannot give us any practical guidance in the consideration of the currency systems of our own day, we may perhaps be right—although the experience of the last decades is indisputable evidence against it—but to invalidate it completely we require something more, we must show either that it is impossible to maintain the presuppositions on which it is based or that its logical structure is inadmissible.

4. *The Cost of Production Theory*

It is not enough, however, to rest content with this purely negative or suspended judgment. On the pretence that the Quantity Theory is refuted by experience, attempts have been made to invent other explanations, all of which, however, suffer from the defect that they ignore the circumstances which are peculiar to money, and at bottom only consist of an attempt to apply the economic laws pertaining to goods in general to a field in which they are in the nature of things incapable of application. Since the naïve idea was abandoned that money possesses an inherent value it became necessary to discover the grounds of this value in something outside money, and in accordance with the theory of the classical school it was supposed to be found in the costs of production of money, i.e. of the precious metals, relative to the costs of other goods. The less the effort and sacrifice required for the production of a certain quantity of gold in comparison with the production of a certain quantity of other goods, the larger the quantity of gold must be which will exchange for one unit of those other goods. In other words, their price rises and the exchange value of gold falls. This is the so-called cost of production theory, or, more correctly expressed, the theory of the comparative cost of the value of money, which was brought to a high degree of theoretical perfection by Senior. Senior maintained that in the case of countries not producing silver and gold to an appreciable extent the costs of procuring, i.e. the costs of producing and transporting not the metals themselves, but the goods for which the desired quantities of the precious metals were to be exchanged, played the same role as the actual costs of production in the mines. He thus found a natural explanation of the fact—very striking in earlier times when communications were still undeveloped

—that in the interior parts of a continent commodity prices were habitually much lower than on the coasts. In Germany one used to speak of "thaler" countries and "gulden" countries, i.e. North Germany on the one hand and South Germany and Austria on the other, in the sense that a thaler in the former was not regarded as having greater purchasing power than a gulden in the latter, although containing 50 to 100 per cent more silver. Even to this day we encounter the same phenomenon in those parts of the world not yet provided with railways. In the interior parts of Germany's African colonies, wages as late as 1915 are said not to have been more than a few pfennigs a day, which must have corresponded to the cost of provisions for a workman or rather a workman's family for one day.

The well-known text-book writer, Ch. Gide, has completely overlooked this when he says that the low cost of transport of gold should result in one gramme of gold having almost the same purchasing power over goods everywhere. This is, of course, false reasoning: it is not possible to obtain gold without sending goods in payment and it is these, usually much larger, transport costs that matter.

There can be no question, as we shall soon see, of a direct relation or exact parallelism between the costs of production of the precious metals and the value of money. Senior also admits this and gives striking examples of how the production of the precious metals has on occasion been made difficult, or even impossible, without any marked change in prices, a circumstance clearly due to the fact that this production, especially in earlier times, was extremely small in proportion to the total stocks of money and precious metal. In contrast to Senior, Karl Marx and his school who generally carry the classical theory of value to its extreme, and consequently to the point of absurdity, adhere to the cost of production theory as a simple and tangible explanation of the value of money and oppose it to the Quantity Theory, which Marx calls an illusion based on the "insipid hypothesis that goods without a price and money without a value enter into the process of circulation, for which reason an aliquot part of grain is subsequently exchanged for an aliquot part of metal". Yet it is not difficult to show that, even from the point of view of the cost of production theory, goods "enter into the process of circulation without price and money, i.e. gold, without value", and that they acquire their relative exchange values just by this process of circulation. Karl Marx is himself compelled to admit that labour is wasted and cannot be counted if it produces nothing useful or if it exceeds the amount of socially necessary labour-time. We only need to carry the argument one stage further to realize that labour, or rather the productive forces in combination, will be rewarded by exactly the market value of its product; in other words that costs of production and price mutually control each other. If, therefore, more gold is produced than the process of circulation can absorb at ruling prices, then the value of gold will fall and the producers of gold will have to content themselves with a smaller income—in other words the costs of production of gold are reduced—unless they prefer to abandon their work.

Moreover, in the case of *extractive* industries such as gold mining, the costs of production, in the sense of amounts of labour and capital employed, are very different for different parts of the product, owing to the abundance or scarcity of gold in the mines or river beds in which the production of gold is profitable at all. Attempts have also been made to improve upon the theory by substituting for the words "costs of production" the words "marginal costs of production", i.e. those incurred in the production of a certain quantity of gold in the least profitable mines or goldfields, which leave no profit after payment of wages and possibly interest on capital. But this margin is itself highly variable; a rise in the value of gold, e.g. due to increased demand for minting or to improved technique of production, may cause mines and goldfields previously regarded as too poor to be worked, again to be exploited; old slag heaps will be gone over again, etc., in other words the margin of production will be extended. On the other hand, a fall in the value of the metal, such as we have seen in our own time in the case of silver as a result of its demonetization, will necessarily cause labour and capital—

in so far as the latter can be released at all—to be withdrawn from the less profitable fields of production, and the margin of production will contract.

On the whole, therefore, the influence of the conditions of production of the precious metals, and nowadays particularly of gold, on the value of money—an influence which is certainly not slight, but in the long run predominating—is to be found in the relative increase or decrease they bring about in the existing quantity of money, in so far as greater ease of production of gold has a tendency to increase the available quantity at a pace more rapid than that of the ever increasing demand for a medium of turnover, whereas increasing difficulties in the production of gold tend to slow down the tempo of the increase in the supply of gold. The cost of production theory is thus fully justified as constituting *an element* in the Quantity Theory. But only one element. Since the annual production of gold, even in the most favourable circumstances, can only increase the existing stocks of gold coin by a few per cent, changes in output will only gradually, and as a rule very slowly, exert their influence, whilst an increase in the production and turnover of goods occasioned by technical improvements, or still more the transition of one or more countries to a gold standard, may sometimes increase the demand for the medium of exchange in a much higher degree. And on the other hand a more intensive employment of the gold stocks available in the banks, whether by means of banknotes, cheques, bills of exchange, current accounts, or by the general development of the credit and banking system, may produce a much greater increase in the media of exchange than the simultaneous production of gold ; on the other hand it may for long periods neutralize the effects of a decrease in gold production. Were this not so, it would be impossible to explain the rapid rise in commodity prices which usually occurs in times of business prosperity and the even more violent setbacks in times of crisis.

The latter circumstances—the physical and virtual velocity of circulation of money which the Quantity Theory is accused, though wrongly, of having overlooked—can, however, find no place in the cost of production theory and is in fact rather cold-shouldered by its consistent advocates. To Marx the velocity of circulation of money is simply an automatic process whereby the existing supplies of money always spontaneously reach equilibrium with the requirements of turnover at a given commodity price level, whilst that price level itself is determined by the comparative costs of production of goods and gold. " One piece of money," he remarks in his picturesque, though precisely on that account unscientific language, " becomes so to speak responsible for another; if it increases its velocity of circulation it cripples that of the other or else it completely vanishes from the sphere of circulation," since the latter at existing prices can only absorb a given quantity of gold. In proof of this, he remarks, it is " only necessary to throw a given number of one pound notes into circulation in order to throw out an equal number of sovereigns—a trick well known to every bank ".

This language is very vague. We need not dispute that up to a point the velocity of circulation of money can sometimes be automatically acclerated or retarded, but the idea that this will always happen to the desired extent leads to absurd results, for it presupposes that merchants and bankers would quite passively submit to seeing their safes filled to overflowing when gold is plentiful, and exhausted when it is scarce, perhaps to the last sovereign, without taking any steps to restore the normal position. As regards the money driven out of circulation, Marx completely forgets to tell us whither it is driven, though he cannot possibly imagine that it is stored up in money-boxes.

As regards the banks' " well-known trick " of " throwing a certain number of one pound notes into circulation in order to throw out an equal number of sovereigns (or metallic money)," we must carefully distinguish between two different points of view. If for one reason or another the banks desire to strengthen their gold reserves, then certainly the issue of banknotes of small denomination is a useful means to that end, as was shown, for example, by the German Reichsbank when it issued 20-mark notes in addition to the 100-mark notes which it had previously issued alone. The public accepts and uses these as willingly as, or even more willingly than, metallic currency, and the banks can then retain the gold which flows into them in daily payment of debts or deposits, while on the other hand they pay out banknotes against discounted bills or their other loans. All this, however, has nothing to do with our immediate problem, since the whole process is nothing more than the substitution of one medium of exchange for another.

It is quite certain that an increased issue of notes, especially of small denomination, tends to drive metallic money out of circulation, not because more money cannot be absorbed, but because the increased supply of the means of turnover will lead to a rise in prices, so that the balance of trade becomes unfavourable and metallic money flows out of the country—all in complete accordance with the Quantity Theory, but in conflict with what Marx wishes to prove. I am assuming here that the notes are issued by the banks by way of loan and as a result of extended or cheap credit, for if the banks should restrict themselves to exchanging notes for gold, so that gold accumulated in their own vaults, then their "trick" would only involve them in losses, since they must themselves provide for and maintain the note circulation.

Of course, the cost of production theory is still more blatantly inadequate when it comes to explaining the exchange value of purely conventional money such as token money, standard money with limited coinage, inconvertible notes, etc. Those who wish at all costs to maintain an "inherent" value of money dependent on its metallic content or costs of production as the basis of its exchange value are driven in this case to the most perverse and fantastic explanations. At one moment it is the image of the actual metallic currency into which the notes were at one time convertible before they were declared legal tender which remains in the mind of the public and thereby to some extent maintains the value of the notes, at another moment it is the hope of the future convertibility of the notes into metal. Support has been sought for the latter view in the fact that the mere announcement of the resumption of convertibility of notes at a certain future date, and also external circumstances, such as political and military success, whereby confidence in the Government is increased, are sufficient to give paper currency a considerably higher value and to diminish the discount against metallic money, although the notes continue to circulate in amounts as great as before, and should thus according to the Quantity Theory maintain their value unchanged.

During the Union War in the United States it was necessary to declare dollar notes inconvertible, and their value sank, so that between 1863–4 the gold premium rose 40 per cent, although the number of notes issued was only increased by 16 per cent. During the Battle of Gettysberg the premium on gold rose to 45 per cent, but owing to its victorious conclusion and to the Battle of Vicksburg, it sank in a few days to 23⅓ per cent (Laughlin).

In fact, however, under such circumstances notes no longer circulate in the same quantities as before or, at any rate, no longer circulate with the same average velocity. The hope of convertibility in the early future at face value affects notes in the same way as an increased bill discount rate in the country of payment affects long-term bills: they are converted (in part) from means of payment into capital investments. Many people hoard banknotes in the hope of gain from an expected conversion at par value, which gain possibly represents a high rate of interest. In this way the average velocity of circulation, and therefore the amount of money actually circulating at any particular time, is retarded, and the increase in value is in complete agreement with the Quantity Theory. It is moreover probable, for various reasons, that it will operate more strongly or at least more rapidly on metallic money in reducing the premium on the latter or the discount on notes than on a lowering of commodity prices proper reckoned in notes. But we need not discuss this question further.

The position will be reversed in times of political instability, when an increased note issue and an ensuing fall in their value is to be feared. Nobody will then hoard notes, but everybody will exchange them for goods or other real wealth as soon as possible (and at practically any price), so that the circulation of money will be accelerated beyond the normal. In extreme cases paper money may under such conditions lose practically all its value—as happened in the case of the French *assignats*—to the extent that business will begin to employ foreign money or revert to pure barter. But this also, as will clearly be seen, is not contrary to the Quantity Theory, for in this case the volume of the purchases effected by the depreciated paper money will be correspondingly reduced.

It may be observed *en passant* that the history of the French *assignats* affords an interesting contribution to the theory of the *funding* of banknotes or paper money. In order to maintain the value of these *assignats* the Government accepted them in payment of the purchase of " national property " (confiscated church property, etc.). Had this been done at a definite predetermined price, e.g. per acre, this object could certainly have been achieved. For if the *assignats* had then begun to fall in value a number of people would have retained them in order at a later date to transact profitable business by purchasing national property. In that way the value of the *assignats* could have been kept almost unchanged and the Government which permitted the payment of taxes in *assignats* might without loss have cancelled the notes which flowed in in payment for purchases.

In fact, however, the national property was sold at auction to the highest bidder, i.e. for the largest sum in *assignats* which it could command. Thereby the brake (which would have existed in the hoarding of these for speculative purposes) on a heavier fall in the value of the *assignats* was obviously removed; since the Government then received payment of taxes in money which had lost its value, it found itself compelled not only to reissue the *assignats* which it received in payment for national property but also to issue large additional quantities with the inevitable consequence that they soon became valueless.

5. *Modern Theories*

The view of this problem which is nowadays advanced even by writers who claim to be rigorously scientific is still less scientific, if possible, than the Marxist and kindred theories.

The cost of production theory does at least, though one-sidedly, find the cause of the change in the value of money in something directly affecting money. But in modern reasoning on general commodity prices, money is not infrequently regarded as a kind of amorphous, infinitely elastic, or plastic mass which adapts itself without any pressure to any price level and is therefore entirely passive in relation to the pricing mechanism, whilst the latter is regulated only by circumstances concerning the commodities themselves. If there occurs such a general and enduring fall of prices as was witnessed in the last three decades before 1890, at any rate as regards world prices, this is found to be sufficiently explained by reference to the progress in the technique of production and transport: goods are produced more cheaply and are transported more cheaply, therefore they are cheaper. If, on the other hand, there is a rise in prices, as in the years immediately before the War, then it is the higher standard of living and increased enterprise which produces an increased demand for goods, unless we also take refuge in the supposed screwing up of prices by cartels and trusts, the greed of middlemen, trade union claims for higher wages, etc.; or else the cause is found in import duties—even though no increase in such duties occurred during the period in question. To such an extent have people accustomed themselves to seeing in the modern credit and banking system a means of satisfying any demand whatever on the part of society for a medium of exchange that they cannot conceive of money influencing prices in one direction or the other. The many apparent inconsistencies between the Quantity Theory (and also the cost of production theory) and the actual facts have completely discredited that theory in the eyes of most people. Some other explanation is sought and the first available one is chosen. But in reality nothing is explained. The reasoning contains an inadmissable generalization; for arguments which are valid only when it is a matter of relative prices are applied without qualification to a field in which they no longer possess any meaning, i.e. to the absolute prices of commodities, expressed in money. That a commodity which can be manufactured more easily will fall in price is at bottom a corollary of the obvious fact that labour and capital, in so far as they can be readily transferred from one branch of production to another, must always tend, each for itself, to obtain an equal return in all branches of production. There is clearly nothing else in the theory of the dependence of relative prices on the cost of production. But how meaningless it is to seek to apply this to concrete prices, to the relation of goods to money, if the conditions of production, or other conditions influencing money are not taken into consideration at all!

From the point of view of the Quantity Theory there is no doubt that increased production tends to depress prices unless it is accompanied by a corresponding increase in the medium of exchange, simply because the velocity of circulation of money cannot be increased at will to any degree whatever. If we believe this possible, then evidently there is nothing to prevent the increased productivity finding expression in a rise along the whole line instead—in wages, rent, and interest on capital, expressed in money—whilst general prices remain undisturbed or even rise. In other words, the relative cheapening of a certain group of commodities owing to easier conditions of production would not produce a perfectly equal fall in its money price but would consist partly of a small increase in the price of all other goods, so that the average price level might perhaps remain unaltered, or, in any case, would not fall.

As regards a fall in the cost of *transport*, it is quite forgotten that this has a twofold effect: a fall in price in the place of destination, the importing country, and a rise in price in the exporting country, or country of production, in consequence of the increased demand from other places. Thus on the whole there is a levelling up rather than a fall in prices. In Senior's view, which as far as it goes is quite correct, lower transport costs have the further result that the non-goldproducing countries can obtain their requirements of gold at a lower cost in goods than before. But this would be the same thing as a fall in the exchange value of gold, i.e. a rise, and not a fall, in commodity prices. In the interior of continents and in remote places improvements in transport have certainly brought about a considerable rise in the general price level. By the great increase of production, exchange and turnover in general which improved transport produces it certainly creates a tendency, on the other hand, to lower prices, if the amount of money is unchanged. But this again takes us back to the Quantity Theory.

The same is true of the other alleged causes of a rise in prices. Import duties and taxes on consumption undoubtedly lead to higher prices of the commodities so taxed, but it is by no means certain that other goods will remain unchanged in price and that therefore the general price level will rise. In any case, there is nothing to prevent the possibility of a simultaneous pressure on and fall in the prices of other goods—as the Quantity Theory would lead us to suppose—so that the average price level would remain unchanged unless there existed some monetary cause for their change. The reader is referred to pp. 138–9 for the effects of a customs union or increased international trade on the prices of duty-free goods and on the commonest index numbers. Trusts and rings, and even middlemen, may undoubtedly raise their price by the monopolization of one commodity or other, though as a rule, demand is reduced thereby, in full accordance with the Quantity Theory. In proportion as trustification extends, however, this procedure would become quite purposeless, as may easily be seen, for the trusts would rather seek to profit by reduced overhead costs, which should result in lower rather than higher prices. Middlemen are as a rule only links in the social division of labour and should consequently assist in lowering the prices of the goods in question. There are, of course, exceptions to this rule, as we have shown in the treatment of retail prices in an earlier section (Vol. I, pp. 86–8). But even superfluous middlemen cannot raise the general price level. The contrary is more probably the case, since goods would then pass through more hands and the same quantity of money would effect a greater number of exchanges.

As regards rises in wages Ricardo, and later John Stuart Mill, have clearly shown that a general rise in wages cannot possibly increase the price of goods produced by the same labour. In this connection it should be sufficient to point out that if more highly paid labour makes all goods more expensive, it must also make gold dearer, since it also is a product of labour. Since, however, gold is the measure of prices, it cannot itself either rise or fall in price. If, therefore, the producers of all other goods could indemnify themselves for increased wages by a higher price for their products, whilst the producers of gold alone could not do so, this must result in a decline in the production of gold. A rise in money wages along the whole line is therefore either equivalent to a fall in the share of the product of the two other factors of production, land, and capital, which must leave the prices of commodities on an average unchanged, or else the general rise in money wages is caused by easier facilities for producing gold, in which case the rise is purely nominal and is only one link in the general rise in the prices of goods which occurs when in accordance with the Quantity Theory or the cost of production theory the production of gold becomes cheaper.

However, this does not prevent a rise in wages caused by an increased (money) demand for labour—a fact which the classical economists perhaps overlooked. This rise in wages in its turn causes a rise in the prices of the goods *already on the market* and thus establishes a higher price level, which will be maintained through the force of inertia even in the future. On the whole, this remains true even if the increased demand for labour originally proceeded from the increased production of gold. If, on the other hand, it has proceeded from extended credit facilities a further inquiry will be necessary, to which we shall return later.

Increased prosperity need not, of course, lead to higher prices. On the contrary the additional well-being may find expression in a greater cheapness of everything, with unchanged income. The view which was formerly so often held—even by a writer such as Ricardo—that a higher standard of living in a country was always combined with a high price level, was an illusion, fostered no doubt by the fact that prices in England, compared with other countries, were unusually high, especially at the beginning of the last century. This, again, was due to the fact that at that time England exported few bulky raw materials, but imported considerable quantities, such as grain, timber, etc., whereas this position is now altered to a large extent, in so far as England exports large quantities of coal, so that it obtains a large part of its imports at low return freights in collieries. And yet perhaps just for that reason the welfare of the great masses of the population of England is incomparably greater than a hundred years ago. Similarly England's free trade has contributed to the lowering of its prices in comparison with those of protectionist countries. Broadly speaking the price of the same commodity cannot vary in two different countries by much more than the import duty and the freight. A factor which certainly tends to raise the cost of living in prosperous countries is the high level of wages and the ensuing higher prices for all personal services and all work done by hand. But this does not appreciably affect commodity prices, or at any rate the prices of those commodities entering into commercial statistics.

Finally, as regards the statement that increased entrepreneurial activity may lead to higher prices, this is often true, but only on the assumptions which we have already indicated and which we shall examine more in detail at a later stage. In itself the increased "spirit of enterprise", i.e. the increased employment of capital in the service of production, only creates an increased demand for certain raw materials which are necessary for the creation of almost all fixed capital, especially iron and steel, bricks, timber, etc., and these are in fact the goods which at the beginning of so-called "good" times first rise in price.[1] But whether this rise in prices will be followed by a rise or a fall in the prices of other commodities cannot be determined in advance. It depends on whether the money market itself has participated in stimulating the spirit of enterprise. If the moneys from which the increased demand for fixed capital, or its components, proceeds are the fruits of *present* savings, then there will be a corresponding decrease in the demand for ordinary consumption goods, and their price should accordingly fall.

[1] The American statistics given by W. C. Mitchell's *Business Cycles* do not seem entirely to confirm this view, especially as regards pig iron. I will not for the moment discuss how this contradiction is to be explained or whether it is only apparent.

The case is quite different where the necessary money capital is partly supplied from metallic reserves which were accumulated and lay idle during previous "bad" times or where they are created by extended credit, in other words, by an accelerated velocity of circulation of money.

6. *The Defects of the Quantity Theory. An Attempt at a Rational Theory*

In the foregoing I have merely wished to point out the folly of supposing that circumstances in which, as in the case of concrete commodity prices, there is an essential relation between two things—goods and money—can ever be satisfactorily explained from the point of view of the changes undergone by only one of them, in this case goods, without reference to the other, money. It is, moreover, evident that it would be useless to dwell on the question at all if this view were not in fact so widespread, not only in business jargon but also in scientific literature, especially German.

In one respect, however, this view is justified and serves a purpose in more detailed investigations into the causes of price changes. Every rise or fall in the price of a particular commodity presupposes a disturbance of the equilibrium between the supply of and the demand for that commodity, whether the disturbance has actually taken place or is merely prospective. What is true *in this respect* of each commodity separately must doubtless be true of all commodities collectively. A general rise in prices is therefore only conceivable on the supposition that the general demand has for some reason become, or is expected to become, greater than the supply. This may sound paradoxical, because we have accustomed ourselves, with J. B. Say, to regard goods themselves as reciprocally constituting and limiting the demand for each other. And indeed *ultimately* they do so; here, however, we are concerned with precisely what occurs, *in the first place*, with the middle link in the final exchange of one good against another, which is formed by the demand of money for goods and the supply of goods against money. Any theory of money worthy of the name must be able to show how and why the monetary or pecuniary demand for goods exceeds or falls short of the supply of goods in given conditions.

The advocates of the Quantity Theory have perhaps not sufficiently considered this point. They usually make the mistake of postulating their assumptions instead of clearly proving them. That a large and a small quantity of money *can* serve the same purposes of turnover if commodity prices rise or fall proportionately to the quantity is one thing. It is another thing to show why such a change of price must always follow a change in the quantity of money and to describe what happens. Nor is this so easy, especially with our modern and extremely complicated monetary and credit systems. Nevertheless, in what follows we shall attempt to do so. In accordance with what has been said above we shall first describe the probable effects of a relative increase or decrease of the quantity of metallic money, and also the analogous phenomena associated with the issue of a State paper currency or inconvertible banknotes. We shall then consider in more detail the conditions of acceleration or retardation of the velocity of circulation and the influence of both on the value of money. In both respects the literature of currency, otherwise so voluminous, leaves much to be desired as regards detail and clearness.

Hume's well-known fiction of our waking up one morning to find double the number of shillings and sovereigns in our pockets, whilst everything else remains unchanged, may seem quite appropriate, but suffers from the defect that it is not a simplification of reality—which is permissible—but relates to a purely paradoxical case, which in the nature of things never can occur. Moreover it is clear that such an eventuality would in no way cause us immediately to begin to offer or demand double prices for what we require or can sell. Only gradually would the *superfluity of cash* dispose us, for example, to effect a purchase earlier than otherwise or to retain our goods longer than usual. In other words, the demand for goods would be stimulated and the supply diminished, whilst at the same time commodity prices would gradually rise until they reached a level corresponding to the increased quantity of money. But since the whole idea contains an assumption contrary to reality, we may perhaps add that the rise in prices required by the Quantity Theory from an increased supply of money is in fact *not* reached in *this* manner.

The matter becomes simpler if we consider the effect which a sudden large increase in gold output would have, and has in fact sometimes had in our own times, on world price conditions. The discovery of rich goldfields or gold mines in, say, a colony immediately attracts a very large part, perhaps the largest part, of an already scanty population to the goldfields and induces it to abandon its usual occupations. The first result will be not only a great superfluity of gold but also a scarcity of goods. The existing stocks will soon be in demand and exhausted, and the consequence will be a rapid rise in prices, often to fantastic heights. Tooke and Newmarch in their *History of Prices* relate how in California in the glorious days of 1848–9 everybody was a buyer at any price, an egg cost a dollar, a pair of boots 100 dollars, medicine such as opium was retailed at 6*d*. a drop, and fine iron pins which the gold diggers were accustomed to use to secure the strips of cloth with which they covered the walls of their log cabins were, to make matters simpler, paid for by their weight in gold. If this were the final result it is clear that it would check or even render impossible the further production of gold. Indeed the inhabitants of such a country would soon come to look upon the lumps of gold scattered about the country with the same indifference as did the nations of America at the time of the first discovery of gold. This preliminary stage soon merges, however, into another. Rumours of the newly discovered wealth attract not only new gold diggers but also consignments of goods from all quarters in order to profit by the high prices, with the result that prices soon revert to normal and at the first shock possibly fall below normal. As early as the year 1851, according to the above authors, bales of valuable goods were scarcely worth the cost of storage in California. What happened and what might have continued to happen for many decades had certain striking features, among which the most important characteristics were the following. Owing to the fall in prices occasioned by the heavy influx of goods, the production of gold again became extremely profitable, but since most of the gold-fields had passed into private ownership they no longer attracted an unlimited amount of labour, but continued on more or less the same scale year after year. The prices of most commodities remained at a level, apart from transport costs, somewhat, though not much, higher than the corresponding level in the non-goldproducing countries, and so they remained during the changes which they subsequently underwent and of which we shall shortly speak. The balance of trade of the country will therefore be passive or unfavourable and gold will continue to flow out, which is quite natural and necessary since it is produced in much larger quantities than the turnover of the country requires.

Meanwhile the constant flow of gold to the non-gold-producing countries causes a progressive increase in prices there, although, owing to their vastness and populousness, this may for a long time not be noticeable or may even be counterbalanced by other causes such as a change of monetary standard or an increased demand for gold. Normally prices would rise in the following manner: exporters of goods whose claims abroad had previously been met either by the sale of bills of exchange drawn by them on their foreign debtors, or by the remittance from abroad of bills drawn on importers of foreign goods, will now be paid partly in gold, and this gold will constitute an addition to what was already in the hands of the public (or was deposited in the banks) for the purchase of goods. If we now revert to our simple schematic example of two commodities, butter and coffee, the imports and exports of which balance, even among those who ultimately produce and consume them—then on the assumption here made this would no longer be the case. At first, the increased demand for and diminished supply of goods from the gold countries causes, directly or indirectly, a rise in the price both of our butter and of the coffee we import, but although the price of commodities rises, yet imports and exports no longer balance. On the contrary, if formerly Sweden imported coffee to the value of forty million crowns and exported butter to the same amount, our butter exports will now rise to, say, forty-two million crowns and our coffee imports to forty-one million crowns, as the remaining million would enter in the form of bullion. In order to make the matter clearer we will assume that the rise in price of both butter and coffee in the first year is 3¾ per cent, so that the increased export value of exported butter is caused partly by an increase in the volume of exports (about 1¼ per cent). For the same reason imports of coffee will be less than before (also 1¼ per cent) in spite of the increased purchase prices. On the whole, this must happen, since a part of the coffee harvest now goes to the gold producers. Since, then, the Swedish population (producers of butter) does not fully satisfy its need for coffee, though it has more than sufficient money income to do so, its demand will immediately lead to a further rise in the price of coffee, and when this increase has reached the producers of coffee through the agency of importers here and exporters in the producing countries it will create among them an increased monetary demand for imported goods (in addition to that which has developed spontaneously there for the same reasons as here). This will directly or indirectly stimulate a further rise in the price of our butter, which will again raise the price of coffee, etc., until the production of gold, which becomes less profitable with every such rise in prices, either ceases or is restricted until it is exactly sufficient for the normal demand for new gold. Again, so long as the extra demand for goods by the gold countries continues, the rise in prices can never cease, for the price equilibrium in our and other markets presupposes, in the main, that imports and exports balance, and that can never happen so long as one part of our exports is paid for in gold beyond the normal requirements of turnover. It is quite different if from the beginning we require gold, e.g. to adopt a gold standard in place of a silver standard, or of paper currency. We should then be in a position either to offer silver abroad or to take up a loan, or to acquire the means by additional taxation, so that consumption within the country would be correspondingly decreased. In all these cases, as will easily be seen, there could be no stimulus to higher prices from our side and gold would simply take the place of silver or paper in business and banking, whereas in the former case it constantly increased the existing supplies of the medium of exchange.

If, on the other hand, the production of gold falls below the normal requirements for new gold, similar phenomena occur, but in the opposite direction: commodity prices constantly fall until the production of gold, which thereby becomes more profitable, is again sufficient for ordinary requirements, or possibly new gold mines are discovered.

This account of the course of events, if correct, may possibly modify the views commonly held of the effects of an increased or diminished production of gold. It is frequently supposed that the newly imported gold only gradually, after arrival, causes a rise in prices. In the meantime, it is supposed to lie idle in safes or in the vaults of banks and the normal consequence of this should be that the sums available as loans would increase beyond requirements. Since the excess of gold is always maintained by continued imports, the result must be that the rising prices would be caused by an unusually low rate of interest, and only when prices had reached the maximum and the turnover absorbed the increased volume of money would interest rates rise again to the normal. And vice versa in the case of a shortage of gold and falling prices.

Experience shows, however—and the opponents of the Quantity Theory have not been slow to point it out—that the position is rather the reverse: periods of rising prices are usually characterized by high interest rates, while falling prices and low interest rates usually coincide. In what follows, when we come to speak of the influence of credit on prices, we shall find what I believe to be a fully satisfactory explanation of this fact. It will be sufficient to say here that even if price fluctuations were caused exclusively by changes in the production of gold—which is certainly not the case—then the contradiction would perhaps not be as great as it appears at first sight. A rise in prices may be conceived as due to increased demand even before the cases of gold have been received in payment for exported goods, perhaps even long before, since even the preparations for gold mining require large amounts of labour and capital, i.e. of goods which will only be paid for in the future by the newly mined gold, and the capital perhaps may only be partly created by actual savings (and thus by a diminished demand for goods) the rest being brought into being by claims on bank credit.[1] Meanwhile a rise in prices becomes possible and may perhaps be caused in the first instance by a freer use of credit, and interest rates will have a tendency to rise rather than fall. The increasing gold stocks would then act as a kind of buttress to the price movement, preventing it from falling back, as it would otherwise sooner or later have to do in consequence of the contraction of credit, i.e. as a prop introduced *later* for a rise in prices which has already started, rather than as its prime cause.

The contrary would be true in the case of diminished gold production if we supposed that the diminished demand for goods from the goldfields led to a fall in prices, for which the existing supplies of the medium of exchange would possibly be quite sufficient. We should then find the curious coincidence which attracted so much attention in the 'seventies and 'eighties and was thought to defy any explanation: diminished gold production and falling commodity prices, but at the same time an excess of loan money and falling rates of interest.

I only mention this, in passing, as a conceivable hypothesis; the phenomena in question have been studied in too little detail for us to be able to express any definite opinion, and in any case the picture is too incomplete if we do not take into account any other cause of the rise in prices than the magnitude of the gold stocks. The very fact that a continuous large increase or decrease of those stocks must *ceteris paribus* have a dominating influence on prices must surely be obvious and will scarcely be disputed by any economist, to deny it would lead to absurd results.

We might explain the heavy fall in the value of money

[1] In proportion as the preparations for mining correspond to real saving and diminished consumption on the part, for example, of those who subscribe for shares in the gold mine, there need be no rise in prices, for the reason stated, until the new gold itself begins to appear in the market.

which is usually the consequence of successive issues of *paper money* in very much the same way. For example, a Government requires the money for heavy expenditure, usually on armaments, and obtains them either by a loan from the Central Bank, which is granted the right to increase its note issue, or by putting into circulation paper money on its own account, which, either from the beginning, or later when metallic money has been withdrawn, is declared legal tender at a compulsory rate. The immediate consequence is that some labour and capital is withdrawn from the production of ordinary consumption-goods for the production of war material, or is directly absorbed by men being conscripted. If, instead, the money required had been obtained by high taxes, then the diminished production of those goods would have coincided with a diminished demand for them by the taxpayers. In that case no rise in prices need occur. But now there is an undiminished monetary purchasing power against the diminished supply of these goods and services, and all prices must rise. In consequence of the rise in prices the normal needs of the Government for money will increase also. If it then issues still more paper we get the endless chain by which paper money may sometimes fall in value until it is worthless.

The somewhat monotonous and unedifying history of paper money in various countries has recently been written by Subercaseaux, whose book is mentioned in the bibliography. It appears that the reason for the issue of paper money, both in earlier and later times, has nearly always been the need of Governments for money in war time. Especially on the outbreak of civil war, when no Government has sufficient authority successfully to levy new taxes, or enjoys sufficient credit to take up bona fide loans, disguised taxation in the form of inconvertible gradually depreciated paper money is the only escape, even though it is an extremely dangerous one. What interests us most is the question to what extent experience of paper money tends to confirm the theory of the value of money which seems *a priori* most tenable, i.e. a more or less modified version of the Quantity Theory. Supported by the statistics prepared by Subercaseaux (*El papel moneda*, p. 126 et seq.) we may assume that, in so far as the issues of paper money are kept within reasonable bounds, the economic forces which resist too violent a decline in its value and which are partly invoked by this very decline operate so strongly that only a slight tendency to depreciation of the paper money is discernible, a tendency which nevertheless appears more marked the more the effort is made to use paper money for foreign payments or to acquire the precious metals. The need for a medium of exchange which grows with the increase in population and volume of transactions, the driving of hard money out of the country and its replacement by paper money, and finally the hoarding of paper money itself in the speculative hope that it will at some future time become convertible at its face value—all these are forces tending to resist the depreciation of the currency.

On the other hand there is no doubt that large and continuous issues of paper money lead to a corresponding fall in the value of the paper money, which, as might be expected, is in exact accordance with the principles of the Quantity Theory. A recent and very striking example is afforded by the Republic of Colombia in South America, whose Government in 1855–1905, and especially during the Civil War in 1899–1902, issued constantly increasing quantities of inconvertible paper money, which fell pro-progressively in value. The first issue, in 1886, amounted to something over three million pesos (= dollars) only, and the gold premium, i.e. the additional value of gold over paper money of the same denomination, amounted to only 35–40 per cent. During the following years the quantity of paper money was increased, and the gold premium rose without interruption—with the single exception of the year 1896—so that when the Civil War broke out in 1899 the total of paper money in circulation amounted to about 50 million pesos and the gold premium to 218–320 per cent. During the war the amount of paper money was multiplied tenfold to 638·6 million pesos in 1903, and the gold premium rose during the war to 20,000–25,000 per cent, i.e. the paper peso had only 1/200th to 1/250th of its gold value. After the war this issue continued, but on a moderate scale, so that in 1905 the amount was 847·2 million pesos. With the return of peace to the country the gold premium sank, it is true, a little, so that during those three years the quotation was 10,000 per cent, i.e. the paper peso stood in relation to the gold peso as 1 : 100. Unless we demand a pedantically complete agreement, these developments in every respect confirm the expectations of the Quantity Theory.

Thus here also the rise in prices is, strictly speaking, primary and the increase of credit media secondary, and it is at least conceivable that under such circumstances any real superfluity of paper money, with a resulting fall in interest rates, will never occur. It actually happens, as Subercaseaux observes, that an inconvenient shortage of money often arises in countries with depreciated paper money, and business men besiege the Government with demands for increased note issues. We must, however, bear in mind that business men and manufacturers as a rule profit, or believe they profit, by a falling value of money, since during the period of a fall they can buy in a cheaper and sell in a dearer market. A fact which complicates this problem still further, and which in connection with a depreciated currency may be of practical importance, is that a rise in prices, when it begins to be regarded by the public as an habitual phenomenon, becomes itself the cause of a rise in interest rates, though at bottom only an apparent one, for 5 per cent interest on money which falls in value or purchasing power by 1 per cent per annum is quite the same as 4 per cent on a currency with a constant value both to the lender and to the borrower. In the same way an expected fall in commodity prices on the occasion of a withdrawal or rehabilitation of paper money will cause an (apparent) fall in interest rates.

7. *The influence of Credit on Commodity Prices. The Dispute between the Currency and the Banking Schools*

We have hitherto only concerned ourselves with the influence exercised by a change in the actual amount of money—principally, but not exclusively, metallic money—on the value of money or commodity prices. Every change in the normal velocity of circulation of money must, however, be regarded as acting in essentially the same way. The best proof of this is the fact that the different kinds of credit used in the course of business, bills of exchange, cheques, banknotes, may be regarded either as real money, competing with or replacing hard cash, or as merely a means of increasing the velocity of circulation of money in the real sense, in so far as we extend the term to include what we have called the *virtual* velocity of circulation. Inconvertible paper money also is sometimes regarded as an instrument of credit (one speaks of the paper currency debts of a Government), though incorrectly, since its conversion belongs to an uncertain future or often never occurs at all and therefore does not as a rule influence its exchange value. It would be more correct to regard it as purely artificial money like token money, or still better like debased silver currency without free minting—what G. F. Knapp calls the "epicentric" medium of payment. On the other hand, paper currency and banknotes are very closely related and may sometimes imperceptibly merge into each other when the convertibility of notes is interrupted or resumed.

It is now our task to examine more closely the effects of *credit*, the great and principal agent in accelerating or retarding the velocity of circulation, and especially to ascertain to what extent the banks or the Government of a country are in a position to regulate the value of money by it, or by similar means, i.e. materially to modify the fluctuations in value which are the consequence of changes in the output of the precious metals. This is admittedly one of the most important questions in the whole of monetary theory, and at the same time the most difficult. It may be said that this question more or less consciously underlies all the controversies in monetary theory which have divided even competent economists, and particularly those of the last century, into radically different camps.

In one respect, however, it may be said that no serious difference of opinion exists, at least among the leading economists, concerning such *paper money* as is issued by Governments themselves or is placed at their disposal by the banks and which is legal tender side by side either with metallic money, or with any substitutes which may have driven the latter out of circulation or out of the country. It is true that with regard to the functions of paper money and the factors which influence its value in relation to the precious metals and to the currency of other countries, there are certain obscure and disputed points; but that a large issue of paper currency progressively depreciates in value and thereby raises the prices of all other commodities, calculated in paper money, has been proved too often in history to be open to doubt. Similarly there are some, though by no means many, examples of a successive withdrawal of paper money rehabilitating its value and causing a fall in commodity prices, in terms of paper money. The rise in price in the former case and the fall in the latter is also easily explained and has already been discussed above. As regards the calling in of paper money, we need only add that it can be effected in the main in two ways, either directly by an *increase of taxation*, by which the revenue of the State is raised above its expenditure, in which case the notes can be partly withdrawn as they flow into the State treasury in payment of taxes, or the State may issue a *loan*, by means of interest-bearing bonds, and commit to the flames the notes received from subscribers. In the former case the taxpayers, in the latter the subscribers to the loan, will have less purchasing power and consequently there will be a reduced monetary demand for goods, so that commodity prices will directly begin to fall *pari passu* with the decreased supply of money. In any case, however, the diminished amount of money will ultimately produce a fall in the prices of all goods, though this may be counteracted, and indeed in many cases is counteracted, by the increased use of bank and other credit, i.e. in effect by an increased velocity of circulation, physical and virtual, of the smaller amount of paper money.

An interesting recent example is afforded by Austria, whose Government paper currency has for decades been regulated at a more or less fixed rate on gold by a periodical issue of interest-bearing State bonds, so-called "Salinenscheine" (because the State salt mines were the original security) and a corresponding withdrawal of paper currency, alternating with the repurchase of "Salinenscheine" in the market, i.e. a re-issue of the paper currency withdrawn.

As regards instruments of credit proper, and especially *the issuing of bank credit* to the public, either in the form of notes or fictitious deposits, their influence on price formation has been much more in dispute. This dispute constitutes the real essence of the discussion concerning the most suitable form of banking organization, which occupied a large part of the nineteenth century and which can still not be said to have terminated. According to one theory, the so-called *Currency Theory*, which had in Ricardo its most distinguished protagonist in the beginning of the nineteenth century and which subsequently found practical expression in Peel's Bank Act of 1844, the banks possess, by the granting of credit, and especially by the issue of notes, an unlimited power to increase the circulating medium and therefore to raise commodity prices. This must especially be the case if the banks, as was the case with the Bank of England in Ricardo's time, are not required to redeem their notes in metal. If, on the other hand, this obligation exists—the only demand Ricardo himself not quite consistently put forward as a condition of a good banking system, and which was established in England by the first Bank Act of Peel in 1819—then naturally a powerful brake is applied to the banks, simply because commodity prices in such a country *can* no longer rise materially above the price-level in all other countries having the same metal as a measure of value, for this would involve the loss of metal to the country, thus compelling the banks to restrict credit facilities. But, on the other hand, as Ricardo also pointed out, it does not prevent the banks in a number of countries from following the same policy and from issuing a number of notes side by side with the metallic money. The general price level might then rise to any height, and since there would then be no reason why metallic money should flow in any particular direction, the convertibility of the notes would no longer constitute a check on the rise of prices, unless it had proceeded so far that the industrial demand for gold began appreciably to diminish the banks' reserves. To this extent Peel's Bank Act, which, as is well known, requires full metallic cover for all notes over a certain fixed amount, and which has been more or less faithfully copied in the banking laws of other countries, represents a consistent adoption of Ricardo's principles.

This measure, however, is of course very imperfect in its social aspects as a means of stabilizing commodity prices, even from the point of view now under discussion. Note issues are only one of the means which the banks have at their disposal for increasing the total amount of exchange media or the velocity of circulation of money and of thereby raising prices, and the example of England shows best to what extent other means may be increasingly employed when the issue of notes is too severely restricted. Of the business transacted through the English banks only a small portion is discharged by notes or cash, by far the greater part consists of payment by cheques on current account. The same developments are to be observed, though to a less extent, in other countries, such as Germany and the U.S.A. But if, on the one hand, current banking law is for this reason unable to prevent an incipient rise in prices as a result of inflationary credit policy—to say nothing of the rise which would be produced by an increase in the supplies of coin itself—on the other hand it imposes unnecessarily severe restrictions on an increase of the note issue at times when such an increase is desirable in order to avoid a heavy fall in the prices of goods and commodities, as, for example, in crises when other credit instruments refuse to function in consequence of a general lack of confidence between individuals. That Peel's Bank Act has not for this reason given rise to greater commercial misfortunes is entirely due to the fact that the banks, and especially the Central Banks, have more and more adopted the practice of keeping in reserve large amounts of unused loan money, a practice which was not contemplated in the original plan of Peel's Bank Act, for which reason it had to be suspended several times during the first period of its operation.

The other view, which usually goes under the name of the Banking principle—a vague name for an essentially vague thing—originated among the opponents of Peel's Bank Act, among whom the most prominent was Thomas Tooke, famous for his great work *The History of Prices*. We cannot here discuss much of the excellent criticism directed by Tooke and Fullarton against the bias of Peel's Bank Act as a practical control of the banking system and especially their emphasis upon the supreme importance of bank reserves, which had been too much neglected by Ricardo and his disciples. We can only consider their view of the influence of bank credit, and more especially of note issues, on prices. This school, or at least its most consistent representatives, denies any such influence so long as the banks only grant credit to the public in the form of *loans* on absolutely sound security. Even if the banks are not compelled to redeem their notes in gold they cannot, says Tooke, *under such conditions* either increase or diminish the total amount of credit instruments in circulation. Whatever the transaction of business requires in this respect is drawn from the banks in the form, for example, of loans, and whatever is not required is returned to the banks in the form of deposits or repayment of loans. This assertion may appear paradoxical, for the banks are theoretically free to call in all their notes and all their loans; but if they did so they would also refuse to satisfy the legitimate demand for loans—which is contrary to the initial assumption.

Tooke based his views on comprehensive statistics, which appeared to show that a large note issue had practically never preceded, but always followed, rising prices. This fact would then prove, in Tooke's opinion, that the volume of exchange media is never the cause, but on the contrary always the effect, of fluctuations in prices and of the requirements of turnover for the medium of exchange. Both Tooke and Fullarton emphatically assert the essential difference, in their opinion, between State paper money, including advances by the banks to the Government in the form of notes, and banknotes proper regularly issued in the form of loans. In the one case, they say, the notes are issued in direct payment for goods and services and do not return to the bank of issue but remain in the hands of the public; in the other they only come into circulation as loans with strict reservations as to repayment and therefore always return to the banks of issue after the lapse of some months. In this respect, however, it may be observed that the return of the banknotes, upon which Fullarton, and many other economists with him, laid such great stress, cannot be of predominant importance if the banks continuously reissue the notes as they are paid in; Government paper money also frequently returns to the issuer in the form of tax payments, and if it remains in the hands of the public, it is because the Government continues to reissue its notes in order to meet its current expenditure. Again, as regards the return of banknotes to the banks in the form of deposits, this can, and often does, occur in the case of paper currency also. In both cases the deposits are made because the public obtains interest (or corresponding advantages) on the money deposited. That the banks give such interest is in turn due to the fact that they intend to release the notes as soon as possible, or as large a part of them as possible, at a higher rate of interest.

Tooke's arguments were developed in a modified form by John Stuart Mill, of whom Marx says, somewhat maliciously, that in his monetary theory he succeeded in simultaneously holding the opinion of his father, James Mill, Ricardo's friend, and the contrary opinion of Tooke. Mill considered that Tooke's view of the innocuousness of the banks as regards price movements was quite correct in normal, tranquil times, when everybody only borrows for his business requirements and only expands his business in proportion as the growth of his own capital or that of the persons associated with him permits it. Under such conditions an increased supply of loan money by the banks would be useless, and even if, by offering a lower rate of interest, they were able to induce borrowers to borrow more than usual the borrowed money would sooner or later come into the hands of somebody who did not require it and would then flow back to the banks as a deposit. On the other hand, in troubled times, when a crisis is approaching, and business men, who have hitherto, by mutual credit, bills of exchange or ordinary credit for goods, succeeded in artificially keeping up prices, must by reason of the loss of confidence, begin to seek other and safer instruments of credit and turn to the banks for loans, the banks, according to Mill, would undoubtedly be in a position by too generous an issue of banknotes or granting of credit, to maintain for a time, and even to add to the artificial rise in prices and thus retard a crisis which is nevertheless inevitable and also necessary if sound business conditions are to be restored. This view held by Mill was accepted by the Germans Nasse and Adolf Wagner and may be said to prevail at the present day among German economists. The practical conclusion from these teachings would be that all restrictions upon banking activity are really an evil, or at any rate can only have reference to banking activity during such times of crisis as are referred to above. The convertibility of banknotes into cash must of course be insisted upon in the interests of the international foreign exchange and for this reason the banks must always be provided with sufficient reserves. As regards note cover proper, ordinary bank commercial bills or other easily realizable securities, should be fully adequate and are most desirable because they combine security and elasticity. In tranquil times the banks must also hold a considerable reserve in gold or notes in order to meet the increased demand for loans when a crisis sets in.

So far as the practical organization of the banking system is concerned the difference between these two schools is not of special importance, and existing banking systems may be said to be the result of a compromise between them, especially if we remember that the right to issue notes, under severe restrictions and regulations, is only a part, and in many countries a very small part, of modern banking activity, which otherwise enjoys almost complete freedom. But as regards the problem which immediately concerns us here—the influence of money and credit on prices under normal conditions—the contrast between the two views is as complete as possible, and this divergence of opinion persists even to-day, despite discussion which has lasted for almost a century.

8. *A Criticism of the Theories of Ricardo and Tooke*

This depressing result is of course due to the fact that neither of the parties has been able to penetrate to the bottom of the questions at issue or to present its views in a manner at once so comprehensible and free from contradiction as completely to silence its opponents by sheer force of logic. That neither of them did so is due to a number of external circumstances. Ricardo, from whose incomparable acumen we should certainly have expected an exhaustive treatment of this subject, only mentions it in passing. He was primarily concerned with showing that the difference between the value of unminted gold and inconvertible notes—in fact, *The high price of bullion,* as his famous first treatise is called—which appeared in the latter part of the period of bank restriction in England, proved beyond a doubt that notes had fallen in value, and that this in turn was caused by too liberal an issue of notes and too generous granting of credit by the note-issuing banks, especially the Bank of England. At a time when even leaders of commerce and statesmen were advancing the vaguest conceptions of units of money, measures of value, exchange rates, etc., the first part of this statement was by no means so axiomatic as it is now. The argument of his opponents was that, on the contrary, gold had risen in value, which of course fundamentally amounted to the same thing. Ricardo's clear and definite examination of this conflict of views, conducted in a language which contrasts favourably by its freshness and directness with his later and much heavier style, is for all time a precious pearl in the literature of political economy. Even the latter part of his thesis could scarcely be disputed, and was not disputed, by Tooke and his school, who emphasized, with Ricardo, the now generally accepted view that the banks, when confronted with a falling rate of exchange and a threatened outflow of gold, and therefore still more with a depreciated paper currency, must as a remedy restrict credit.

Ricardo's exposition was, however, only completely convincing on the question of the relation of notes to gold, i.e. with the possibility of their being at a discount. Their relation to goods, or the changes in the commodity price level, is not necessarily the same thing. Too liberal credit on the part of the banks by means of lower discount rates may cause a flight of domestic capital and consequently, as we may well assume, an outflow of gold, even if, meanwhile, the domestic price level does not simultaneously undergo any fluctuations. It has indeed been fully proved, among other things by Tooke's inquiry into prices, that during that period there really occurred a great rise in commodity prices in England, both in terms of gold and, naturally, also in terms of notes. But this rise in prices had begun before any premium on gold had appeared and in those days of permanent war it may very well have had many other causes, such as high freights, which constituted, in consequence of the composition of England's imports and exports at that time, a very important factor in the balance of payments. Ricardo's proof on this point is all too slender, and even superficial. He wishes to show that an excessive issue of notes and a real excess of gold have the same effect on commodity prices, and for this purpose he has recourse to the picture of an imaginary goldfield discovered in the vaults of the Bank of England (in the "Reply to Mr. Bosanquet"). Just as this hoard of gold, either minted, or in the form of notes based upon it, would within a short time circulate in the hands of the public and there produce a rise in commodity prices, so also, he thinks, it must be possible for the banks to circulate these inconvertible notes or unbacked notes to an unlimited amount, if only they are willing to issue them. To the objection of his opponents that there must be an essential difference between notes—and, they might have added, the gold coinage originating from the Bank's imaginary goldmine—which were only loaned and must be repaid, and the actually freshly produced gold which belongs *ab initio* to the holders and is mainly used for the purchase of goods, Ricardo answers that there is no difference, since it is the function of even the freshly produced gold to be loaned out. If this is not done immediately by the owner of the gold, the gold will sooner or later come into the possession of persons who will lend it. This answer is not satisfactory. The gold which reaches Europe from the countries of production does not as a rule arrive in the form of capital to be loaned, but in payment for goods, and it therefore continues to function directly for the exchange of goods just as other remittances do. Even if the pieces of gold were lodged in a bank *in corpore*, they would immediately release for circulation a corresponding amount of notes or cheques, the former exchanged for gold and the latter drawn on these gold deposits. Here therefore we find the obvious and indisputable tendency to higher prices, though not in the case of money which primarily leaves the banks in the form of loans.

Ricardo assumes, as we have just done, the case of a number of countries which have previously only had metallic currency, instituting banks with the right to issue notes "on the same principles as the Bank of England", i.e. with the right to issue unbacked notes (but payable on demand). If this occurred at the same time, he says, the metallic money could not be driven out, since it would have nowhere to go, and the banks would accordingly be able to add to an already adequate circulation a further amount of credit instruments. If this is admitted, he continues, the problem is solved; if it is denied he asks how unbacked banknotes could ever originate and come into circulation. But this argument is not quite conclusive either. Banknotes might, after all, have been issued at times when the supply of currency was not adequate for business, because an increase of population or a growth of turnover required more unless prices fell. Or they might have been issued to Governments, without any liability to redeem them, and their influence on rising prices in *that* case is not disputed by anybody. It is remarkable that Ricardo never examined in detail by what means the banks could succeed in putting a larger amount of their stocks of money or notes into circulation and especially what effects the lowering of the loan rate would have on the demand for credit instruments and on the level of prices. This is probably due to the fact that in his day interest rates were legally fixed at a maximum of 5 per cent. As soon as the banks reached this maximum they could not restrict their credit facilities by raising the rate of interest but had to do so directly by refusing facilities to certain customers, even though they offered first-class security. During the eighteenth century, when the

Bank of England was obliged to redeem its notes in gold, this measure was often resorted to if for one reason or another the bank's gold reserves were threatened with exhaustion. Once freed from the obligation of note redemption, however, the banks no longer needed to refuse facilities to their customers and on principle did not do so if sufficient security was offered. It was precisely in this circumstance that Ricardo found the principal cause of the depreciation of the banknotes.

It appears, however, from one passage in his work that he was himself not entirely clear as to the effect of changes in the rate of interest on prices. Those who denied that a surfeit of paper money was the cause of the depreciation of banknotes insisted, among other things, that if such a surfeit existed it would show itself in an abnormally low rate of interest. Against this Ricardo rightly insists that a fall in money interest can only take place so long as the surfeit of money has not led to a corresponding increase in prices. As soon as this occurs there no longer exists any surfeit of money, relatively to the requirements of turnover, and consequently there is no reason to keep interest rates below the normal level, which, he remarks, is regulated by the supply of and demand for real capital.

So far so good. But in order further to emphasize the impossibility of a permanent lowering of interest rates he attempts a further proof by a *reductio ad absurdum* which is much less convincing. If such a permanent lowering were possible, he says, "then the banks would be powerful engines indeed. By printing paper money and lending it at 2 or 3 per cent below the open market rate the banks would reduce business profits in the same proportion and if they were patriotic enough to lend their money at so low a rate of interest that it only sufficed to cover the costs of printing, profits would be still further reduced. No nation could then compete with us, except by adopting similar measures; we should absorb the whole trade of the world. To what absurdities," he continues, "would not such a theory lead us; the profits of capital can only be reduced by competition with the capital which does not consist of media of exchange (real capital), but as the increase of banknotes does not increase this kind of capital, since it adds neither to the volume of our exports, machinery, or raw materials, it cannot add to our profits or lower the rate of interest."

Even the form of this argument is peculiar, for at the beginning, and subsequently, he refers to a lowering of business profits, but at the end he seems to be referring to the possibility of raising them. This may, however, be due to inaccurate expression, though the whole argument that the forcing down of business profits would improve the competitive powers of a country in general is superficial and is in complete conflict with the well-known theory of international trade which Ricardo himself later adopted and which bears his name. Nobody has shown more clearly than Ricardo that the exchange of commodities between nations is regulated not by the absolute but by the relative costs of production. A country which by reason of its technical or natural resources can produce all commodities with less labour than other countries and is therefore technically superior at every point will nevertheless be commercially inferior in the fields in which its technical superiority is relatively least. And especially as far as the effect of increased accumulation of capital and the resulting reduction in rates of interest and profits on capital are concerned, this certainly produces a cheapening of those articles for the production of which an especially large amount of capital is required, but also *eo ipso* an increase in the cost of articles which require comparatively little capital. Excluding the rent of land, a fall in the profits of capital is, as Ricardo so clearly shows elsewhere, the same as an increased share of labour in the product, i.e. an increase of wages; but higher wages make all those goods dearer which are mainly the product of manual labour and do not require the employment of much capital. A fall in the rate of interest caused by increased capital wealth thus causes fluctuations in the relative prices of both these groups of commodities, but cannot exercise a depressing influence on the general price-level except in so far as it increases the actual volume of goods, the value of money remaining stable, and possibly gives rise to a slower circulation of money. From the point of view of the comparative cost theory of the value of money, a fall in the rate of interest would only tend to lower prices if the production of gold required less capital proportionately to labour in other branches of production, but it would tend to raise prices in the opposite case. We need not for the moment consider which of these assumptions accords best with the facts.

Much less can a fall in the loan rate which had its sole origin in increased credit facilities on the part of the monetary institutions have such an effect. This would conflict with the whole conception of currency and of price formation which Ricardo defends elsewhere, and not least in these works. Let us take the extreme and drastic example of the discovery of a gold mine within the Bank of England. In order to bring into circulation the increased volume of money, which, be it noted, would still be done by means of loans, the Bank must, temporarily at least, lower its loan rate or its discount rate on bills below the previous level. This is admitted by Ricardo. If, now, this reduction in the rate of interest should result in lower costs of production and consequently *lower* prices, then the need for credit instruments would be diminished and not increased, a part of the money already in circulation would flow back to the banks, and from them to the Bank of England, and *a fortiori* it would be impossible for the banks to bring even the smallest part of their excessive gold stocks into circulation among the public. If this point of view is not to be self-contradictory we must assume that a spontaneous lowering of the loan rate by the banks—i.e. a lowering not caused by a fall in the real rate of interest—will produce *higher* costs of production and higher prices, so that the ability of the country to export abroad will be diminished and not increased. And this is in full accord with Ricardo's general view, which can scarcely be disputed, that an increased issue of notes, whether by the Government or through a lowering of the discount and other loan rates by the banks, leads to an outflow of metal and an inflow of foreign goods in payment for it. But Ricardo's argument by no means explains why, how, and to what extent a lower rate of interest has this effect, which is the essence of the whole problem. In his zeal to provide a striking proof of a fundamentally self-evident thesis Ricardo advanced a vague and partially erroneous argument, which could not fail to exercise an unfavourable influence on the subsequent discussion of the subject.

When restrictions on the rate of interest were removed, as happened in England in 1833, and the banks acquired a big instrument for increasing or decreasing their loans at will by being able to raise or lower their rate of interest, the question of the influence of interest rates on commodity prices came more into the foreground, and one of the chief arguments in favour of Peel's Bank Act was precisely that it would compel the banks to raise their rates in good time when commodity prices became too high and a resultant adverse trade balance was threatened. Tooke had, indeed, shown by what were regarded as irrefutable statistics that high commodity prices were scarcely ever a consequence of inflated note issues, but as a rule preceded them. This, however, did not really prove much, since, as Tooke himself explains, big business at that time mainly made use of other media than coin or notes. If, therefore, the banks contributed by too low a loan rate to a rise in prices they themselves thus created the increased demand for the *medium of turnover* which might eventually lead to an increased demand for notes also, especially when the rise in prices became general and penetrated into those branches of business (in England, the live-stock business among others) which prefer to use notes.

Tooke, however, absolutely denies that a lowering of interest rates tends to raise prices. As usual, he starts in the first place from empirical reality and points out that rising commodity prices usually coincide with high and rising interest rates, and not vice versa. The correctness of this observation is beyond dispute; later statistics have frequently fully confirmed this fact, though how it is to be correctly interpreted we shall see later. But Tooke goes still further and maintains that the effect of a lowering of interest rates would be the exact contrary to what the original defenders of Peel's Bank Act supposed. "A general reduction of the rate of interest," he says,[1] is equivalent to, or rather constitutes, a reduction in the costs of production;

[1] *Inquiry into the Currency Principle*, 3rd ed., p. 81.

this is in particular, and quite evidently, a necessary effect where much fixed capital is employed, as in the case of manufactures. But it is also true in all cases where capital expenditure is required owing to the time which usually elapses before the commodities, whether raw materials or finished articles, are brought to market. The resulting lower costs of production should by the competition of producers inevitably cause a fall in the price of all those articles into the cost of which interest on money entered as a factor. We must therefore assume," he adds, " that the considerably lower rate of interest which has prevailed during the last two years has been a contributory cause of the great reduction in price of some of our most important factory goods which has occurred simultaneously with the reduction of interest."

The final conclusion may be quite correct if we emphasize the words "factory goods", i.e. if the goods in question are such as required an especially large amount of (in this case fixed) capital. In general, however, Tooke's thesis is certainly wrong; it is of exactly the same kind as the view put forward by Ricardo, which we have just criticized, with the difference, however, that whereas in Ricardo it appears as a hasty interpolation and has no connection with his general point of view, in Tooke it is the foundation and forefront of his theory. The argument is based on the inadmissible, not to say impossible, assumption that wages and rent would at the same time remain constant, whereas in reality a lowering of the rate of interest is equivalent to a raising of the shares of the other factors of production in the product. Indeed, as Ricardo (and more recently Böhm-Bawerk) proved, and as experience has often shown, a rise in wages or rent constitutes *ceteris paribus* just the necessary condition for the profitable employment of more capital in the service of production. A fall in loan rates caused by increased supplies of real capital (increased savings) should thus in itself cause neither a rise nor a fall in the average price level.

In the present case, however, there is no question of an increase of real capital, at any rate not at the outset—but of artificial capital created by bank credit, an increased purchasing power against which there exists for the moment an unchanged quantity of goods and labour: a combination which can scarcely fail to produce a general rise in prices. All this will, I hope, become clearer in what follows.

In certain situations, however, it is not impossible for a lower loan rate, due to whatever cause, to be the occasion of a fall in prices—not indeed of present prices, but of future prices calculated at present; such would be the case where an entrepreneur has undertaken to execute certain work, such as a building, to be finished within a year or two at an agreed price. If he calculates his own costs on the assumption that wages and the price of materials will remain unchanged, then a lower rate of interest will more easily induce him to undertake the work at a lower price than he would otherwise have done. But frequently he will discover to his sorrow that he has calculated wrongly if at the same time an increased demand from other entrepreneurs has caused a rise in the price of labour and materials, as will presumably happen.

Tooke was of course not unfamiliar with the common argument that a low bank rate is an "inducement to speculation" and consequently to higher prices, but he attempts to blunt its point by the objection that speculation in goods is scarcely ever effected on the basis of borrowed capital save when the expected rise in prices is so great, and the profit can be realized in so short a time, that a higher or lower interest rate or discount rate is a matter of quite secondary importance. In another connection he argues that the increased purchasing power which under such circumstances merchants must employ need not be provided by the banks at all. Ordinary commercial credit may under such conditions afford speculators the opportunity of providing themselves with quantities of goods in glaring disproportion to the amount of their own capital. He advances some very striking and often quoted examples from England's tea and grain trade at the end of the 'thirties and beginning of the 'forties.

Tooke has, however, confused two essentially different phenomena. The examples which he gives of speculation in goods are those in which, owing to political events, failure of harvests etc., a future rise in price can be foreseen with more or less certainty. That in such cases a rise in present prices through the competition of speculators should occur is not surprising, and for such speculation the inducement of low interest rates is certainly quite unnecessary. On the contrary, speculators of this kind, if they are not afraid of the risk of miscalculation, are usually in a position to offer a rate of interest much higher than the normal in order to procure a short term credit. The influence of interest rates on prices is quite a different matter, however, as regards the element of speculation which necessarily enters into all business transactions and into all capitalistic production. Business men as a rule do not count on rising prices in the future, but, on the contrary, normally proceed on the assumption that present prices of commodities will remain constant. If, nevertheless, present goods and services, *for which payment need only be made in the future*, fetch on the average a higher price corresponding to the level of loan interest—and this is the essence of every loan transaction and every advance of money—this is due simply to the ordinary laws of interest or to the fact that labour and land, if their fruits are not to be consumed immediately, may assume such forms as give to them a greater (marginal) productivity, a greater yield in consumable commodities, than in their present form. If banks or lenders generally demand exactly the higher price corresponding to this difference in value (= the marginal productivity of waiting) then equilibrium will be attained and the cash price of goods and services will remain, at any rate under otherwise stationary conditions, unchanged year after year. If, again, they offer cheaper loans, then evidently the entrepreneurs, even with current prices as the foundation of their calculation of future prices, will be able, without encroaching on the usual profits of enterprise, to pay a somewhat higher price for raw materials, labour, and land, and by competition among themselves they will be more or less compelled to do so: in this way the present price level will be raised indirectly and therefore the future price level also. Thus there is no question of rousing such more or less speculative enterprise as is occasioned by the blasts of the trade cycle, but of a slow and continuous pressure on normal economic developments in a certain direction. One business is, let us say, on the point of expanding its activities and is stimulated to do so by the availability of capital at cheaper rates than usual; another is perhaps about to restrict its activities or to close down altogether, but is kept going by the low loan rate of interest. A tendency to increased enterprise, to an increased demand for goods and services, and therefore directly and indirectly to rising prices, thus undoubtedly underlies every *spontaneous* lowering of the loan rate, whether caused by increased supplies of money or merely by the increased employment of bank credit.

But, of course, this is not the only factor. Exactly the same effects would be visible with an unchanged, or even a higher, rate of interest, if meanwhile the expected profit on capital had considerably increased, owing, for example, to technical improvements in production or increased demand for capital (i.e. a general increase in the marginal productivity of waiting). It is by neglect of the complex nature of this phenomenon that what are essentially different phases of the same thing have been represented as irreconcilable opposites. It is clearly a support for Ricardo's theory, and a stumbling block for Tooke's, that the banks always lower their loan rates when money is abundant and raise them when it is scarce, and especially that a flow of the precious metals abroad regularly leads to a raising of the discount rate. If Tooke's view were correct we should be confronted by the curious situation, used as an argument against him even in his own day, that in order to improve the discount rate and the balance of trade, the banks would take steps which, on his theory, would lead to higher costs of production and higher prices and to a further restriction of the already too limited export of goods. Tooke's reply to this is that the raising of the discount rates in such cases is usually of too short a duration to influence the cost of production of goods; and that, on the other hand, it creates an immediate credit stringency, with the usual consequence of failures and forced sales, as well as falling prices, so that exports are encouraged, the demand for credit instruments is decreased, and gold flows back to the banks.

This reasoning is certainly somewhat distorted—forced sales and failures are at best only one element in the forced offers of present goods caused by a high loan rate. It would surely have been better to argue that a high discount rate leads to the influx of foreign capital and a prolongation of commercial debts outstanding as well as an improvement, even if only fortuitous, of the balance of trade, even with no change in the price level. But nevertheless the contrast remains, as we have already observed when speaking of the inconsistencies in Ricardo's theory. A persistent low discount rate on the part of the banks would, according to this theory, lead to a reduction, and not an increase, in the demand for loans by business people, money would flow into the banks and would cause a further reduction of interest rates, and so on, until the rate fell to nil. On the other hand, if interest rates which are too high remained long in operation, they would, by increasing the cost of production and commodity prices, create a continuously increasing demand for money, and in the vain attempt to maintain their reserves and their gold holdings the banks would force up rates of interest ever higher. In other words, the money rate of interest would be in a state of unstable equilibrium, every move away from the proper rate would be accelerated in a perpetual vicious circle.

None of Tooke's disciples has, so far as I know, devoted himself to this side of his reasoning. They have been content to insist on the supposed powerlessness of the banks as regards commodity prices and the demand for credit instruments. Thus Nasse in his earlier monetary writings (in his later work he has, though somewhat inconsistently, tended to the opposite view) and Adolf Wagner in his well known work *Geld- und Credittheorie der Peel'schen Bankacte.* Nasse relies mainly on experience, according to which low interest rates have often proved incapable of increasing turnover and bringing the available resources of the banks into circulation. Wagner, again, seeks to strengthen his position by the following lines of argument. He remarks that the requirements of business for credit instruments is a somewhat vague conception, and he admits that an increased offer of credit by the banks, e.g. by a discount rate lower than usual in relation to the rate of the open market, may itself create an increased demand for bank credit and especially for notes. But, he says, " the corrective lies at hand ; a bank which continues to make advances on a large scale below the market rate will soon find its notes returning to it *for redemption*,[1] partly because the volume of the note issues soon awakens distrust and partly because the turnover in all probability does not require the increased number of notes." This argument is clearly erroneous : a run on the banks caused by distrust of their power to redeem their notes in gold is nowadays an exceptional occurrence and may be regarded as a thing of the past. Again, the view that business men, if they do not require such an amount of credit instruments, will exchange them for gold coin involves, unless the balance of payments has meanwhile become worse, a contradiction, for gold coin would then take the place of the superfluous notes. Rather would the superfluous notes flow back to the banks in the form of deposits ; but if this occurred in the bank of issue it would suffer no injury ; it could reissue them, profiting meanwhile by the difference between the deposit rate and loan rate.

But what is of greater importance, as Wagner proceeds to add, is that if among a number of note-issuing banks in a country one or more endeavoured to increase the amount of their loans by lowering their own loan rate, then their notes would soon reach the other banks and be presented by them for payment or give rise to interest-bearing claims on current account. This is undoubtedly true, not only of note-issuing banks but also of banks in general. A single bank cannot discount at materially lower rates than other banks ; it would thereby acquire a number of borrowing customers but no (real) deposits to a corresponding amount. It could not clear its cheques with the other banks and would therefore soon be insolvent, or at any rate illiquid. But this applies only to each individual bank as against the others, and not

[1] Italics mine.

to the whole banking system of a country, if all the banks simultaneously observe the same discount policy.

What is it then which ultimately regulates the money-rate and which prevents banks in one country from arbitrarily lowering their rates of interest by common agreement? If we accept the view that this would lead to a *continuous rise in commodity prices* in that country, then the answer is clear: where there are no notes of small denomination and where metallic money is used in business, then on this assumption the increased demand for gold for internal business would soon empty the bank's vaults. In addition, and this applies also to countries which only use notes, the position with respect to foreign countries would soon be rendered untenable by an unfavourable movement in the balance of trade. If, on the other hand, we deny the effect of low money rates on commodity prices it is possible that a reaction might conceivably occur, in so far as the low interest rates would drive domestic capital out of the country; bank deposits would be withdrawn in gold, or notes would be cashed for gold, which would be sent abroad for capital investment. This, of course, is only to evade the whole question. If we go further and suppose a simultaneous reduction of the money-rate by all the banks in the whole of the commercial world, it is difficult to see where and how, according to this view, the reaction would arise. On the contrary we must assume, ***nolens volens***, that such a reduction might be effected to any extent whatever without having any unbearable consequences. The dissatisfaction of depositors with such an arrangement would actually be great, but at the same time they would be impotent, for since they could nowhere obtain a higher rate of interest on their money than that which pleased the banks, they would have no reason to withdraw their deposits. And even if they did so in order to use their money in some way or other themselves it would *on the assumption that turnover could not absorb more of the medium* of exchange, soon flow back to the banks. The beneficial consequences to all non-capitalists would on the other hand be evident: business would have the advantage of operating with extremely cheap capital; the rewards of enterprise, and wages, would rise, and production would increase to the maximum, the highest degree of prosperity would be attained, and all in consequence of the alteration of a few figures in the books of the banks. Proudhon's ideal, *le crédit gratuit*, would be realized!

9. *The Positive Solution*

It is not easy to find the right solution in this chaos of vague conceptions, in which diametrically opposed and sometimes self-contradictory views are defended by the most famous writers. A solution is perhaps in some respects at present impossible, at any rate, if it is expected to be directly verifiable by experience. Concrete reality is altogether too shifting and complex for us to be able directly to appeal to its testimony: an isolation of the phenomena is both difficult and doubtful. The only experimental proof which would be really satisfactory would be for all the banks of the world after common agreement, in the interests of pure theory to initiate a heavy rise or fall in their interest rates and continue these rates in operation for some years at least, so that the effects on commodity prices might reveal themselves. But we shall have to wait a long time for such an experiment. The only immediate escape, therefore, is to appeal to generally accepted economic principles: in order to be believed, a view which is in evident conflict with them, will require much greater support than one which is in full agreement with them. The latter can, if it is itself free from contradiction and is not manifestly refuted by experience, lay claim to be a working hypothesis and a provisional theory capable of guiding us in a more detailed investigation of the facts.

It is a well recognized principle of this kind that in the last analysis the money rate of interest depends upon the supply of and demand for *real capital*, or, as Adam Smith, and later Ricardo, expressed it, that the rate of interest is regulated by the profits from the employment of capital itself and not by the number or quality of the pieces of metal which facilitate the turnover of its products. This is, on the whole, incontrovertible, and the reasons are known to everybody. Money does not itself enter into the processes of production: it is in itself, as Aristotle showed, quite sterile. He who borrows money at interest does not as a rule intend to keep it, but to exchange it at the first suitable opportunity for goods and services, by the productive use of which he hopes to be able to acquire not merely the equivalent of their price, but also a surplus value, which constitutes the real rate of interest and more or less corresponds to the interest on the loan which he must himself pay.

In simple credit between man and man the connection between interest on capital on the one hand and interest on money on the other is easy to understand. The lender also has the alternative of employing his money productively, and if the borrower fails adequately to satisfy him he may prefer to do so. As a rule, it is true, the borrower's ability, or opportunity, is in this respect greater than the lender's, because often the latter cannot, or is unwilling, to run the risk attached to every productive undertaking. Indeed, this is the reason why a loan transaction which is otherwise sound must be of mutual advantage. But the difference in this respect need not be very considerable: a person who is himself unable to administer a concern has nowadays opportunities for participation as a shareholder, debenture holder, etc. In addition there is another circumstance which makes the real and loan rates more or less coincide, i.e. the competition among entrepreneurs for loan capital.

A complete correspondence is of course not to be expected, if only for the reason that profit on capital is far from being a uniform conception, but varies greatly in different undertakings according as they are more or less successful. In addition there is the difference between interest on short and interest on long dated loans, of which only the latter corresponds to the real rate. In many private accommodation loans no interest is usually paid, partly because the borrower can only secure a minor advantage from it, and partly because the lender frequently cannot find any productive use for his money in the meantime. This difference is to a large extent levelled out by the credit market, though not completely, as is to be seen from a comparison of the ordinary discount rate and the interest on mortgages and debentures. Yet it may be remarked that the so-called private discount rate (open market rate) by no means corresponds to the average rate, even on short loans. It is there a question of first class securities, bills with a banker's acceptance or endorsement, etc., which, since they can be converted into ready money at any time, are more readily employed as cash reserves than as the medium for the investment of capital in the real sense.

That loan rate, which is a direct expression of the real rate, we call the normal rate. In order more precisely to grasp and to define this conception we must first clearly understand the term real capital. Of course, we are not here primarily concerned with capital which is more or less fixed or tied up in production, such as buildings, ships, machinery, etc., for its yield has only an indirect influence on interest rates in so far as it can attract or repel the employment of new capital in production. It is the latter mobile capital in its free and uninvested form with which we are concerned.

But of what does this capital consist ? In this connection it is usual to think of the *stocks of goods* in the warehouses of merchants and manufacturers' stocks of articles ready for consumption, or of raw materials, or semi-manufactured goods. But this is not correct. The magnitude of stocks of goods is of little importance to the real phenomenon of capital, although in certain circumstances it may become so (cf. p. 251). On the contrary, on a first approximation we may completely ignore the existence of stocks and assume that all products, consumption goods, raw materials, and machinery find a market as soon as they are ready either for consumption or for further processes of production. Under such circumstances free capital will not really have any material form at all—quite naturally, as it only exists for the moment. The accumulation of capital consists in the resolve of those who save to abstain from the consumption of a part of their income in the immediate future. Owing to their diminished demand, or cessation of demand, for consumption goods, the labour and land which would otherwise have been required in their production is set free for the creation of fixed capital for future production and consumption and is employed by entrepreneurs for that purpose with the help of the money placed at their disposal by savings. Of course, this process presupposes an adaptability and a degree of foresight in the reorganization of production which is far from existing in reality, though this is as a rule of secondary importance in comparison with the main phenomenon.

The rate of interest at which *the demand for loan capital and the supply of savings* exactly agree, and which more or less corresponds to the expected yield on the newly created capital, will then be the normal or natural real rate. It is essentially variable. If the prospects of the employment of capital become more promising, demand will increase and will at first exceed supply; interest rates will then rise and stimulate further saving at the same time as the demand from entrepreneurs contracts until a new equilibrium is reached at a slightly higher rate of interest. And at the same time equilibrium must *ipso facto* obtain—broadly speaking, and if it is not disturbed by other causes—in the market for goods and services, so that wages and prices will remain unchanged. The *sum* of money incomes will then usually exceed the money value of the consumption goods annually produced, but the excess of income—i.e. what is annually saved and invested in production—will not produce any demand for present goods but only for labour and land for future production.

What has been said applies, however, only to credit as between man and man, and even so with many exceptions in reality. In certain cases a great rise in prices may, in fact, be maintained by private credit alone, i.e. by the substitution of credit on goods for money transactions. At bottom this phenomenon also comes under the general rule which we are now beginning to develop. A person who procures goods or services on credit might for one reason or another offer a higher rate of interest without loss, if the chances of profit have increased. If, however, the seller only demands the usual interest, or, in the case of a short loan, no interest at all, then the buyer might instead offer a higher price for purchased goods; indeed, he will more or less be forced to do so owing to competition from other buyers. If to this we add organized credit, and especially the activity of the banks, the connection between loan interest and interest on capital will become much less simple; indeed, it will then only exist at all by virtue of the connecting link of price movements, as we shall now see. Banks are not, like private persons, restricted in their lending to their own funds or even to the means placed at their disposal by savings. By the concentration in their hands of private cash holdings, which are constantly replenished by in-payments as fast as they are depleted by out-payments, they possess a fund for loans which is always elastic and, on certain assumptions, inexhaustible. With a pure credit system the banks can always satisfy any demand whatever for loans and at rates of interest however low, at least as far as the internal market is concerned. But the same would apply even under the existing monetary system, in so far as the assumption is correct that a lowering of the bank rate does not exercise any influence on commodity prices (and naturally still more so if its influence were exercised in the manner supposed by Tooke). This assumption must therefore be wrong, and it is not difficult to prove directly that it really is wrong. If the banks lend their money at materially lower rates than the normal rate as above defined, then in the first place saving will be discouraged and for that reason there will be an increased demand for goods and services for present consumption. In the second place, the profit opportunities of entrepreneurs will thus be increased and the demand for goods and services, as well as for raw materials already in the market for future production, will evidently increase to the same extent as it had previously been held in check by the higher rate of interest. Owing to the increased income thus accruing to the workers, landowners, and the owners of raw materials, etc.,[1] the prices of consumption goods will begin to rise, the more so as the factors of production previously available are now withdrawn for the purposes of future production.

[1] The extra profits of entrepreneurs need not be considered here, as they arise at a future time and correspond more or less to the diminished interest received by bank depositors. Cf. *Geldzins und Güterpreise*, p. 124 *et seq.*

Equilibrium in the market for goods and services will therefore be disturbed. As against an increased demand in two directions there will be an unchanged or even diminished supply, which must result in an increase in wages (rent) and, directly or indirectly, in prices.

It is, of course, not impossible for the rise in prices to be counteracted to a certain extent by an increase in production, for example if previously there had been unemployment, or if higher wages had induced longer working hours, or even by the increasing roundaboutness which is undoubtedly invoked by a fall in interest rates, even if it occurs artificially. But all these are secondary considerations. As a first approximation we are entitled to assume that all production forces are already fully employed, so that the increased monetary demand principally takes the form of rivalry between employers for labour, raw materials and natural facilities, etc., which consequently leads to an increase in their price, and indirectly, owing to the increased money income of labour and landlords and the increased demand for commodities, to a rise in the price of all consumption goods in addition to that which arises from diminished savings.

How great this rise might be in a certain period, say during the first year after the fall in the rate of interest, is difficult or even impossible to determine *a priori*. Neither is it distributed uniformly over the whole range of commodities, at any rate not at first. It evidently becomes greatest in respect of goods and services intended for capital investments of longer duration, such as the building of railways, houses, shops, etc., though on the other hand it is necessary that the reduction of interest rates by the banks should be for a sufficiently long period to influence the rate on long term loans also, as will sooner or later be the case. A fall in the discount rate on three-months' bills from four to three per cent per annum would, as will easily be seen, directly raise the price of goods purchased by one-quarter per cent at the most, but if this low discount rate persists and gradually brings about a reduction in the rate on mortgages and debentures from, say, five to four per cent, then builders, railway companies, etc., would be able to offer up to twenty-five per cent more for wages and raw material, since four per cent on 125 Kr. is the same as five per cent on 100 Kr. What is still more important is that the rise in prices, whether small or great at first, can never cease so long as the cause which gave rise to it continues to operate; in other words, so long as the loan rate remains below the normal rate. If a rise in prices has occurred over the whole range of goods and services, then a new price level will be created, which in its turn will constitute the foundation and starting point for all economic calculations and agreements. Entrepreneurs who see their expected additional profits vanishing owing to the rise in price of raw materials and labour will wholly or partly realize these profits, thanks to the rise—which has already taken place—in the prices of the goods they produce, whereas workmen and landlords whose incomes are apparently increased only to a small extent will derive no benefit because the stocks of the commodities in demand are limited. The gains they actually reap correspond *in this case* principally to the positive losses suffered by the other consumers, borrowers, pensioners, and others, whose money income has not been increased at all in the process. On the basis of these new prices the future is judged. Entrepreneurs who until how have been able to offer workmen, owners of raw material, etc., higher prices simply because they are themselves able to borrow money at cheap rates without expecting more than normal prices for their products, will now, *even if bank rate reverts to the normal natural rate*, on an average be able to offer the same high price, because they have reason to expect the same increased prices for their own products (or rents or freights, etc.) in the future. If, therefore, the banks maintain the lower rate of interest, it will act as a tempting extra profit to entrepreneurs and by competition between them will force up still further the price of labour and materials and indirectly of consumption goods, and so on. Thus the great and decisive difference between relative commodity prices on the one hand and the general price level on the other is, as I have already explained in my book, *Geldzins und Güterpreise*, that the equilibrium of the former is usually stable and is to be likened to a freely suspended pendulum, or a ball at the bottom of a bowl. If by an accident they are driven out of the position of equilibrium they tend themselves, i.e. through the force of gravity, to resume their former position. The general price level on the other hand is, on the assumption of a monetary system of unlimited elasticity, in a position of, so to speak, indifferent equilibrium of the same kind as that of a ball or cylinder on a plane, though somewhat restricted, surface: the ball does not move itself further, but from inertia and friction remains where it has been placed; if forces of sufficient strength to drive it from its position of equilibrium are brought into play, it has no tendency to resume that position, but if the forces which set it in motion—i.e. in this case the difference between the normal or real rate and the actual loan rate—cease to operate they will remain in a new and also indifferent position of equilibrium.

One consequence is that a rise in prices brought about in this manner must in the long run necessarily outweigh the tendencies to lower prices which may exist, in certain goods and in certain cases, with a low money rate, since these at least operate only once for all and are not cumulative. A general tendency of this kind, as pointed out, among others, by Mangoldt, is that with low interest rates, especially in primitive conditions, a number of people, for reasons of convenience or fear of taking risks, prefer to have large sums of money idle rather than to lend them, so that the velocity of circulation is retarded. The truth of this observation can scarcely be disputed, but even this circumstance could only exercise a pressure on prices up to a certain point, whereas the pressure we are now discussing tends to raise prices without limit, so long as the difference between the bank and the normal rate continues.

This conclusion may appear surprising, and even artificial and improbable, but we should not forget that it is in full agreement with what would occur if prices rose in consequence of an actual superfluity of gold, if the new gold came into the hands of the public in the form of loans from the banks. This is certainly not usually the case, for gold flows into the country from abroad to some extent directly in payment for goods. In such a case it should immediately give rise to an increase in commodity prices, and this increase may even precede the arrival of the gold, so that in relation to the continually rising price level there may be no excess of gold and consequently no reason for lowering the rate of interest. But to some extent also the new gold enters the country and finds its way to the banks as "capital", i.e. the owner of the gold has not purchased goods for the amount and has no immediate intention of doing so, but wishes to lend the money out at interest. If we now assume, as we may, that large quantities of this gold are deposited in the banks by domestic and foreign capitalists, then the banks, in order to put it—or an equal amount of notes—in circulation must inevitably lower their loan rate, and in accordance with our argument we may further assume that they will succeed in their object, i.e. all commodity prices will rise and business will thus require more media of exchange. As soon as that happens there will be an end to the relative excess of money, the banks will again raise their rates to the normal, i.e. to correspond with the real rate, and at that rate the prices already raised will be maintained. The gold which has once left the bank will in reality not return there, but will remain in the hands of the public. The condition on which the banks could maintain a rate of interest permanently below the real rate would therefore be an incessant flow to them of new gold, and under such circumstances commodity prices would also rise continuously. If this be admitted, there can scarcely be any difference if for gold we substitute banknotes, fictitious deposits, or other bank credit. The *causa efficiens*, the direct and active cause, is in both cases the same, namely a rate of loan interest below the normal, and in both cases the consequences must be the same.

The objection has been raised to the whole of the above reasoning that a lowering of the loan rate must also depress the real rate so that the difference between them is more and more levelled out and thus the stimulus to a continued rise in prices is eliminated. This possibility certainly cannot be entirely rejected. *Ceteris paribus* a lowering of the real rate unconditionally demands new real capital, i.e. increased saving. But this would certainly occur, even if involuntarily, owing to the fact that higher prices would compel a restriction of consumption on the part of those people who had fixed money incomes, such as civil servants, unless they were able to secure increases in their salaries corresponding to the rise in prices. Against this, however, would have to be set the decrease in voluntary saving which a lowering of interest rates tends to produce. But if the former influence prevails, and if production is unable to absorb unlimited quantities of new capital without a reduction in net yield, then the incipient rise in prices, though it would certainly not recede, might yet be arrested, unless the banks reduced their rate still further. Professor Davidson has suggested a further objection. He thinks that the same things might happen if the lowering of the rate of interest were caused by an excess of metallic currency of the same nature.[1] He remarks that if the output of production has grown by reason of new discoveries and inventions such as would increase the yield of real capital, pressure will be felt on the prices of all, or almost all, commodities—unless one assumes unlimited elasticity in the currency system. Thus the profits of entrepreneurs will remain at the old level and no increase whatever in the real rate of interest will actually occur. To this it may be answered that increased production belongs, in the nature of things, to the future, whereas the increased demand for raw materials and labour belongs to the present. For that reason an increased supply of goods will at most counteract in the future the cumulative rise in prices which has already begun. But even if the effects of such an increased supply of commodities were immediately visible, the disappearance of the extra profits of entrepreneurs, in spite of increased productivity, would, broadly speaking, necessarily presuppose a corresponding rise in real wages and therefore in the real capital from which these increased wages are paid. If, however, real capital has increased, no matter how, and the real rate has consequently fallen, then there would exist from the beginning no difference between the lower real rate and the banks' loan rate, which is contrary to our assumption.

[1] *Ekonomisk Tidskrift*, p. 11 *et seq.* (1909). Cf. my reply in the same year, p. 61 *et seqq.*

In spite of the difficulty of satisfactorily isolating phenomena which both in reality and in the public mind are so clearly connected with each other as real capital and its money value on the one hand and interest on capital and loan interest on the other, we may assume that the above-mentioned counteracting forces may be referred to what we have described as the secondary factors of the problem. In practice, moreover, it is of no importance if one conceives a price movement as continued infinitely in one direction or another, if it is caused by the difference between the two rates of interest. What is alone of importance is that it is strong enough to explain actual price fluctuations which manifestly cannot be due to variations in the quantity of gold and to guarantee the possibility of regulating the price level by the interest policy of the banks, if metallic gold ceases, as at present, to be the measure of prices.

Professor Davidson has also adduced in his essay a very interesting example (overlooked by me) from Ricardo (*Principles*, ed. 1888, ch. xxvii, p. 220) which is very much on the same lines as the theory I have developed.

In the same way the banks can theoretically bring about an unlimited fall in prices by maintaining a rate of interest above the normal rate. It is true that they must at the same time raise their rate on deposits in a corresponding degree, as they would otherwise, even under a pure system of credit, lose all lucrative business, because private loans would take the place of their own. (The paying out of metallic money would not be essential, and all money transactions could still be effected by book entries; the greater part of the deposits, however, would be withdrawn and loans paid in, so that bank balances would merely correspond to the amount of the ready cash necessary. Credit obligations which had previously been effected by the banks would remain between private individuals and would therefore bring no profit to the banks.) As has been shown in the preceding section, it is sometimes also necessary even for the Central Banks to give interest in one form or another on deposits when it is necessary to control the loan market and to improve the balance of trade.

If we take as our starting point the view that a lowering of the loan rate below the normal rate (determined by the existing demand for capital and the volume of saving) in itself tends to bring about a progressive rise in all commodity prices, and a spontaneous rise in loan rate a continuous fall in prices, both of which would go beyond all limits in practice, then all monetary phenomena would be extraordinarily clear and simple and at the same time the obligation of the banks to maintain the rate of interest in agreement with the normal or real rate of interest would be obvious. Not only would an arbitrary raising or lowering of the discount rate lead to an untenable shifting of the balance of payments through the medium of price changes (unless foreign banks followed suit), but it would also prove impossible for internal trade, especially when gold continues to be used on a large scale as is the case in most of the great trading countries. A raising of interest rates, with a consequent lowering of prices, would cause some gold to flow out of circulation and into the banks, and on this money the banks could not refuse to pay interest if they wished to avoid the loss of their bill-discounting. In a word, they would be forced to pay interest on money which they could not lend out, and the only remedy would clearly be to reduce loan rates. Again, too low a rate would lead to successively rising prices and the cash requirements of business for smaller payments would soon withdraw all gold from the banks or cause the statutory limit for note issues to be exceeded, a contingency only to be met by a raising of interest rates.

We sometimes hear it stated that the banks of the great trading countries are comparatively insensitive to withdrawals of gold so long as this gold only appears to be needed for internal requirements, but are much more sensitive to an outflow of gold abroad. In this connection, however, what is thought of is only the movements of gold in the internal market which are the result of periodically recurrent but transient increases in the requirements for business at certain times, such as quarter-days. No bank, however, can be indifferent to a progressive and continuous increase in the internal demand for gold.

(Cf. Helfferich's remarks, quoted on p. 122, on the increases of the discount rate of the German Reichsbank.)

On the other hand, it appears from the above that the compulsion laid upon the banks in respect of their interest rates depends mainly upon purely conventional circumstances, such as the prohibition of notes of small denomination in certain countries, so that the public is compelled to use coin, and in general the legislation regarding the issue of notes. This may be considered a good thing so far as it prevents the banks from causing unwelcome fluctuations in the price level by an arbitrary interest policy, but it is just the opposite if it also hinders them in *preventing* such fluctuations as are a consequence of changes in the demand for gold or in the conditions of its production. We shall shortly return to this question.

There still remains, however, the most important objection to this theory—an objection which the members of the Tooke school have triumphantly produced at every opportunity as a support for their theory and which the Ricardians have hitherto passed over in silence. It is the fact, which we have already met with in dealing with the influence of the amount of gold on prices, that rising prices very rarely coincide with low or falling interest rates, but much more frequently with rising or high rates.

It has, it is true, been objected that rising prices usually begin when interest rates have reached their maximum, and vice versa. But this rather indicates that either Tooke's theory, by which rising or falling rates of interest are the cause of rising or falling commodity prices, is right, or that changes in the rate of interest are caused by those of commodity prices, and not vice versa. For in both cases the lowest points of both these movements should coincide in time, whereas it might appear as if according to our theory the maximum of the one would coincide with the minimum of the other, or vice versa.

A careful study of Fig. 4, which explains itself, shows that the parallelism under discussion is by no means complete. But the general rule should be the one we have given.

But this apparently crushing objection loses all its significance, indeed it becomes a support for the view which it

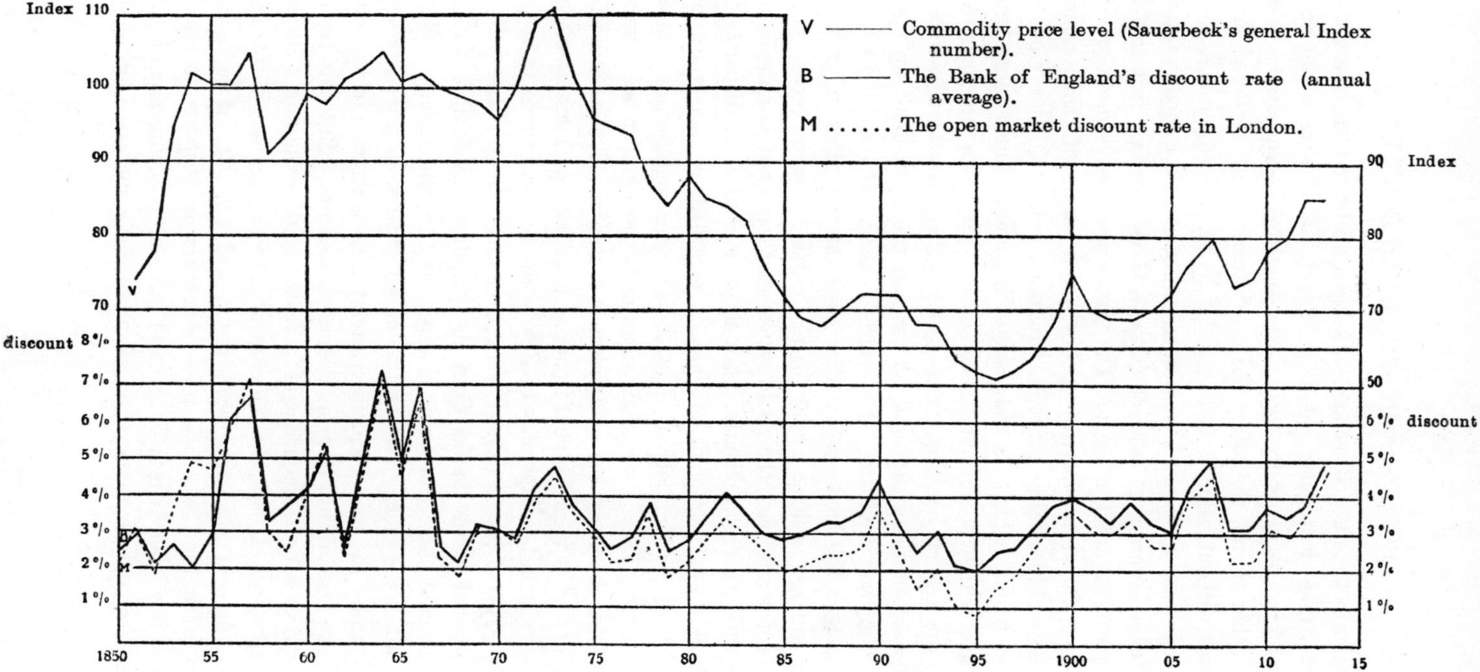
Index 110
100
90
80
70
discount 8 %
7 %
6 %
5 %
4 %
3 %
2 %
1 %
V
B
M
V —— Commodity price level (Sauerbeck's general Index number).
B —— The Bank of England's discount rate (annual average).
M ...... The open market discount rate in London.
90 Index
80
70
50
6 % discount
5 %
4 %
3 %
2 %
1 %
1850
55
60
65
70
75
80
85
90
95
1900
05
10
15

FIG. 4.

pretends to refute, if we ask ourselves on what do the changes in the banks' loan rates actually depend. If it were a fact that such changes generally spring from the banks themselves; that, in other words, the latter quite arbitrarily raise or lower their rates without being forced to do so by market conditions, then there would certainly be reason to expect rising commodity prices after a lowering of interest rates, and vice versa. But this is apparently not the case. The banks are always more or less *bound* in their interest policy, and even if this policy presumably could, through common action on the part of the banks which is nowadays becoming more prevalent, move within somewhat elastic limits, yet there predominates in the field of banking, more perhaps than elsewhere, precisely because of the great sums at stake, a procedure built up upon custom and tradition, in a word—*routine*. It may, indeed, be said that the banks never alter their interest rates unless they are induced to do so by the force of outside circumstances. They raise the rate when their gold stocks are threatened with depletion or their current obligations are so great that their disparity in relation to their gold holdings is regarded as dangerous, or, still more, where both of these things occur together, as is often the case. They lower their rates of interest under the reverse conditions: increased gold holdings or diminished commitments, or both. It is probable, of course, that such an increase of the banks' gold holdings may be due to the receipt of gold from the countries of production or from foreign countries, if this gold is deposited in the banks from the beginning as capital, and in such case there can be no doubt that the consequence will be a fall in the money rate and a consequent rise in prices, though naturally the banks will successively raise their rate to the level of the normal rate in proportion as prices rise. But this is not the necessary consequence of increased gold production. Higher market prices may, on the contrary, be the primary factor and the flow of gold the secondary; and a matter of equal importance for the actual price structure is that an increased quantity of gold may in general have no influence on prices if the demand for money has simultaneously increased owing to the growth of population or to a more widespread social division of labour or a more extended use of money.

The fluctuations in commodity prices which are not directly caused by *changes in gold production* must therefore have another cause in many cases, namely the changes which occur from time to time in the *real rate of interest*. This is not to be understood as meaning that the level of this interest makes commodities on the average either cheaper or dearer, for that, as we have seen is generally not the case, *but because the loan rate does not adapt itself quickly enough to these changes*, so that the influence of the banks on commodity prices is in fact a consequence of their passivity, and not of their activity, in the loan market. In other words, the difference between the actual loan and normal rates, which we have already designated as a major cause of fluctuations in commodity prices, arises less frequently because the loan rate changes spontaneously whilst the normal or real rate remains unchanged but on the contrary because the normal rate rises or falls whilst the loan rate remains unchanged or only tardily follows it. In the discussion of these questions this consideration has been almost entirely overlooked, probably owing to the fact that the theory of interest has hitherto remained in a rudimentary stage and has only in our own days been placed on secure foundations by the epoch-making work of Böhm Bawerk. The natural rate of interest, the real yield of capital in production, is, like everything else, exposed to changes—sometimes very strong. It falls when, other things being equal, capital increases by continuous saving, for as it becomes more and more difficult to find profitable employment for the new capital, competition with existing capital lowers the rate of interest whilst wages and rents rise in consequence. We must not forget, however, that even if, *ceteris paribus*, the rate of interest exercises a determining influence on the volume of saving, it is also affected by a number of other causes, such as increasing prosperity, increased legal security, increased forethought and a higher level of civilization. In some cases, too, a lower rate of interest may even stimulate saving, though this must be regarded as an exception to the rule.

Conversely, the rate of interest rises when the amount of

capital diminishes, either relatively, for example, through an increase of population and the resulting increased demand for capital in excess of current savings,[1] or absolutely, as the result of a destructive war or some catastrophe of nature. But the rate of interest may also rise for a time in consequence of some technical discovery which opens up a hitherto unknown profitable employment for capital and which at the same time usually requires more capital for its realization. If, for any of these reasons, or for all together, a change occurs in the natural rate, what will be the consequences? The money rate should, in accordance with general economic theory, undergo a corresponding change, but there exists, at least in our complex modern monetary system, no other connection between the two than the *variations in commodity prices* caused by the difference between them. And this link is elastic, just like the spiral springs often fitted between the body of a coach and the axles. An increase in the real rate does not therefore immediately cause a corresponding rise in the bank's rates, but the latter remain unchanged for a time and with them the loan rates between individuals. The money rate therefore becomes abnormally low in relation to the real capital rate, and this naturally has just the same effect as if the money rate had been spontaneously reduced with an unchanged interest on capital—which seldom happens. Frequently commodity prices therefore rise continuously, business requires greater cash holdings, bank loans increase without corresponding deposits, bank reserves, and often bullion reserves, begin to fall and the banks are compelled to raise their rates somewhat,

[1] An increase in the population of a country thus has a double tendency in relation to the movements of prices. A tendency to lower prices because it increases the production of goods and the volume of turnover, and hence the demand for money and a tendency to raise prices through its influence on the real rate of interest. Only in proportion as the first tendency is neutralized by continued production of gold and by continued gold imports, and also by the development of banking technique (cheques and clearing business) can the latter tendency operate unhindered. This would be still more the case in a pure credit system in which the banks could easily satisfy even the largest demands for currency needed for internal trade.

In modern society the concentration of the population in towns contributes to the maintenance of the rate of interest more than the actual increase in the population, because the development of the town and everything pertaining to it, such as new buildings and means of communication, absorbs the greater part of freshly accumulated capital.

though this does not prevent the continuous rise in prices, until the interest rates have reached the level of the normal rate. Indeed, if the rise in prices itself gives birth to exaggerated hopes of future gains, as often happens, the demand for bank credit may far exceed the normal, and in order to protect themselves the banks may be forced to raise their rates even above the level of the natural rate or the normal loan rate. Still more is this true if signs of a crisis have already appeared; confidence begins to be shaken and the credit of the big monetary institutions is the only credit accepted. The converse will naturally occur with a falling natural (or real) rate which is only followed gradually and at a distance by a corresponding fall of the banks' rates. Our conclusion is that rising prices are accompanied by high and rising rates of interest, and falling commodity prices by low rates of interest—which is in full agreement with our theory, and yet adduced as the main disproof of the *connection between the money rate and commodity prices* which we have assumed.

It is a common experience that "good times", when business is active and everybody is earning, or believes or hopes he can earn, a good profit, are also times of rising prices. Good times and a generally hopeful tone in the business world are created by the prospects of gain, and the real foundation is doubtless the gain already obtained in certain enterprises, as a result, for example, of technical or commercial progress. The real rate of interest, therefore, is high, and is expected to remain so in the immediate future, whilst the loan rate remains for the moment unchanged. The element of a rise in prices is therefore present, according to our theory, but it is equally clear that sooner or later the banks will be induced to raise their rates, since the technical discoveries have not brought them any additional supplies of money and neither the velocity of circulation of money nor the perfection of banking technique can be raised to an unlimited extent. Higher prices and an increased volume of business, on the contrary, require a larger amount of hard cash or banknotes in circulation. And the contrary is the case in "bad times".

It might therefore be supposed that the fluctuations in the bank or money rate of interest are sometimes the cause of fluctuations in commodity prices and sometimes, more frequently, caused by them. In this view, which is actually held by many writers, there is nothing essentially unreasonable, for it is not surprising that the movements of prices and the interest rate occur in the same direction in the latter case and in opposite directions in the former case; there are parallels to be found in many other economic phenomena which merely illustrate the general law of effect and counter-effect. Thus, for example, an increased demand for a commodity may sometimes be associated with a rising, and sometimes with a falling price, according to whether the change in price is caused by the increased demand or itself caused the latter. What is unsatisfactory, however, is that the very cause of a rise or fall in the general price level is still unexplained in the case, extremely important in practice, where it is not due to a change in the supply of gold or to an increased demand for goods from the gold countries. From what has been said, however, it should be clear that both phenomena, the influence of prices on the money rate and the influence of the money rate on prices, follow the same law. The primary cause of price fluctuations in both cases is the same, namely the difference arising no matter how, between the normal and actual money or loan rates. A lowering of interest rates by the banks causes rising prices, and a raising of them causes falling prices, only when the loan rate thereby falls below or rises above the normal rate which in its turn is connected with the natural rate. In the same way the fluctuations in the latter, which we regard as the essence of good and bad times so-called, influence prices only so long as they are not accompanied by a corresponding modification of interest rates. If on the other hand changes in the loan rate take place simultaneously and uniformly with corresponding changes in the real rate of interest then—apart from the direct influence of gold production—no change in the level of commodity prices, and least of all a progressive, cumulative change, can occur.

Note on Trade Cycles and Crises.

The above views, so far as they relate to price movements in " good " and " bad " times, are connected with a view of the nature and causes of trade cycles which I have not had the opportunity of developing further since I put it forward in a lecture to the Norwegian Statsökonomiska Förening (Economic Club), published in *Statsökonomisk Tidskrift*, 1907. The lecture does not claim to give a definitive explanation of the puzzling phenomena of the trade cycle, but does point out a necessary and hitherto often neglected clue to a full explanation. Moreover my view closely agrees with that of Professor Spiethoff. Its main feature is that it ascribes trade cycles to *real* causes independent of movements in commodity price, so that the latter become of only secondary importance, although in real life they nevertheless play an important and even a dominating part in the development of crises.

Since rising prices almost always accompany prosperous times and falling prices times of depression, it is natural—though in my opinion wrong—to regard such a rise in prices as the cause of good times, and falling prices as the cause of depressions, just as according to Clément Juglar—who may well be right here—the cause of crises, or rather the crises themselves, consist of the sudden cessation of the rise in commodity prices.

A consistent statement of this point of view is contained, for example, in Sombart's well-known assertion that, historically, prosperous times are always associated with increased gold production.

That such a general rise in prices, or rather a rise caused in such a way, may act as an incentive to increased business activity and thus to conversion on a large scale of liquid capital into fixed capital, which, as all agree, is the outstanding characteristic of good times, need not be disputed. But if the formation of the real capital which is then absolutely essential is only based on the rise in prices itself, i.e. is due to diminished consumption on the part of those persons or classes of society with fixed money incomes, then the increased prosperity could scarcely be very great or enduring. Moreover, the constant parallelism between largely increasing gold production and boom periods which advocates of this view have observed is disputed, and in my opinion rightly, by others, for example by Spiethoff.

Still less can we accept the view first put forward by Tugan Baronowski, and later adopted by Lescure (in his work on crises) according to which both a rise in prices in good times and a fall in prices during and after a crisis have no relation to the currency system and are caused exclusively by the phenomena of production and of the market. Thus, for example, in this view increased production and the resulting increase in the supply of certain kinds of goods, especially of those for which the demand is not very elastic, such as foodstuffs, would lead to a heavy fall in the prices of such goods, and since sellers would then obtain smaller amounts of money with which to demand other goods, the fall in prices would extend to these also and depression and crisis would result (*surproduction généralisée* in contrast to *surproduction générale*, formerly the commonest theoretical explanation of crises, but now mostly abandoned).

Clearly the fact is here overlooked that the purchasing power which on this assumption would be reduced in the case of the sellers of the former goods would be increased to a corresponding degree in the case of the buyers. If the latter only have to offer a smaller part of their income in order to satisfy their needs for the goods or classes of goods in question, then they have a correspondingly greater amount left for their demand for other goods, and it is not impossible that these other goods—quite contrary to the theory—would *rise* in price and thereby perhaps compensate for the fall in price of the cheapened goods.

On the whole it is vain here, as in the general theory of prices, to explain any particular movement without regard to the one thing which constitutes a basis of comparison in all price-formation, namely money and its substitutes, or the means of hastening its velocity of circulation, credit. In pure theory we are at liberty to invent any measure of prices we please. Let us suppose, for example, that instead of 0·4 grammes of gold, as in Sweden, we select as our unit of money value one kg. of pig-iron. Then, since of all commodities pig-iron usually shows the most violent fluctuations in price before and after a crisis, the choice of this measure of value would mean that the prices of all goods (except pig-iron, which would remain constant) would *fall* in good times and *rise* in the subsequent depression. That price movements in fact occur in the opposite direction can only be explained by the choice of the measure of prices—gold, and not pig-iron. Yet the difference does not consist in the fact that gold as a commodity, i.e. in industrial use, is less in demand in good than in bad times —the opposite is certainly true—but in the fact that its quality as a commodity remains in an indifferent relation to the other factors influencing its value. The utility of gold in its technical employment is, unlike that of pig-iron, at any rate during the short periods here under consideration, of too little importance to be able to offer any resistance to the changes in its exchange value which are caused by an acceleration or retardation of the velocity of circulation of minted gold or by the expansion or contraction of credit.

It is true, of course, that the last-mentioned factor is of some influence between individuals, apart from any measures taken by the banks. The general tone of confidence produced by a boom no doubt has the effect of considerably expanding the volume of claims and debts on ordinary current account between merchants—and vice versa in times of depression— but in the main and especially nowadays it is probably the banks who by their discounting of bills and other credit facilities regulate the amount of circulating medium. And after what we have said above we may take it for granted that that which primarily determines the extent to which this bank credit is taken must be its price, its relative price, the bank rate, in relation to the yield or expected yield of capital employed in production and turnover.

Our conclusion is therefore that the changes in the purchasing power of money caused by credit are under existing conditions certainly ultimately bound up with industrial fluctuations and undoubtedly affect them, especially in causing crises, though we need not assume any necessary connection between the phenomena.

The principal and sufficient cause of cyclical fluctuations should rather be sought in the fact that in its very nature technical or commercial advance cannot maintain the same even progress as does, in our days, the increase in needs—especially owing to the organic phenomenon of increase of population—but is sometimes precipitate, sometimes delayed. It is natural and at the same time economically justifiable that in the former case people seek to exploit the favourable situation as quickly as possible, and since the new discoveries, inventions, and other improvements nearly always require various kinds of preparatory work for their realization, there occurs the conversion of large masses of liquid into fixed capital which is an inevitable preliminary to every boom and indeed is probably the only fully characteristic sign, or at any rate one which cannot conceivably be absent.

If, again, these technical improvements are already in operation and no others are available, or at any rate none which have been sufficiently tested or promise a profit in excess of the margin of risk attaching to all new enterprises, there will come a period of depression; people will not venture to the capital which is now being accumulated in such a fixed form, but will retain it as far as possible in a liquid, available form.

It is not difficult to understand that in the former case such goods (raw materials) as serve in the construction of fixed capital—bricks, timber, iron, etc.—would be in great demand and rise in price, and that in a period of depression they would be in slight demand and fall in price. But this rise or fall in price should under ordinary conditions be accompanied by a movement in the opposite direction of the price of other goods, so that the average level of prices would remain unchanged. This would probably be the case if the banks at the beginning of a boom raised their interest rates sufficiently and on the other hand finally lowered them at the beginning of a depression. In that case presumably the real element of the crisis would be eliminated and what remained would be merely an even fluctuation between periods in which the newly formed capital would assume, and, economically speaking, should assume, other forms, of which we shall now speak, but which have been almost completely ignored in all previous theories of the trade cycle.

Since the demand for new capital in an upward swing of the trade cycle is frequently much too great to be satisfied by contemporaneous saving, even if it is stimulated by a higher rate of interest, and since, on the other hand, in bad times this demand is practically nil, though saving does not nevertheless entirely cease, the rise in rates of interest and commodity prices in good times and their fall in bad times would presumably be much more severe than now, if it were not that the replenishment and depletion of stocks in all branches of production producing durable goods, acted as a regulator or " parachute ". When demand falls, manufacturers, unless they wish to dismiss their workers or work half-time, have no alternative but to work for stock, and usually they do so, since wages have generally fallen and the rise in prices which they expect to occur later on will more than cover the loss of keeping goods in stock even for several years. (In some years the price of bricks has varied from 25 to 40 Kr. per 1,000. If rent and warehousing are estimated at 10 per cent per annum for the whole output—which is an exaggeration—then the holding of stocks for even five years would be economically possible, if the higher price were assured at the end of the period.) The accumulation of stocks is probably the most important form of fresh capital accumulation in bad times. In subsequent good times the largely increased demand for raw materials and finished goods for production and consumption is largely satisfied from these stocks, both directly and by exchange for the products of other countries.

Clearly, working for stock would be much facilitated if the banks offered sufficient cheap credit. Manufacturers would then not need to wait for a fall in wages or in the prices of raw materials, but even a moderate fall in the prices of their own products would, in combination with low loan rates, make it profitable for them to increase their stocks in order to reduce them after some years by selling at normal prices.

Earlier theory has in my opinion turned the whole matter as it were upside down in so far as it assumes that stocks are increased in good times and are depleted in bad times (the so-called theory of over-production). It is not easy to understand whence the surplus in the former case or the shortage in the latter case should come. In point of fact consumption increases in good times and much labour and land is withdrawn from the production of present commodities. Nor can we understand why practical business men should habitually choose such a topsy-turvy procedure as to complete their stocks when costs of production are high in order to sell them when prices are low. Not even the assumption of widespread unemployment (or short time) in depressions suffices as an explanation, for, quite apart from the fact that this argument is exaggerated, unemployment itself implies greatly reduced consumption.

Unfortunately here also we lack the detailed commercial statistics which alone can finally solve this problem. Yet from inquiry among business men I have learned that it is just in periods of depression that they are forced to work for stock, and that they can never do so in good times, since they are then often not in a position fully to meet the demand for their goods. And this appears probable *a priori*. If we ask *when* a manufacturer may reasonably describe loans as good and take steps to expand his output, the answer must be when the demand for his goods begins to exceed his production capacity. But that is the moment at which his stocks, which he had previously enlarged, begin to be depleted, that is, mathematically, when they have reached their maximum, and not their minimum dimensions. An apparent argument against this is the heavy fall in prices which usually accompanies a crisis, but the cause of this need not be sought in the accumulation of stocks. No manufacturer is disposed to sell his wares at a slump price just because his warehouses are full. But if he is refused credit and if he is compelled to obtain ready cash, then he will be compelled to dispose of his goods at any price at all, whether his stocks be large or small.

In the absence of comprehensive statistics, however, we must content ourselves with a weighing of arguments. Spiethoff (in his discussions in the transactions of the *Verein für Sozialpolitik*, 1903) mentions as a well-known fact that in bad times manufacturers' stock rooms are filled from floor to ceiling. Herkner (in the article " Krisen " in the *Handwörterbuch der Staatswissenschaften*, 3rd ed.) disputes this fact by reference to Esslen and Merovich. Esslen's work, however, gives no information on this point and Merovich's work is still, so far as I know, unpublished. How little this important point has hitherto been considered may be seen from the fact that the comprehensive questionnaire which the *Verein für Sozialpolitik* at one time sent out, and which is the foundation of the inquiry into the crisis of 1900, did not contain any question as to the magnitude of stocks.

10. *Conclusions. The Practical Organization of Currency*

If we sum up what has been said, it will be found that there are two essential causes of change in the commodity price level.

Firstly the demand for goods from the countries producing the precious metals, especially gold, followed by shipments of gold in payment thereof, a demand which, if it is greater than that corresponding to the demand of the non-goldproducing countries for new gold at ruling commodity prices—whether for industrial purposes or by reason of increased population or the increased use of money—must necessarily cause a rise in prices, and if it is less than that demand a fall in prices in the latter countries. Both are accompanied by an absolute and usually increased quantity of money and therefore of money in circulation, but relatively to turnover it is increased in the former case and decreased in the latter.

Secondly, the fact that interest on borrowed money is for one reason or another either below or above the level which would normally be governed by the real rate ruling at the time, a circumstance which, so long as it lasts, must cause a progressive rise or fall in prices and during which the *medium of turnover* is adapted to the changed demand, not by an increase or decrease in the quantity of money (gold), but by an increase or decrease in the (physical or virtual) velocity of circulation of money through the agency of credit.

It is not possible to subsume these two causes under a common cause (as I tried to do in my earlier work, *Geldzins und Güterpreise*, following Ricardo's example), since the quantity of money and the velocity of circulation of money are two different things, even if they both have an influence on the price level. Only in so far as new gold is deposited in the banks in the form of " capital ", i.e. without being drawn out in cheques and notes soon after, can it give rise to a lowering of interest rates and in that way affect prices. But this need not happen, and, contrary to Ricardo's view, does not happen as a rule. Rather most of the gold flows in in payment for goods and should then, in proportion as it exceeds the demand for new gold, have a direct influence in raising prices without lowering interest rates. Indeed, this effect may, on the hypothesis we have developed above, even precede the inflow of gold, in which case its influence on interest rates will rather be in the contrary direction.

We evidently possess no control of *this* cause of price change so long as gold production remains in the hands of private enterprise and the free minting of gold for private account is retained. The only possibility of a rational control of the price level must lie in another direction, in the proper regulation of the interest policy of the banks. Theoretically such steps should under all circumstances be sufficient, for a spontaneous raising or lowering of the discount rate should in the long run have a more powerful influence on prices than any other cause. But in practice, nevertheless, it encounters under existing conditions almost insurmountable difficulties.

This method is comparatively simple in those cases which in times gone by caused economists the greatest difficulty, namely in cases of a diminished flow of gold from the producing countries and a threatened shortage of gold. An adequate lowering of interest rates should successfully counteract the otherwise inevitable pressure on prices; the only obstacle to its realization would be the fact that the banks' supplies of gold would no longer suffice to fill the vacuum in the circulation of gold among the public which would be caused by the diminished production of gold. But the proper remedy for this is to be found partly in the issue of notes of lower denomination even in the larger trading countries, as was proposed in several places in the 'eighties, when the shortage of gold was threatened, and as could probably have been effected if the shortage had continued,[1] and partly in an increased use of bank credit, in proportion

[1] It cannot be said that the lowering of the denomination of bank notes which occurred in Germany before the war was occasioned by a shortage of gold. The step was rather taken for private economic reasons, or for public economic reasons in the narrower sense. On price developments on the whole it had rather an unfavourable effect, i.e. it contributed to the accentuation of the rise in prices produced by the large increase in gold production.

as the habit of keeping a banking account spreads more widely among the population. So much as regards the needs of internal business. As regards international payments, the necessity of maintaining large gold reserves for eventual payment abroad might be reduced to almost any extent if, instead, the banks held deposits in foreign banks, a development which is already in progress and which is quite natural in itself in so far as foreign payments are concentrated in the hands of the banks. In a country such as Sweden in particular, and in general where the gold reserves are not employed in the transaction of internal business, there is no doubt that foreign bills might take the place of gold without any danger to the legally prescribed note cover, The higher price which these bills would command in the market with an unfavourable balance of payments and also the interest which the banks themselves would be obliged to pay for the credits by which they would strengthen their foreign holdings in case of need, or the falling values of the scrip which they must export in order to obtain such holdings, would make it as compelling a necessity for the banks to raise their interest rates in order to restore equilibrium as the threatened outflow of gold, unless foreign countries achieved the same effect by lowering their interest rates.

The only real limit to the substitution of credit for gold would appear when gold production had fallen so low that it did not meet the demand of industry for gold, which would then turn to the remaining stocks in the banks and would soon decimate them. In this case, in so far as it is still desired to prevent commodity prices from falling, nothing else would avail but a removal of the obligation of the banks to redeem their notes in gold, in other words, the introduction of an inconvertible paper currency; this is a step to which we shall shortly return, but which for the moment and in the immediate future need not be regarded as likely.[1]

On the other hand, the position is much more difficult when there is an excessive supply of gold and a consequent rise in prices for all goods and services. It has not been

[1] [Written before the World War.—EDITOR.]

discussed much, though from all appearances it must have been imminent in 1906. A correction might exist in a contraction of bank credit, but this is much more difficult to effect than an expansion, as it runs contrary to the developments which economic forces are seeking to bring about. In the countries which have notes of small denomination a withdrawal of such notes would certainly leave room for gold in general circulation, but naturally at the sacrifice of the profit which in such countries nowadays usually goes to the State, and with a resulting extra burden on the tax-payer. In the chief European countries, again, this remedy is not possible, since gold is already largely in circulation there. A withdrawal of the English five-pound note and the German 100-mark notes, so that the lowest denomination would be £10 or 200 marks, would only inconvenience business and would perhaps have no effect, since notes, especially in England, are being more or less replaced by cheques. As regards the proposal sometimes made to demand of the non-issuing banks the maintenance of large gold reserves as a guarantee for their deposits and current accounts, such a measure, if it were not required by a real need for increased security and soundness of the banks (which would be difficult to prove), must be regarded as an unnecessary and costly restraint.

Therefore, unless we are prepared to accept the consequences as regards commodity prices, since they must ultimately adjust themselves to an equilibrium with the demand for gold, though at a considerably higher price level, there is scarcely any other fully satisfactory remedy against a great and persistent increase in gold production than the one which has been applied almost everywhere in the past with regard to silver, namely the *cessation of free minting* on private account.[1] There can scarcely be any

[1] Another alternative is also conceivable, namely whilst retaining free gold minting to relieve the banks of their obligation to redeem their notes in gold or to accept gold at a fixed price. Gold coinage would, in other words, be converted into a mere money of exchange which would change hands at varying rates of exchange, as was formerly the case with the silver countries. The measure of value would then become the banknote and it would be the business of the Central Banks to maintain its value both in reference to goods and to the currency of other countries in a manner which we shall shortly endeavour to explain. In a way, perhaps, the latter method is the most rational, for it is at bottom a reasonable demand that the State should maintain a gold

reasonable doubt that such a step would be fully effective for the maintenance and preservation of the present price level and purchasing power in goods and services if we look at the influence which the cessation of free minting in Holland and British India—in which countries most of the hard cash consists of silver—has had on the value of money in those countries. Without any difficulty whatever silver is held at parity with gold, in Holland at the old ratio of 1 : 15½, in India at the new ratio 1 : 22, and consequently any other variations in terms of goods than those which gold undergoes, and therefore such as might have been caused by the subsequent heavy fall in the value of silver are eliminated. From an economic point of view this measure would constitute a great saving and would be much preferable to an attempt to maintain the value of money at its present level by contracting credit, whilst retaining free minting, for in that way, as Davidson rightly observes, the production of gold would also be maintained on its present excessive scale and might even be increased. That would be wasteful of capital and labour, which might from the point of view of economy be more profitably employed.

The only people who could complain would be the shareholders in the gold mines, whose vast capital sunk in them would no longer give the expected yield: in some cases, indeed, it might yield nothing at all. This, however, is a secondary consideration. The interest of gold-producers cannot, or at least should not, be decisive in this question, nor should it set aside much more important and more comprehensive interests any more than the interests of the owners of silver mines in keeping up silver prices were allowed to prevent the abolition of the free minting of silver or the repeal of the Bland and Sherman Bills in the U.S.A.

We now come to the main question. Is such a step possible

coinage guaranteed in fineness and weight, whereas there is no obvious justification for the demand that its gold coins should also regulate all economic estimates and agreements. On the other hand the inconvenience in everyday affairs of using money with an uncertain and variable purchasing power is so great that the alternative mentioned above, restricted minting, is to be preferred.

without sacrificing the advantages of gold monometallism with free minting and especially the advantages of an *international* medium of exchange which it now possesses and which is, rightly, valued highly? A single nation, however important, which on its own account introduced such a measure would of course cut itself off from the existing fixed currency parity and the relative stability of foreign exchange rates. Its currency, gold coinage with no free minting on private account, would as a rule have a higher, perhaps much higher value than the gold currency of other countries, but at the same time it would be an unstable value. With an occasional unfavourable balance of payments abroad, the gold coin of the country could not be used as a medium of payment abroad, or at least only in a case of extreme need and after a heavy fall in its internal value; in order to effect payment it would be necessary to use first stocks of unminted gold and foreign coin held by the banks or by private individuals who had acquired it in speculation for this purpose, and second, and most important, existing holdings abroad, such as securities, etc. Indeed, this method of payment is finding wider employment even under present conditions, and experience has shown that both old silver countries, after the abolition of free silver minting, and paper currency countries, such as Austria in recent times, have been able, by a rational use of minting, note issue, and discount policy, successfully to maintain their conventional money at parity with the gold currency of other countries. There could therefore be no special difficulty in maintaining it in a country which, by the abolition of free gold minting, had already imparted a higher value to its gold currency than its metallic value, i.e. in preventing occasional and unnecessary disturbances. Of course it would never remain quite stable in relation to the currency of other countries, for the purpose of the abolition of free minting was just to prevent the value of money from following foreign currency in the anticipated fall in value of metallic and free minted gold. That would be an inconvenience which the country in question would have to submit to for the benefit of possessing within the country a fixed measure of value and an average price level for commodities and services which is as constant as possible.

If other nations should follow this example—though at first gradually—and the value of gold should meanwhile continue to fall, then there would be the inconvenience that we should possibly have a whole series of gold currencies in different countries whose value in relation to goods, and therefore their internal value, would depend on conditions quite other than their weight and fineness. This is more or less what happened to the silver currencies of various countries, such as the French 5-franc piece, the German thaler, the old Austrian silver gulden, the Russian silver rouble, the Indian rupee, and the Mexican dollar; they all had different values in relation to their silver content. Undoubtedly the simplest and best course would be for the abolition of free minting of gold—assuming sufficient reason for this measure existed—to occur simultaneously by agreement between the principal Great Powers, in which case the remaining countries would certainly follow suit. In such case there would seem to be no insurmountable obstacle to retaining all the advantages of the present system whilst avoiding its inconveniences, by combining, as it were, a constant value of money in space with that in time.

As regards the first half of our problem—the maintenance of a constant internal value between the gold currencies of different countries, the relation of which would be the same as the relation between their gold content, even if they had all risen above the value of the metallic gold, one might at first suppose that it might be done by an international agreement similar to that of the Latin Union in regard to silver, so that the gold currency of the various countries would be legal tender, or would at any rate be accepted by the public treasuries in each country. But this would scarcely be feasible, for it would require common regulations as regards the minting, of gold, which could only be permitted up to a certain maximum, related in some way, for example, to the population. Otherwise some State might avail itself of the low price of gold to mint large quantities of money and to flood other countries with it in payment for goods—an extremely profitable business. But restrictions of this kind are difficult, and even impossible to introduce, as the requirements of currency per head differ so much in different countries and at different times. The best thing would therefore seem to be to leave the regulation of international monetary values to the institutions which at present control them, namely the discount policy of the great banks, though so long as metallic money remains the measure of value it must be supported by the currency policy of the Governments. Nothing is more absolutely necessary than agreements between the central banks of the various countries, of the kind which we have described—and which have actually existed between the central banks of the Scandinavian countries—to redeem at par each other's drafts and notes (and of course each other's gold currency, though this would not then be of major importance) in their own currency and notes. It would then be the banks' own affair to determine how they would exchange or account for these notes and drafts and to what extent and at what rate of interest they would accord each other credit for longer periods. In this way the currency and notes of each country would continue to be legal tender only in the country itself, but they could nevertheless be used for foreign payments, along with the *drafts* of the banks, and, like them, without any loss on the exchange, as they would always be redeemed at par by the central banks and their branches, and in all probability very soon by other banks also.

There remains the much more difficult problem of the maintenance of a constant value of money in *time*, a stable purchasing power of money in terms of goods. It is evident that this could not be achieved by any country alone if the mint parity between countries were maintained the whole time. It must be achieved rather by common measures on the part of all countries and more particularly on the part of their central banks—though from what has been said it is difficult to say of what kind. We have already seen that the system here proposed would by no means release the central banks of the various countries from the necessity of making changes from time to time in their interest rates in order to counteract movements either occasional or more persistent, in the balance of foreign payments. This necessity would remain, though the fact is often overlooked, under any system, however intimate the monetary unions into which the different countries may enter, and even if the proposal for a common world paper currency, issued by one central bank, were adopted. But such rises and falls in interest rates are by nature relative; they are always made on the basis of foreign interest rates. The same result may therefore be obtained in two different ways: by raising the discount rate in the country which has an unfavourable balance of payments and by a lowering of it in those countries which have a favourable balance at the same time. The system has, therefore, to borrow a term from mechanics—*two degrees of freedom*: side by side with the interest policy of the banks with reference to each other, which has the function of producing equilibrium between the debits and credits of the various countries, there should be a common policy, a raising or lowering of bank rates throughout the world from time to time in order to depress the commodity price level when it showed a tendency to rise and to raise it when it showed a tendency to fall. Such an arrangement would in reality be less artificial than one would suppose, for the point round which interest rates in the various countries would oscillate and to which they would be more or less anchored would, as has already been shown, be just the normal or real rate ruling on any particular occasion in any particular country. There is in addition another reason for leaving this function to the interest policy of the central banks instead of, as one might imagine, to a common currency policy of Governments. So long as the production of gold continues to be abundant, the Governments are, it is true, able by restricted minting to raise the value of their coinage to any height whatever above its metallic value. But if the gold mines and the goldfields at some future time should again be exhausted and metallic gold rise to the same value as that of minted gold, or even above it, then a rise in the value of money and a fall in commodity prices could not be prevented by any such measure. The prohibition of the melting down of gold is practically useless, as history shows, and for good reasons. In such a case it would ultimately be for the banks, by an increased note issue or some other expansion of credit to counteract the shortage in *the medium of turnover* in order to raise prices, and it would only be beneficial if by mutual agreement and the habit of common action they were prepared for all eventualities. From a higher economic point of view, moreover, the use of such a costly material as gold is pure waste. The minted gold of the world, calculated at 40 milliards of kronor, would naturally be used to greater advantage if it were placed at the disposal of industry, and even if from a purely commercial point of view gold would then have to be sold at a loss it would be an economic advantage to be rid of it. As an independent measure of value, independent of material substance, whether gold or silver, and kept stable in value both in space and time in the manner described above, the banknote, or in more general terms bank money, is undoubtedly the ideal which currency systems should endeavour to approach.

Finally, as regards the technical difficulties of introducing such reforms, there is no reason either to underestimate or to exaggerate them. That existing price statistics are not sufficiently developed for a precise or reliable calculation of the fluctuations in prices is only too true, and even if they were as complete as is conceivable a regulation of prices and exchanges, especially if it is to be effective throughout the whole world, can only be approximate and to a certain extent purely conventional. But such difficulties must, here as always, be measured and weighed against the urgency of the need which it is proposed to satisfy and the evils which require a remedy. If gold production should again be reduced, or the excess of gold is absorbed—as happened in the 'nineties—by the countries which have not yet found it necessary to acquire large stocks of gold, and if in consequence commodity prices in the immediate future only show a small or uncertain change, then perhaps it would be folly to attempt to reform the existing monometallic gold system, which is without doubt theoretically the most simple and has great and real advantages in practice. But if we are confronted with a real plethora of gold, if the future price level shows an unmistakable and persistent upward trend with all the resultant social inconveniences, and even if the reverse—a great shortage of gold—should happen, then the need for reform of the existing currency system will presumably be so clearly felt that it will be impossible to reject it, and the practical means for its achievement will be discovered, even if they do not at the beginning reach the height of perfection.

Note on Irving Fisher's Proposal for the Regulation of the Purchasing Power of Money[1]

A proposal for the regulation of the value of money which has lately been much discussed is that of the American professor, Irving Fisher, which he first indicated in his *The Purchasing Power of Money*, and later in articles in various journals, especially *The Quarterly Journal of Economics*, March, 1913, where he develops a plan for a " compensated dollar ". Under this plan the free minting of gold is retained, though not, as now, with the deduction only of the costs of minting (*brassage*), but with the introduction of a more or less significant seignorage, which at any given moment would in principle be so determined that the metallic gold actually exchanged for a minted dollar (or other gold coin or notes of gold denomination) would stand in inverse proportion to the current purchasing power of gold in terms of other goods. In this way, according to Irving Fisher, we should retain *a stable purchasing power* in terms of goods, and the average level of commodity prices, calculated in minted gold, would therefore remain stable. On the other hand national treasuries would be under an obligation to redeem gold coins or notes on demand for as much metallic gold as corresponded at any given time to their purchasing power. The profits which would be made by the treasuries in times of rising prices, calculated in metallic

[1] As the author indicates in the preface to the second Swedish edition, this note constitutes a brief résumé of his essay on " The Regulation of the Value of Money " in *Ekon. Tidskrift*, xv, 134–142 (1913). Cf. also pp. 224–7, in which he says that an essay by Professor Davidson had led him to realize " the essential shortcomings " of Fisher's plan.

gold, i.e. from a falling value of gold, would form a fund which would assist them, without sacrifice, to fulfil their obligation to redeem in case the demand for metallic gold should exceed the quantities simultaneously offered to the State for minting. In order to prevent speculation in rising and falling values of gold the seignorage would, according to Irving Fisher, be altered successively by such small degrees that these changes would be counterbalanced by the loss in interest to those who otherwise might be inclined to hold either gold coin (or notes) on speculation for a future profitable conversion into metallic gold or coin or notes.

It is evident, and this is admitted by Fisher, that this method could only be employed on the assumption that metallic gold remains *lower* in price than at the time of the introduction of the reform, so that the seignorage would always be positive. In the opposite case the State would be compelled to mint money of greater weight than corresponded to the metallic gold offered to the State for minting, which is inconceivable, since it would soon lead to a smelting down of coin and new offers of gold to the mint for minting.

But apart from this disadvantage the method has another drawback, which neither Fisher nor the majority of his critics appear to have noticed. It clearly assumes that the exchange value of the *metallic* gold in terms of goods is *not* materially affected by the seignorage. As far as a particular country of the size of the U.S.A. is concerned, this assumption may be made, up to a point, but in that case the whole measure would only amount to a kind of limited minting within that country, and metallic gold as a whole—or in proportion as it was not absorbed for industrial purposes—would flow to those countries where it could still be freely minted at the old ratio, i.e. without seignorage. In other words, the country would then have solved the problem of maintaining the purchasing power of money in terms of goods within the country itself—or what we have called constancy in *time*—but by sacrificing constancy in space, i.e. as against the currency of other countries.

The conditions would be quite different if all countries should adopt the same plan, which is, of course, Fisher's purpose, or, what amounts to the same thing, if it is conceived as being introduced in an *isolated* country producing its own gold. In that case, of course, the exchange value of metallic gold would also be influenced by the seignorage, which to that extent would constitute an obstacle to the intended raising of the purchasing power of minted gold.

Fisher does not altogether deny this, but he assumes, without further reason, that a fall in the value of metallic gold would only constitute about *half* of the seignorage, so that the remaining half would in any case produce a corresponding rise in the purchasing power of minted gold. This, however, is only a guess, and an improbable one at that. If, as Fisher always does in other places, we take the point of view of the Quantity Theory, then it is clear that this measure can only influence the level of commodity prices in proportion as it successfully brings about a diminution, or prevents an otherwise impending increase, of the whole quantity of money in existence in the country. Now the annual quantity of gold produced, and still more the quantity available for minting purposes, is only a small fraction of the existing quantity of coin. The seignorage, therefore, when it is first imposed or altered, would have a very slight influence indeed on the total quantity of money. Its influence on the total quantity of coin or notes, and consequently on the price level, would be limited to a *fraction of a fraction*, or in practice it would be nil; for which reason the value of metallic gold would presumably fall by practically the whole amount of the seignorage when imposed or changed.

On the other hand this pressure on the exchange value of the metal would of course make the production of gold less profitable in the long run and at the same time increase the industrial consumption of gold. In the long run therefore Fisher's method would doubtless prove effective, i.e. it would achieve somewhat earlier equilibrium between production and consumption which sooner or later, though more slowly, the unchecked rise in commodity prices would itself have produced. But the idea that in this manner anything like a stable price level could be achieved must be rejected as illusory.

In crises, as the Belgian, Ansiaux, has pointed out, the Fisher method might have fatal results. In the upward swing of the trade cycle, when commodity prices are rising by means of the granting of credit, the State and the central banks would, on Fisher's plan, endeavour by successive increase of the seignorage to counteract this rise in prices, though certainly only with partial success. When the crisis occurred and credit was contracted, and there came into being an increased demand for gold coin and notes, the banks would have cut themselves off from the possibility of issuing sufficient quantities of them, since the rate of seignorage already levied could only be slowly altered. The crises might thereby become even more acute.

Various other observations of a practical and technical kind may be made, and have been made, against Fisher's plan, but its theoretical foundations are, if the above criticism is accepted, much too weak for us to attribute to it any real importance.

At most it may be admitted that the plan is a step in the right direction, though even this is of doubtful advantage if, as seems to be the case here, the step or steps in question are so small that they effect little or nothing of what is required, whilst on the other hand their effects are prolonged into a period when contrary measures are indicated.

The real advantage of Fisher's method is that, externally, everything would continue as at present, so that the general public would not even notice the change.[1] Such an *argumentum ad ignoratum* seems, however, of doubtful value. The very substance of the proposed reform is to raise something *else* to the position of a *measure of value*, and not gold, as is now the case. Why not, therefore, go the whole way, and choose something different by which the goal in view, a stable price level, may be secured with reasonable certainty ?

[1] This and the following lines are omitted from the German edition.

THE END

AUTHORS INDEX

SUBJECT INDEX